Praise for *All Hallows*

Customer reviews on Amaz

'Exciting, masterfully written, and left me c...._ _
scowling at, all the characters within, while gleefully enjoying the twists and
surprises of the story and character development.'

'I will not forget this novel anytime soon.'

'I found the characters in *All Hallows at Eyre Hall* richly drawn, and the
descriptions that maintain the period of the piece well researched and in
perfect continuity to the original book.'

'At times I thought Charlotte Brontë was writing this; that is how fabulous
a writer Luccia Gray is.'

'Whether you liked or disliked the original *Jane Eyre*, you will find this
sequel alternately engaging, surprising and impossible to put down.'

'*All Hallows at Eyre Hall* is graced with postmodern, postcolonial views that
remove the naivety that whitewashed even the darkest moments of Brontë's
original.'

'I found I could not put the pages away.'

'Absolutely AMAZING!!! A stellar read. I fell in love with Jane Eyre all
over again. A definite red-bleary-eyed, up all night, because I could not put it
down, awesome read.'

'I suggest when reading be prepared for plenty of hours of addictive
reading....enjoy to the fullest and become enraptured with Jane Eyre again.'

'I feel I've been given a new Jane Eyre. She's more imperfect, but I like the
way she's developed, and I'm looking forward to book two!'

'I'd definitely recommend it, whether you've read *Jane Eyre* or not.'

'Incredible continuation of a timeless classic.'

Rediscover the world of Jane Eyre...

Twenty-two years after her marriage to Edward Rochester, Jane is coping with the imminent death of her bedridden husband, and the revelation of his unspeakable secrets.

Richard Mason has returned, instigating a sequence of events which will expose Rochester's disloyalty to Jane, his murderous plots, and innumerable other sins. Drawn into a complex conspiracy, everything Jane holds dear is threatened. Who was the man she thought she loved? What is she prepared to do to safeguard her family and preserve her own stability?

All Hallows at Eyre Hall is the first volume of the *Eyre Hall Trilogy*. Its multiple narrators explore the evolution of the original characters, and bring to life new and intriguing ones, spinning an original and absorbing narrative.

The Eyre Hall Trilogy

Book One

All Hallows at Eyre Hall

Luccia Gray

ISBN: 978-84-617-1009-6

Printed in the U.S.A.

Dedication

For Elsa Margaret, who had started a novel she would have finished if she had survived, and for Elsa Luna, who may inherit her great-aunt and grandmother's insatiable love of stories.

For Sister Catherine, whose sweet and patient voice introduced me to the mysterious, delectable, and delightfully mischievous, Victorians.

Finally, for my mother, Lucía, and my father, Eliseo, whose courage and determination have always inspired me.

Part One: All Is Not Gold

Part Two: The Germs of Love

Part Three: Like a Dream

Part One: All Is Not Gold

"Is it really for love he is going to marry you?" she asked.

I was so hurt by her coldness and scepticism that the tears rose to my eyes.

"I am sorry to grieve you," pursued the widow; "but you are so young, and so little acquainted with men, I wished to put you on your guard. It is an old saying that 'all is not gold that glitters;' and in this case, I do fear there will be something found to be different to what either you or I expect."

Jane Eyre, Chapter 24.

Chapter I

Mr. Mason's Visit

Sunday, 29ᵗʰ October, 1865.

The carriage swayed its way up the birch lined driveway towards Eyre Hall, tunnelling through the ghostly morning mist. The muggy air reeked of wilting foliage and soggy earth as the carriage halted abruptly, and the coachman closed and barred the heavy yard gates. The vehicle rocked as he leapt on, spurring the horses back into movement. Seconds later, I stepped out unsteadily onto crunchy gravel, adjusted my cloak and hat, and looked up to the rebuilt mansion for the first time.

Twenty-three years had passed since my last visit to another house in this same spot, when I was bitten by a raging lioness fighting to preserve her offspring and her reason. My bones shivered. My sister had been wronged, my niece had been wronged, and my mission was to settle the injustice before the funeral. The sharp smell of burning coal seeped into my frosty chest, and I thanked God there were fireplaces in this gloomy, damp climate, in which I cannot envisage my ancestors ever having lived.

The top floor and tower were still wrapped in a vaporous cloud, but the ground floor casements, which seemed to rise up from the ground, symmetrically sliced into squares, stood out like prison bars. I could sense the witch was there watching me. I fancied her slight shadow floating over the curtains, and imagined curious fingers pulling back the heavy dark fabric, in an effort to catch a glimpse of my arrival. I had received no answer to my message requesting an encounter, but I prayed she would be curious enough to converse with me.

He had arrived. I would have gasped and convulsed had I not challenged myself hours earlier, when I received his note, to firmly control any hint of emotion. I would not give him the pleasure of guessing how his visit had driven me to yet another sleepless night inhabited by unearthly beings.

Michael, my valet, announced my visitor. I was unimpressed. The person who stood before me was barely a shadow of the fine looking man I had met twenty-three years earlier at Thornfield Hall. His visage repelled me. The nose had become more aquiline, pointing directly at his extended chin, and his face had lost its ovalness and melted into a shapeless mass of puffy fat. His furred olive green cloak hung loosely over his drooping shoulders, awkwardly resting on his protruding contour, while a sardonic smile dressed his gaunt lips. His eyes, blanker and darker, had merged to the expressionless colour of his dull iris. He bowed stiffly, while a smooth, swollen hand made a sharp rising movement to remove the hat, which he thrust towards my robust, fine looking valet towering over him. It took all my self-control not to smirk at the strands of lank white hair he uncovered, as I endeavoured with every visible muscle in my body to hide any emotions from the devil's messenger who stood before me.

I was grateful for the embroidered French cuffs, which hid my fists as my nails clawed into my palms, while I reluctantly remembered the last time I had seen him. He had ruined my life, destroyed my wedding day, and driven me away from my beloved Edward and from my dear Thornfield Hall.

I extended my hand limply, took a deep breath, and braced for what was to come, anticipating uneasily that once again my life would change irreversibly after his undesired visit. He bowed, brushed his lips over my embroidered mitts, and then took a step backwards, reinforcing his position as adversary. There was no doubt in my mind that he meant to

3

trouble me with ghoulish memories. I turned to my vigilant valet and asked him to leave before addressing my displeasing visitor.

"What brings you here, Mr. Mason?" I asked coolly.

I took a few seconds to reply, taken aback by her unprecedented assertiveness and waiting for the defiant looking servant to leave.

"I heard you finally became Mrs. Rochester." I examined her carefully. She was still as slight and elflike as the last time I had seen her, a trembling debutante underneath her pathetic white veil.

"Indeed. After your sister's unfortunate death, Mr. Rochester and I married, as we both wished."

She hadn't fooled me then, and she wasn't going to fool me now. I knew that her innocent, demure expression hid a determined and ambitious viper, "Not so unfortunate for you…"

"Have you come here to insult me, Mr. Mason? Because if that is the case, it will not be tolerated and I must ask you to leave at once."

Be careful, Richard, I reminded myself. She had employed over twenty years to enhance her wicked skills. "Pardon me, madam. It was not my wish. I merely pointed out that by her death she opened many doors…. for both of you."

I saw her left eyebrow rise slightly, and she blinked a shade quicker before replying.

"Have I wronged you in any way, Mr. Mason?"

Her complexion was pale and flawless, and although her look was stiff and almost expressionless, her smooth face was pleasing to look upon, "Indeed you have not, madam."

"Did I not respect your sister's existence and abandon Thornfield as soon as I learned of her presence?"

"That is so, madam."

Her thin brown lips pursed as she tightened her jaw. Can she really believe she's innocent? Can she not see it was all her fault? She killed my sister as surely as if she had thrown her off the buttery that tragic night. Bertha had been accused of setting the house on fire, but no one

4

had seen her do it. They also accused her of committing suicide, therefore, her interment was without ceremony, and even so, I was not allowed to attend. It was all obviously a scheme set up by her husband to be rid of her. Edward would have done anything to be a free man and recover this enticing little sorceress.

"Can you or anyone reproach anything in my behaviour?"

I smirked as she insisted on her innocence and scuttled away like a scared mouse. It was easy to imagine how they had both planned their revenge. He had rid himself of my poor, wretched sister, and she had returned to a free man.

I had decided that her curiosity by far outweighed her hatred of me, or she wouldn't have agreed to see me. Or perhaps it was fear? In any case, I decided to play furthermore.

"Indeed, Mrs. Rochester. I have nothing to reproach … you."

"Explain yourself, Mr. Mason. I have many matters to attend this morning."

I had been informed by his agent that she had been attending to legal and financial matters in provision of her husband's foreseeable death. Did she really think she was going to get away with it? Did she think that she, a plain and penniless governess, would inherit all his wealth and property, while he shunned and murdered my sister, who was a beautiful heiress?

"Of course, madam. It is Mr. Rochester with whom I have matters to resolve."

"Mr. Mason, you must be aware that Mr. Rochester is unwell."

"It pains me to hear such news."

"Allow me to doubt your sincerity on this matter."

"Please, madam, accept my sympathy for your personal pain and your son's."

She shot a piercing look, moved her lips as if to speak, hesitated, then seemed to change her mind before finally speaking, "Your sympathy is accepted, because it would be unchristian to reject it."

I envisioned the proud and uncouth Saxon who lay on his deathbed. I never understood what my sister or any of his women ever saw in his stocky figure or irksome character. I will no longer have to deal with him, thank God. She will be my new business associate, although she is not yet aware of our inevitable partnership.

"I am honoured, madam, that it should be accepted."

"Will you now tell me what is your business, Mr. Mason?"

Did her lips curl slightly? Was she so easy to entice? Or was I being enticed? Her face did seem most pleasant, especially when the vexation ceased. I insisted more mildly on this occasion, "I have some urgent business with Mr. Rochester."

"He is not receiving any visitors at the moment."

"Yet, I must speak to him."

"That will not be possible. In any case, I cannot imagine what business you should have with my husband."

She had been suitably lured and was eager to discover the reason for my visit, "I would not wish to bother you with certain unpleasant matters, madam."

"I am afraid you will have to deal with me from now on, Mr. Mason, so proceed."

I wondered how much she had already discovered about her husband's finances and offences. He was a dark horse, if ever there was one.

"Please sit down, Mr. Mason."

She pointed to two high-backed Regency chairs on either side of a red teak table. Dark. In spite of the rebuilding, and modern furnishings, the house was as gloomy and distasteful as the last time I had seen it while my sister still lived. It was so different to my bright colonial mansion, where one can drink iced lemonade in the mornings and dark rum in the evenings, on the verandah, inhaling the ocean breeze.

In spite of the unfortunate and occasional insurrection of the local slaves, now called workers, who were usually pleasing and compliant, it is far more beautiful than this dreary land will ever be. For a moment, I imagined pale, petite Jane in a colourful colonial dress with ample cleavage, her hair free and carelessly caressing her bare shoulders, smiling and twirling while carrying a parasol to keep the sun out of her flushed face. She would make a splendid widow. I wondered how soon she would remarry after the sick beast's death.

"Thank you, madam."

"Please continue."

"The matter is pertaining to his first wife, my sister Bertha Antoinette née Mason and died Rochester."

"The lady died twenty-three years ago, sir. There can be no further matter to discuss."

"Oh, but there is madam, and a very serious one indeed."

"I trust it is not a financial matter, Mr. Mason. My husband and I have nothing more to discuss with the Mason family in this respect."

"I'm afraid you do, madam."

"You tire me with your games. Explain yourself once and for all or abandon my house."

Perhaps I ought to speak now. I wonder how she will react. Will she faint? Or have a hysterical fit, as most women would due to the inferior size of their brains? Might she call the constable and have me arrested? Or call her stalwart servant to throw me out of the house?

"Mr. Mason, whatever agreement you may have had with my husband will have to be authorized by me henceforth."

"Mr. Rochester has broken an agreement we had. There is the matter of a certain sum of money that has not been received in the last few months."

"Indeed? I have been supervising Mr. Rochester's finances, and I do not recall your name on any of the transactions."

"I have been informed that you have cancelled a transfer to Spanish Town, Jamaica."

"That is so, to the Convent of Saint Mary. We are Church of England, sir. I cannot imagine why my husband should continue sending money to a Roman Catholic convent in Jamaica."

"Did you not ask your husband about the matter?"

"Indeed, I did."

"Did he not tell you that you were to continue making the payments after his death?"

"He did not. He told me it was an old matter dating from his youth, and I needn't carry his burden any further."

"Is that so? I cannot understand why he should act in such a dishonourable manner."

She surprised me by suddenly jumping up from her chair and rushing to the door. I got up immediately, wondering what she was going to do next. She spun around and spat out the words.

"How dare you speak to me of honour? My husband is the most honourable man I have ever met."

"Your loyalty is touching, madam. You have been wronged, as my sister was before you. Mr. Rochester is not, has never been, an honest man."

"I beg you, order you, not to speak of my husband disrespectfully in his own house."

Her voice had gradually risen during our last exchange. I smiled in the security right then that my news would destroy any illusion of happiness or ounce of tranquillity she might have had in her years with Rochester.

"I doubt you will be of the same opinion when I tell you the reason for my visit. I do not wish to distress you, madam, but what I have to say may trouble you."

I looked into his false face, in the knowledge I would have to listen once more to his version of the truth, which had to be a lie. Edward had once told me Mason came from a long line of liars and slave traders.

"Why do you always bring me such bad news?"

"I humbly ask your forgiveness before I convey the tidings I must bring you."

I sighed and returned to my seat in anticipation of what I had no choice but to hear.

"To the point, if you please, Mr. Mason."

She looked away from me, absently caressing the folds on her pale blue day dress.

"There is someone Mr. Rochester must see before he dies."

"No more games. You are to leave. My husband will not be molested by anyone in his final moments."

"Not even by his daughter?"

"What!"

She cried, as she jumped out of her chair and ran to the window, breathing heavily. I could not see her face, but her shoulders were hunched, and she seemed to be trembling. I wondered if she might be crying and waited a few minutes before continuing.

"She would like to meet her father before he dies." I said the words I had come to say slowly and softly. I wanted to make sure she heard them clearly.

We both heard the instants pass, as the small steel second hand ticked around the inner circle of the long clock standing majestically between the bay windows. Her eyes were fixed on the watery pane. Abruptly she straightened her back and lifted her head, as if she were looking for something in the sky. It was a damp dismal morning, and the cloud burdened sky loured heavily above the laurel orchard. Her palms repeated the ritual. She straightened her dress and swirled around towards me, surprisingly composed after her initial shock. She spoke slowly and resolutely.

"What trick is this, Mr. Mason?"

I walked towards her, putting on my most earnest voice.

"The infant was born in Thornfield Hall twenty-three years ago, in March, 1843, and taken to the Convent of Saint Mary in Spanish Town, Jamaica a few months later."

"Impossible!"

"I took her myself. That was the object of my visit, when we first met at Thornfield Hall. Surely you remember the extraordinary events you yourself witnessed?"

⸻⟡⸻

Of course I remembered the night I had walked up the chill gallery and the dark, low corridor of the haunted third storey on my way to the tapestried room, where I nursed him at Thornfield Hall. His shoulder and arm were soaked in blood. He had been attacked with a knife and bitten by the murderous monster. I heard the unearthly cries, which seemed to belong to more than one person or fiend lurking behind the wall. I remember looking up to the dying Christ on an ebon crucifix above the panelled cabinet doors and praying for protection and strength to fulfil my gruesome task. Mason's eyes were dull with pain and horror while I dipped my hand again and again in the basin of blood and water, and wiped away the trickling gore. He said she had sucked his blood. What kind of a monster or monsters inhabited therein? Edward had left me alone to look after Mason while he fetched the doctor. As the hours passed and the candle waned, I thought he was dying. At last the master of the house returned with Dr. Carter, who dressed the wounds and took him to his house to be fully cured, so the rest of the guests would not see what had happened.

"I saw no child."

"You did not see my sister and she was there, too. Both of them were with Grace Poole in the concealed chamber, a few feet away from us while we waited for Dr. Carter to arrive. Did you not hear the cries of the madwoman and the child?"

"I heard the cries, but I saw neither."

"Precisely."

"But Edward never mentioned a child, nobody has…"

"Can you be surprised, madam? Edward Rochester's honesty on such matters is easy to doubt. On the other hand, his ability to buy anyone, and cover up his wrongdoings, is notorious."

"How dare you?"

"What do you know about Adele's mother or about his relationship with Blanche Ingram?"

"That was before we were married."

"Come, come, madam. Were you not aware that he continued to visit Miss Ingram after your marriage, even when she became Lady Carrington? Or that he rented rooms in Sloane Square for his friends in

London, such as Mrs. Annabel Beresford, Louisa, Lady Edgeworth? And Miss Daisy Pickering?"

How could he know? If he knew, it had to be common knowledge, in London, in Millcote, in Hay, at Eyre Hall. Nobody ever told me! I never suspected anything until I took over the supervision of our finance. I must have seemed so innocent, and so easy to deceive for so many years.

As soon as Edward recovered his eyesight, he started visiting London on his own. During the London season he would stay there for months, returning occasionally for a brief family interlude, when he recounted his trips to the theatre or the opera. Very occasionally I would accompany him to visit my editor or attend dinner parties with his friends or distant relatives. I never objected to his frequent trips, not being much taken by fashionable London life, finding it too superficial and oppressive.

During the hunting season he would stay at Ferndean on his own. Even though he could not hunt, his left arm having been mutilated into a mere stump by the fire, he enjoyed accompanying his friends who engaged in the sport. I knew the Ingrams and the Carringtons visited, but his visits had never concerned me, because I disliked hunting, and in any case, I was busy with our son.

We would have liked to have more children, but I had a miscarriage and a still born daughter in the following years, and I gave up hope. I moved to another bedroom to put an end to his sleepless nights with young John. I never allowed any of the maids to sleep with my son, or any of the governesses to instruct him. I wanted him to be brought up with the mother's love I had so longed for myself. Only Adele was allowed to take part in his education. His father did not agree, considering it inappropriate for landed gentry, and I reminded him that he had married the governess, Jane Eyre, not a wallflower.

I educated my son until he left home to study at Rugby, when he was twelve, then moved to Oxford five years later. In the next elections, when Mr. Crowley retires, we expect he will be elected Member of Parliament for our constituency. There is much to do to improve our country. There is too much poverty and misery to be

Christianly tolerated. I know he has it in his heart to improve our world.

The ten o'clock chime startled me back to my present predicament.

"That was a long time ago," I replied feebly.

"Well, he is hardly in a position to go gallivanting at present."

I pressed my palm against the casement in the hope that a refreshed hand would somehow energize my mind. It did not. Mason was waiting for an answer. There was no point in lying to this man. He knew everything about Edward and me, he knew even more than I did about my husband. I acknowledged hopelessly that there would be no use in setting up a farce. No more lies, they were too exhausting.

"I see you are well informed, sir. May I ask you how it is you know so much about my husband's affairs?"

"Lord Ingram and my father were acquainted, madam."

"He knew of your sister's existence?"

"Naturally he did."

"And you did not disapprove of their marriage?"

"Miss Ingram was a rich and noble heiress, she would have added to our fortune and position."

"Of course she is very noble. Is her husband of the same opinion, I wonder?"

"Marriages are very… personal contracts, madam."

"Why should I believe you?"

"I never lied to you, madam. I merely exposed the truth. Mr Rochester had received a plentiful dowry for marrying my sister, and instead of honouring her, he locked her away in his cold, damp attic with a drunken idiot as a keeper."

"Your sister was a lunatic."

"It is not difficult to become a lunatic, if one is confined and tortured for ten years. Let us imagine the contrary had happened. Let us imagine you were taken by force to Jamaica and locked away in a hot, damp basement, with no one to speak to, not even a mirror to look at yourself and comb your hair. Would you not have gone mad, madam?"

Those were his only true words. Of course I had thought about that poor woman, who became a beastly monster. I knew that before her transformation she had been a beautiful and happy girl, living a life of gaiety in the warmth of her colonial plantation. Thornfield had destroyed her as much as it had transformed me.

I heard her cries at night, listened to her footsteps in the corridor, once I even saw her reflection in my chamber mirror, and her ghostly contour approached me with a candle. I thought I was dreaming and she was my nightmare, but I was wrong. We met that night for the first time. She was deranged, in agony, and nobody helped her, not her husband, her brother, or her servants. They were all in connivance to destroy her. And now he is telling me that they stole her daughter!

"Why didn't you come and rescue her, if you were so concerned about her welfare?"

"I was in Jamaica. I received letters regularly from Mr. Rochester with news about Bertha. I understood matters were normal. Until one day, I received a letter advising me that Mr. Rochester was to marry a certain Jane Eyre, at the local parish church. Naturally, it was my duty to come and speak up for my sister, that is, my stepsister and her daughter."

"What do you mean?"

"The day after you left, I discussed the matter with Mr. Rochester. He agreed to continue sending maintenance for the child, if I promised to keep his secret."

"What?"

"You must remember how you left in the middle of the night the day after the wedding farce. Edward was distraught, quite out of his mind. He said he'd kill Bertha with his own bare hands, but fortunately we were able to hold him down. He made me promise to keep the child a secret. The child was still in Millcote with a wet nurse at the time. After the incident, I took her with me back to Spanish Town."

⁓⦂⦂⁓

It was a pleasure to watch her tormented expression wrench her previously demure countenance.

"Yes, madam, your husband has been sending his daughter money every month. She has been brought up as fits her status, and our family. She is a well bred, well educated, well mannered and beautiful young lady."

"It's not possible!"

"May I ask you to speak to Dr. Carter, or his agent in London, Mr. Cooper? They will both confirm the nature of the regular financial transfers to Spanish Town, Jamaica, and the reason."

"Your business then is financial, sir."

"I wish a guarantee that my niece will continue to receive a lifelong allowance, when her father has died, and that she will be procured a suitable husband, dowry, and a place in English society."

"How can you prove it? Who will believe you?"

"You are quite right, madam. I cannot prove it with documents, but I can sow the seeds of doubt, which would be very unfortunate for your son. I understand you have a son? A fortunate young man, as I have heard, who is studying Law at Oxford and wishes to make an honest living at Parliament, no doubt he will be a peer one day. You must be very proud of him. He has such a promising future. I also understand he is engaged to Lady Elizabeth Harwood, Judge Harwood's daughter."

"You are well informed, sir. He is an honest man. Would you ruin his life by disseminating this scandal?"

"Of course not." I paused before adding coolly. "What would I gain by doing so?"

"What is your proposal then, sir?"

"She will be introduced to everyone as Mr. Rochester's niece and mine, which is her official status. She will become your ward. She will be given a fitting dowry for a suitable husband, and the Convent of Saint Mary will continue to receive funding regularly."

"What does she know?"

"Originally, I contrived imaginary parents for her. She was informed that her mother, Sybil, had died in childbirth, and her father, Henry

Mason, a fictional brother I created for myself and Bertha, had died shortly after. However, she has recently been informed she is Bertha and Rochester's daughter. Nevertheless..." I paused and almost heard her muscles as they wrenched before continuing gravely, "she is prepared to continue to play the role of niece to Mr. Rochester, her wealthy uncle and benefactor. It is her wish to see him and thank him before he passes away."

I looked out to the dismal day and wondered why the man I had loved so much had brought me so much pain. How could I look after another clandestine daughter, once more, as my own ward after his death?

When I had first arrived at Thornfield twenty-four years ago, I had been governess to Adele, born as a result of his affair with the French opera singer, Céline Varens. Adele cannot be held responsible for her mother's faults, and she was my reason for arriving at Thornfield, so I will always be grateful for her existence. We took to each other from our first meeting, and over the years I have grown to love Adele, who has become a pleasing and obliging companion. However, Bertha's daughter was an unexpected and unbearable burden.

"Well, Mrs. Rochester, will you agree to Annette's humble request?"

My head was spinning. Annette's request! She has a name! She exists! She is a girl! She is his flesh and blood! Or could it be a trick? What could I do? Who could I turn to for consolation and advice?

"Madam?" She was quiet for a few minutes. I approached her, but she held up her hand like a shield, and small and delicate as it was, I kept my distance.

"I will speak to Mr. Rochester about this matter," she started feebly, "and if he agrees to a meeting, there will be a meeting."

"We are staying at the Rochester Arms, in Hay. It would be more appropriate if we were to visit Mr. Rochester as soon as possible and receive an invitation to stay here, at Eyre Hall, while we find appropriate accommodations for Miss Annette Mason."

She shot a daggered look and dismissed me curtly.

"Goodbye, Mr. Mason. I will discuss the matter with my husband, and I will send you a message forthwith."

I have learned from experience that in a hunt wounded animals can be unpredictably dangerous. I should make sure not to lower my guard in future negotiations.

"Good day, madam." I bowed, as dainty fingers gently shook a bone china bell, at the sound, a tall, sour looking, young valet entered far too soon, and bowed to the shattered mistress of the house. I felt proud I had been the inflictor of such pain. It was a just repayment for my sister's degradation and death.

"Simon? Where is Michael?"

"He is with Mrs. Leah, in her office, madam."

"Please show Mr. Mason out, and tell Michael to bring me some tea and see to the fireplace, it's very cold in here."

Lanky, awkward legs led the way out into the chilly sombre hall. I looked around and up the dark oak staircase. She had managed to rebuild the house to its previous shadiness. English houses, so heartless and frozen, like their dwellers.

The boy's sluggish, wiry arms pulled open the heavy front door. "Good day, Mr. Mason."

"Damn it! It's raining again! Where the devil is my driver?"

"Dunno, sir."

"Well, what are you waiting for? Go and get him you idle idiot! I want my carriage at the door! Now!"

———⁂———

I'm only the footman! How'd I know where his driver was? He was probably in the stables with Joseph, or at the back chatting up the maids. I looked down at me only pair of shoes. If I stepped on the muddy walk, I wouldn't be able to go back into the house through the front door. I'd have to walk all the way to the back and in through the kitchen. Me clothes would be soaked, too, so I'd have to polish me shoes and change me uniform, which meant I wouldn't be able to serve lunch for the Master on time. I'd get scolded again by Leah, the housekeeper, or rather Mrs. Leah as she likes to be called, although it's not her surname and she's not married. Who would have her with her scrawny face and glum temper?

"Move man! Get my driver!" Shouted the chafed toff before he walloped me with his stick.

When I came back with his driver, soaking wet as I was, the mad rake was whipping poor little Flossy, who was coiled up in a corner whimpering. I never thought I'd ever hear a visitor at Eyre Hall curse like he did. When I bends down to pick her up, he tells me she bit him. Flossy! The gentlest of dogs! I was about to tell him she ain't never bit no one, when I feels his mucky boot smack me face. I rolls over down the steps and onto the gravel while Flossy jumps up and scampers towards the stables for cover.

"That bitch deserved to have her head torn off!" He shouts before getting into his carriage and banging the door, like he wants it to fall apart. I hope I never see him again. We ain't used to people like him here.

Back in the kitchen they was all waiting for me to tell them what I'd seened and what I'd heard, except Mrs. Leah, who's in her office, milady's pet, Michael, who's delivering her tea, and his sister Susan, who's teaching at Sunday school this morning. I bribed Christy and Beth to polish me shoes and brush me uniform while I acted the conversation I'd overheard behind the curtains that divide the drawing room from the dining room. Margaret, the cook, called her husband, Joseph, and they all listened, gasped, laughed, and clapped, while I exaggerated some of the details and dramatized the conversation, taking the mickey out of the mistress and her vicious, foul mouthed visitor.

They all screamed as I took cook's tea towel and put it up to me nose, as if it were a dainty handkerchief, and knocked me head, as I pretended to faint, as I played her part on hearing she will have to look after his mad wife's daughter. I was only rehearsing, my big act would come at the Rochester Arms and then the George Inn at Millcote, where me mates'd pass round the box while I acted the scene a few more times.

I was practically born in a ditch. My mother was the wickedest hedge-whore nobody ever seened in the world. Said I was her curse, but more like it she was mine. She was goosed all day. Drank four glasses of liquor before breakfast she did, and bashed me every time I came near her hand. I run away and became a vagabond, labourer, errand-boy, sweep... I did anything and everything to get by, and nobody threwed me out a rope, except Miss Pickering, she took pity on me, after I had an accident and broke a leg, that's why I limps a bit when it's cold. She said I should get a proper job, so she sent me to work with the master in this gloomy house.

The master's a ratty old toad, and this place is in the middle of nowhere, but the mistress is as kind as cream, I eats well, sleeps warm, and usually gets Sunday afternoon off. I been here six years, but I ain't staying here forever. One day, I'll be famous enough to get a job on the stage. I sneaked in to see Hamlet, once as a boy, by a travelling actor's group. I knew then I'd be a player. I always wanted to avenge the death of my father by the bitch of my mother. He's the character I want to play.

Mrs. Leah was not amused when she came in and caught me in the act. She told me I'd get myself into trouble for nosing about other folks lives 'cause they was important people. What does I care? I'm going to London to be an actor, as soon as I gathers up enough chink.

⌐⌐✦⌐⌐

Chapter II

Adele's Letters

I flew to the window to see why Flossy was howling so peculiarly, and caught a glimpse of coach wheels grinding the muddy gravel, as a carriage drove away. I had not heard it arrive, so engrossed was I with the letter I had received from Mr. Greenwood earlier in the morning. I wondered who had come. It was not Dr. Carter's car, nor Mr. Wood, the curate's, nor anyone I knew. Life at Eyre Hall was so boring of late. We did not often receive visitors now that Monsieur was so ill, and Jane was preoccupied with bookkeeping and lost in her own private thoughts. I had found my escape route in my eloquent and affectionate correspondent, the man I had fallen in love with, after exchanging eight passionate letters and two books of poems.

I wanted to reply immediately to his last letter, but I decided it was time to read it to Jane and tell her about my secret suitor. I dashed out of the room, clasping the letter in one hand and holding my skirt up in the other, as it brushed down the staircase. My goodness! I would have to send for some more dresses and sashes from London before my journey! I almost tripped down the polished stairs with excitement at the thought of finally meeting Mr. Greenwood face to face! I couldn't wait to tell Jane. I started screaming "Jane!" halfway down the second staircase, and I saw her rush out of the drawing room with her hand against her breast, looking deathly pale.

"Adele? What is the matter?"

"Jane! I have received a letter from Mr. Greenwood!"

"Is he all right?"

"Yes! He's coming! He's coming to visit! He wants to meet me! And you and Mr. Rochester of course! He wants to take me to Venice with him! Perhaps he wants to marry me!"

I heard Jane say, "Dear God!" before collapsing with a loud thump near the staircase in the hallway. I screamed her name so loudly that everyone rushed up from downstairs.

"Bring the salts from her dressing table!" Shouted Leah, and I saw Michael turn deathly pale and whisper in my ear, "I'll get Dr. Carter" before running out the front door.

"Get water girls!" Added cook, breathless and unable to rush back down the stairs.

Christy flew up to the bedroom while Beth rushed back down to the kitchen.

"Pick her up and bring her into the drawing room, Simon," ordered Leah. Simon obeyed clumsily and I heard her shout angrily, "Be careful Simon, she's not a sack of flour!"

<hr />

Leah, always shouting at me. I was doing me best! I laid her on the fancy couch, accidentally bumping her head on the headrest, and cook waved her dirty apron against her face while first Christy and then Beth brought the water and salts. The salts did the trick. She coughed and opened her eyes. I smiled thinking of my interpretation at the inn on my next night off.

"My dearest Jane! My darling! Are you all right? What has happened?" Fussed Miss Adele, like a flustered chicken with her curls and ribbons dangling around her flushed face. The mistress insisted she was all right and told us to go back to our chores, so we did, except Miss Adele, who stayed with her in the drawing room.

<hr />

"Jane, if you're feeling better, can I read you the letter from Mr. Greenwood? I'm sure it will cheer you up!"

I had inadvertently crushed the letter in my hand, so I straightened it out and laid it on the tea table before us.

"Why not?" Jane said wearily.

It was a strange answer coming from Jane, as if she didn't care. She had always been so interested and comforting, as I had confided some aspects of my correspondence with my poet. Jane had always been sympathetic to my suitors, although she later confessed she never liked any of them, once our brief courtships had terminated. When I asked her why she had not told me before, she always said I had to realize what they were really like and make my own decisions. Several, such as Mr. Percy and Mr. Brook, had been Monsieur's local friends, in an effort no doubt to humour him and take me away from Eyre Hall, but I had seen through their intentions easily. I had met a French Count while in Monsieur's villa in the south of France, but he lost interest once he came to Eyre Hall and learnt I was not the heiress he had imagined. Monsieur had provisioned a splendid dowry, but I was not officially a Rochester, and the Count was disappointed.

My father never forgave my mother's infidelities. He brought me to England as his ward, but I was never acknowledged as his daughter. The Count made me understand this circumstance would make it difficult for me to find a suitable husband. I was distraught at first, until Jane's baby died at birth and she became so ill I had to look after John, and I had no more time to worry about suitors.

The years passed and Monsieur's friends were all too old, or too boring, or wanted to live in the distant New Territories, so I lost hope in finding a husband until I received a letter from my mother, Céline Varens, whom Monsieur had told me was dead. I was devastated by the news, but also excited. My mother wanted me to visit her in Venice, so I prayed every night that God should allow me to make the journey, and God did answer my prayers one afternoon, as I sat reading the Monthly Magazine in the drawing room. It was love at first sight.

Mrs. Greenwood was a famous poet, whose sonnets I had read many times. When I saw Mr. Greenwood's poignant picture by her grave in Italy, I fell in love with the sad widower and decided to gain his acquaintance. He had returned to England some months after his wife's death, so although he was still in mourning, he was almost free to commence another relationship.

He replied to my first letter by sending me a signed copy of his poems, which I read immediately. I wrote back at once to inform him of my delight in reading them. He replied with a poem entitled *Imaginary Angel*, as he had no clue as to my appearance, so I sent him a second letter with a small portrait of myself. He then sent me another poem called *Angel Discovered*. As a result, our letters became more passionate until he told me we could wait no longer and implored me to agree to a meeting, so I invited him to Eyre Hall, and he has agreed to come this week! However, I have not told Jane anything about his visit, yet, and although I was upset that she did not seem the least bit interested in his letter, I started reading in the hope that it would liven her spirits.

My Dearest Miss Varens,

I must thank you for your earnest and affectionate letter, which was a joy to receive coming home last night from a tedious day's business in London. I most heartily and fervently reciprocate your interest and affection. Your letters are among the few which I most care to receive and best love.

I have received your invitation with the utmost pleasure and believe me I fully intended to come to you. I should come as you suggested, next week. You wonder in your letter if I should be displeased at leaving such a major city as London, and I must reply that nothing excites me more than the anticipation of meeting you, at last. I would gladly spend a week walking away from London to gaze upon your face and hear your voice for the first time.

I dined yesterday with the editors of the Monthly Magazine, which is to publish my latest poems, inspired completely by the portrait you so kindly sent in your last letter, Mon Ange. They were impressed by the poems, but moreover, by your exquisite visage. My darling, you are already loved and known in London.

Last week I was at an Italian Opera at Drury Lane, where the greatest artists of the moment sang beautifully, but all I could think of was your face and your endearing words. You are constantly in my mind and in my heart to such an extent that in spite of the cool weather, I walked home feeling a burning warmth that accompanied me through the freezing night. I dearly wish that in the very near future we shall go to the opera together in the land where it first flourished and listen together in the most beautiful city in the world.

I am heartily pleased you enjoyed the poems I sent you, and that you set so much store by my humble dedication. A poem is a small token compared to the works of art that you truly deserve. I wish I could draw fine paintings to express my feelings, so the walls of London would be covered with my admiration for you.

I cannot tell you how grieved I was to know you are suffering with Mr. Rochester's deteriorating health, and I wish him a prompt recovery. I am anxious to meet Mrs Rochester, famous in London as a respected novelist and gracious lady.

I hope to have the immense pleasure and undeserved honour of meeting you very soon.

God bless you and yours, your faithful and affectionate admirer,

Mr. William Greenwood.

"It is a lovely letter, Adele. Mr. Greenwood is a very courteous gentleman, and he writes charmingly."

"He's a great poet Jane, and he's a widower. I'm sure I love him."

"Be careful, Adele. You're so impulsive, my dear. You don't know him. I mean, you haven't met him yet."

"I do know him, Jane. We've been exchanging letters for months!"

"Months?"

"Jane, please forgive me for not confiding in you. He has sent me a letter a week for two months."

"So you have eight letters?"

"And four sonnets. He has dedicated them to me. I am his muse, Jane. He hadn't written anything for months after his wife died, and I have given him the inspiration he needed. He needs me!"

"And you have written to him, too, I suppose?" I nodded. "How many letters?"

"Many." I knew Jane would be displeased when she heard the truth.

"More than eight?"

"Yes. Please don't be angry with me, Jane. I only want to be happy."

"I want you to be happy, too, Adele, but you can't throw yourself at him in this manner."

Jane was still lying on her couch, and I sat beside her with my head beside hers. She stroked my hair softly, and I closed my eyes and remembered how she had been like a mother to me, when I was a lonely child in sombre Thornfield Hall. She taught me how to speak English, like an English lady, how to play the piano, and draw. When I was a boisterous, spoilt child, she was always patient in spite of my lack of enthusiasm for learning, and my slow progress. When she married Monsieur, she made sure I completed my education at a pleasant boarding school, and then a finishing school in Belgium, and as an adult, she was always caring and attentive to my needs. She was less communicative lately, no doubt worried about our future after Monsieur's death.

"I sent him poems, too." I added timidly, afraid of more reproaches.

"You write poems now, Adele?"

"I started writing poems three months ago, when I received the letter from my mother. I was so depressed, and when I told Mr. Greenwood, he told me to write about my feelings. He sent me his late wife's poems and told me to read them and try and do the same. So I did, and I sent him my poems."

"How did you become acquainted with him?"

"I read about him in one of your literary magazines, and when Mr. Cooper came from London to visit you, I asked him to deliver my first letter to Mr. Greenwood personally. Shortly after, he sent me a copy of his poems by post. I fell in love with them, I mean with him."

"I have heard of Mr. Greenwood. Tell me about him."

"Mr. William Greenwood was born in London. His mother was a music teacher, and his father was a prosperous banker. He was educated at home and has read all the classics. He's frightfully clever! He published his first book of poems in his early twenties. He corresponded with the poetess Ellen Berry, and they eloped to Italy."

"Goodness! Why did they do that?"

"Well, it seems her father was opposed to their marriage, because his family was not wealthy enough, or perhaps he thought a poet would not be a suitable husband. They both continued to write poetry, and their reputation grew after publishing many more books. They were married almost twenty years. When Ellen died six months ago, she was buried in Venice, and he returned to England."

"Did they have any children?"

"They had a son, a young man, Dante, who is a painter and still lives in Venice."

"He seems an honest person, although eloping with his wife was rather daring and most inconsiderate to her family."

"It was the only way, Jane. Sometimes transgressions are inevitable in search of love and happiness."

"Perhaps." She became introspective again, her look far away beyond the clouds. "He knows you."

"I'm sure he does not."

"He has written to me about you. He read your novel and thinks it is a very respectable work."

"Does he?" She shrugged.

"He told me Daphne is the ideal companion every man would want to have, intelligent, loyal and honest. She was the only person who stood by Leonard, when everyone else thought he had killed his wife. He considers she is an example to all women."

"I wrote it a long time ago. I'm not sure if I agree with that description anymore."

"What do you mean?"

"I do not think Leonard is as innocent as Daphne thought, and as most readers seem to think. Perhaps he really did kill his wife, after all, and Daphne just helped him conceal the crime."

"Surely not!"

"Who knows? I am not sure anymore."

"But you wrote it, you must know what really happened!"

"I'm afraid characters in novels are like children, you bring them up and you think you know them, but they develop a life of their own, a life you cannot control."

"You are speaking very strangely, Jane. Surely a writer controls his characters, just like God controls the world?"

"Perhaps that is what happened to God. He gave us too much free will, and we turned into something he did not expect, and it is too late now to remedy the situation."

"Jane, you are talking in riddles. I do not understand you. I hope Dr. Carter is not long in coming."

She did not reply. Her eyes wandered out of the window and up to the steel sky, as if she were watching something. Could she be losing her mind again?

"Mr. Greenwood considers you should write another novel. Why have you not written any more, Jane?"

"I have other, more important business to attend to now: the Sunday school, the parish schools, my husband, my son, Eyre Hall and the Estate, among others."

She answered my question, but she was not with me, she was in her own ethereal world, in which nobody could enter.

"Jane, are you upset I invited Mr. Greenwood to Eyre Hall without conferring with you first?"

She finally turned back to me, "This is your house, also, Adele, but I am disappointed that you did not mention your correspondence or your plans. I did not expect secrets from you, too."

"Forgive me, Jane. I do so want to meet my mother. I had thought she was dead, and the idea of meeting her has become an obsession. I need to know who she is, but I have never travelled to Italy, and I cannot go alone. When Mr. Greenwood told me he had a house in Venice and would gladly be my companion, I was so excited, I dared not tell anyone in case the spell should break. Jane, don't you see? He will take me to Italy."

"I do not object to his invitation, but you cannot go to Italy with him alone."

"Susan! Can Susan come with me?"

"Susan? Why Susan?"

"Susan is so kind, polite, and well spoken. I would feel more comfortable if she came."

"It could be possible, but I will have to find another teacher. Adele, vex me not now, dear. I cannot plan too far ahead at present. There is a heavy load on my mind."

"Tell me your worries."

"Not now, Adele."

"De la discussion jaillit la lumière, n'est ce pas, Jane?"

"Perhaps. It's a long and old story..."

"Was it the visitor who just left? Who is he?"

"Not now, Adele. I will tell you, and you will meet him in due time. Do not worry about it at present. Let's talk about other more exciting events. You must humour me and answer a question now. How did you send and receive the letters without anyone knowing?"

"Michael helped me."

She gasped and jumped up from the couch. "Michael? Michael helped you to hide correspondence from me?"

"Don't be angry with him, Jane. I made him promise not to tell anyone. He helped me write the poems, too."

"Michael writes poems?"

"No, at least I don't know. He's very clever, you know. He helped me with some words. He's very good with words."

She moved to the window, putting both hands on the casements, as if she wanted to press the panes out into the garden.

"It makes sense, he reads a great deal. I've often seen him reading. Susan tells me they read the Bible together every night. His mother must have taught him. She had been a governess before she married his father."

"What happened to them?"

"His father was in the Navy and died when he was an infant, and his mother died when he was twelve and Susan was fourteen."

"How terrible! What happened then?"

"I believe they were in some sort of institution, near London, until my cousin, Diana, who had been acquainted with their mother, asked if I could employ them together or they would be separated, and I agreed."

"Where is Susan? I haven't seen her today?"

"She is at Sunday school this morning covering for Miss Brookwell, who had to nurse her ailing mother. She is a wonderful girl. I have no doubts she will be a great teacher."

"I think Michael would be a great teacher, too. He's wasting his time here as a valet. He could do so much more, although it is nice to have such a handsome and intelligent servant, much better than that dreadful idiot Simon!"

Jane returned to the couch and sat down looking exhausted, "Quite! I need Michael at Eyre Hall. We'll see about his future, once we provide for Susan. When she returns from Italy, I may be able to find her a permanent position as a teacher at a charity school. She may like that more than being a governess, which is often such an ungrateful task. Times are changing, and teachers are more necessary than governesses."

"So, she can come with me to Italy?"

"She can, if she wants to."

"I'm sure she will. Can I tell her this evening?"

"Perhaps we should tell Michael first. They are very close."

"I'm so glad you took them in, Jane. You do such good work. I wish I could be like you. I can't speak to those dirty children at the parish school, or the girls at the institution for governesses. I don't understand them. I don't understand Simon most of the time, or the new girl, Christy. They look unclean and sick. I'm disgusted and afraid of them. Am I unchristian for feeling that way?"

"No, you are not. You help them by helping me. Thanks to your assistance looking after Edward and John, I have had the time to pursue my charity work. I could not have done it without your generous support. You cannot help your nature, we are not all called for the same type of sacrifice in life."

"You make us all feel so good, Jane." I hugged her, like I used to when I was a child. She made me feel so safe. "Nothing can happen to us while you are with us. Monsieur is right, you are like an angel."

Chapter III

Michael

When I entered the drawing room with Dr. Carter, Mrs. Rochester and Adele were entwined in a tearful embrace. These were hard times for my mistress. The master lay on his deathbed. Adele had become infatuated with a London poet, and she was determined to travel to Italy in search of her mother, whom she had believed dead. Furthermore, last night, the carriage driver from the inn had delivered an urgent message after supper. I handed it to her myself and saw the tortured expression, which crossed her face as she read it. I should have resisted temptation, but when she retired, I returned to the drawing room with the excuse of putting out the fire. I removed the message from the drawer, where she had left it, and read the contents: *Mr. Mason, from Spanish Town, Jamaica, respectfully requests an interview with Mr. Edward Rochester tomorrow morning, to discuss a matter of utmost urgency.*

This morning shortly after his visit, when I saw her lying on the floor, I could hardly hold my thumping heart in my chest. I had to save her life, so I rushed for the doctor. On my return, I feared the worst, but when both women broke their embrace and started laughing, I felt relieved. My mistress's damp face tilted up towards us. She still looked paler than usual, but she was no longer concerned. Her eyes sparkled as they smiled, and wisps of freed hair tickled her smooth forehead and plump cheeks.

First, she spoke to the surgeon, "Thank you for coming, Dr. Carter." Then she turned to me, "How kind of you to bring him so quickly, Michael."

"I was worried...we all were. Are you recovered, madam?"

"Yes, thank you. I am much recovered, in fact, I have worked up an appetite after this eventful morning. Could you bring us some tea and scones please, Michael?" Her radiant eyes rested on mine, and her lips spread and rose at the corners, giving shape to a silky smile. I was thankful that she esteemed I was useful.

Mrs. Rochester, mistress, as I call her in my dreams, is the most beautiful and most delicate woman I have ever seen in my life. I fell in love with her the first time I saw her five years ago at Mr. and Mrs. Fitzjames's house. My father had served under Colonel Fitzjames before he died in battle in a foreign shore, when I was only eight. My mother, my sister Susan, and I moved to Morton from London and rented a room in a modest household, thanks to a small annuity the Navy supplied, and my mother's work laundering and sewing for Mrs. Fitzjames, Mrs. Rochester's cousin.

When my poor mother died of exhaustion, sadness, and consumption, six years later, having no relatives, we were sent to a poor house near London. We were lodged there for nearly two years. Mrs Fitzjames kindly invited us to spend two weeks at Christmas, a week at Easter, and a week in summer with her every year, because she was very fond of our mother.

Fortunately for us, the Boxing Day Mrs. Rochester visited her cousin, we had washed and were wearing clean clothes, or she would have been too disgusted to even look at us. We were in the study reading the tenth stage at the end of Book One of *Pilgrim's Progress*, when Ignorance appears before the gates of Celestial City without the required certificate and he is thrown out, while Christian and Hopeful pass through the dangerous Enchanted Ground into the Land of Beulah, where they cross the River of Death on foot to Mount Zion and the Celestial City: *Christian then saw that there was a way to hell, even from the gate of Heaven, as well as from the City of Destruction. So he awoke and behold it was a dream.* I was contemplating the dream, when Mrs. Fitzjames called us into the drawing room.

We entered shyly. Experience had taught us to be wary of strangers, especially adults. She was standing at the other end of the room, looking out of the window. The sun was shining directly on her profile, and I caught a glimpse of her grey satin dress and russet hair. She looked like a saint with a halo. I was curious to look up at her face, but we lowered our heads instinctively, as we were introduced. She walked towards us and said cheerfully, "Would you like to come and work at my house, Eyre Hall? I need a valet and a maid." I couldn't help turning my head towards her face. I was not yet fully grown, so we were equal in height and our faces met evenly. I looked into her soft, watery eyes and saw that she too was missing someone.

I would have done anything not to go back to the poor house and not be parted from my sister, but if she had asked me to, I would have crossed the ten circles of Dante's Inferno. She had saved my life and my sister's. I decided there and then that I would never leave her side. Susan and I read the Bible every night, as our mother had taught us, and I used to cry myself to sleep praying for her to return, until that moment. That very instant, I stopped mourning my mother or feeling sorry for myself, because I understood that my mother had put Mrs. Rochester in our path, or perhaps she had even had to die so that I would meet and serve my mistress.

"Have you ever worked?" she asked us, and Susan told her we had done the workhouse chores, such as oakam breaking, which made our fingers bleed. She had not heard of it before, so Susan told her how we had to tease out fibres from old ropes to produce lots of thin loose fibres. "Whatever for?" she asked, quite aghast, and Susan told her the strings were later sold to ship builders, where they were mixed with tar and used to seal the lining of wooden vessels.

Susan told her I was a strong boy and used to hard work, because I often cracked granite rocks with a heavy hammer ten hours a day. Again, she asked horror struck for the reasons, Susan told her the chippings were carted away by older men, who were not strong enough to crack them, and probably used in construction works. Susan proudly explained that with the pennies earned, usually not a shilling a day between us, we were able to buy food, some clothes, and borrow books and magazines to read by candlelight.

When she asked how long we had been there, Mrs. Rochester was again appalled to hear we had been there for two years, since our mother had died. She asked her about our life prior to our mother's death, and Susan explained we had lived in a rented room in Morton.

She looked at me sadly and asked if I did not speak, and I could only gaze at her face and think how very kind and beautiful she was. Susan told her I was shy, but that I spoke, read, and wrote, very well, because our mother had taught both of us to do so. My mistress put her hand up to my face, lightly touching my cheek, and sighed, looking straight into my eyes, as if she were searching for something. It was the moment I fell under her spell. No one had ever touched me like that before, with such concern and affection. Not even my mother, who had been too sad and overworked to bestow such warmth. Then Mrs. Rochester spoke to Susan and said someone would teach us our new jobs at her house.

I don't remember ever being happier than at Eyre Hall. Not even when my mother was alive. Mrs. Rochester was very kind to me from the first day we arrived. She allowed me to use the library and borrow any books I wanted to read. I loved the library. It was my favourite place in the house. The walls were panelled with countless leather bound books, and there was a mahogany ladder to climb up to the top shelves, where the oldest books were kept. There was a large desk, situated in front of the window, with drawers where the household records and accounts were kept. The fireplace stood on the wall to the right of the desk, with two tapestry upholstered chairs and a small oak table with the books or literary magazines Mrs. Rochester read. Since my arrival, Mr. Rochester had not used the rooms downstairs, because he was confined to his bed. I knew my mistress used the room as a retreat on occasions, because nobody else ever entered.

I have served Mrs. Rochester every day since then. I was grateful that I was in her company most of the day. I lit her fire, brought her tea, her lunch, her dinner, and did her errands. We hardly ever talked, except about daily household matters, because it would not be considered adequate, but I longed to converse with her, as I did with Miss Adele, about poetry and literature. Miss Adele confided in me, as if I were a friend. She said she didn't trust the maids, because she thought they were too fond of gossip, and she was right. I enjoyed our conversations, although she was of a capricious and moody nature, sometimes kind and sometimes quite spiteful. My mistress smiled at me frequently, even when I knew she was upset due to her ailing husband's health, or even today with such an accumulation of bad news, she found the kindness to smile, and that was more than enough to make my day.

When we started working at Eyre Hall, it pained me to learn that my mistress was an unloved wife. I was apprenticed to Simon, who was only a year older than me, but he had already been employed for some years. He informed me he had been recommended by a friend of Mr. Rochester's, an actress by the name of Miss Daisy Pickering. As a child, Simon was employed by the Royal Theatre, in London, to sweep the stage after the performances. He also used to deliver flowers and notes from admirers to the actresses' dressing rooms, including Mr. Rochester's, to the fickle and much desired actress. Simon said she had saved his life after a pub brawl, in which he had been seriously injured, by convincing Mr. Rochester to employ him at Eyre Hall.

The master, who was attended by Simon, was mostly unwell in bed, except for occasional walks around the orchard, always accompanied by Mrs. Rochester. She would read to him for almost an hour twice a day, apart from that, they led separate lives. Mrs. Rochester slept in the top tower room on the third floor. When I asked about the master's illness, Simon told me it was to do with the dire women he had frequented. I was shocked that any man, who had my mistress as a wife, would ever even look at another woman, but Simon seemed to think it was quite normal.

I soon learned my trade, and as Simon served the master, I was allocated the care of Mrs. Rochester and Miss Adele whenever they were downstairs. Neither of them employed a maid, they were very close and helped each other dress, in spite of Miss Adele being the master's illegitimate child by a French opera singer, so Mrs. Leah had told us.

When we first arrived, Susan was undermaid and spent most of the time at Eyre Hall scrubbing the floors, polishing the silver, and washing the clothes in the damp scullery. One day Mrs. Rochester heard us reading together on our Sunday afternoon off and was most impressed. She asked Susan some questions about the Bible and Pilgrim's Progress, and was so delighted with her replies that she told her she would find her a better occupation than cleaning. She asked Susan if she would like to be an apprentice to a parish school teacher, and Susan agreed on the condition that she could stay at Eyre Hall, because we did not want to be parted. It was agreed, and Susan is very contented with her occupation. She teaches mostly poor orphans and the farmer's children to read and write at Millcote Parish School.

About a year ago Susan met Jenny Rosset, a widow with two young children, Nell and Thomas. They cannot attend the parish school, because they must help their mother to earn a living cooking and cleaning at the only hotel and largest tavern in the town, the George Inn. Jenny went to the parish school and asked Susan if she could teach her children to read and write on Sunday evenings, as she could not do so herself, and they could not go to school. Susan asked the mistress for permission to do so and Mrs. Rochester agreed. I often accompanied her, so she would not have to travel alone.

Jenny is roughly my mistress's age. She is tall and well built with a wholesome complexion and a pleasant, round face with fleshy smiling lips. Most of the time, she earns enough to pay the bills and feed her family. However, in the winter, when she requires more coal and warm clothes, and there are fewer clients at the hotel, I had heard she might take on a gentleman friend to implement her meagre income. I had never noticed any such happenings while we were there. She always showed herself to be very polite and very keen that her children should be apprentices to an honest job.

While Susan was teaching the children, I would take a walk or visit the library. Sometimes I would accompany Jenny to the George Inn, where she worked. I once asked her if she could write, and she answered only her name and a few more words, so I offered to teach her. We would sit in empty rooms at the inn, where there was quiet, and we should not be interrupted. She offered to darn our clothes and baked us tasty cakes on occasions, but we expected nothing, knowing that she had nothing to offer. When I passed my twenty-first birthday,

I plucked up enough courage to tell her about an overbearing problem I had, in the hope that she might give me a solution.

I told her I was in love and needed to court the lady, but due to my lack of experience I dared not approach her.

"Do you love her?" she asked me, and I nodded. "Does she love you?" I answered that I didn't know yet.

"Does she like you?" I told her once more that I did not know, and she embarrassed me by saying she was sure she did, because she knew women found me attractive.

"The important thing is you love her, because you will have to make the first move. You will soon learn if she likes you or not."

"She is the most beautiful face I see all day."

"Then it will be easy. Ask the young girl out for a walk, and when you are alone together, tell her you love her and ask for permission to kiss her. The rest will come naturally. Follow your instincts. There is nothing to teach."

"She's not a young girl, Jenny."

"If she's married, put her out of your mind. You will end up in a duel or in bigger trouble." She sighed and added, "There are plenty of single girls out there."

"She's a widow. She has had experience and I have none. I need to know how to please her. She is not an innocent young country girl."

"What kind of a woman is she?"

"What do you mean?"

"There are two kinds of women to my knowledge, those that like it rough and don't mind a little knocking about, and those that need patience and a tender hand. Which do you think she is?"

I had seen and heard disgusting and unnatural acts nightly at the workhouse, men and women who behaved like stray dogs or bitches in heat. Sometimes gangs tried to force unaccompanied women or young girls. Sometimes they were solitary drunks or simply dehumanized scoundrels. Their cries and insults filled my head with awe as I trembled with disgust and shame. Mandrakes pursued young boys, and I was thankful that I was fourteen, almost fully grown, and strong when I arrived, or I could have been prey to the unscrupulous and degraded savages.

I had to kill one of them one night with my own bare hands. He was an animal who stalked Susan. I was only fifteen, but I mustered all my courage and imagined he was a granite block I had to destroy, and I did. I crushed his skull until I felt it sag and crumble. I heard the snap of the bone crack, and I felt the softness underneath as crimson blood trickled out of his ears. His eyes swirled up, revealing only whiteness, and I heard his last gasp of wickedness leave his wretched body. I would have killed him a hundred times over to protect my sister. I had promised my father I would look after my mother and my sister while he was away. Before he left for battle he reminded me that I was the man of the house. He told me never to shy away from another man in defence of honour and righteousness. He also told me I should treat women kindly as our Lord had wished.

"Tender, definitely." I finally answered. "I could only treat her gently."

"Are you sure that's what she wants? What she's used to?" I thought about her choleric, moody husband and decided perhaps he had not been a tender and considerate lover, but I was adamant I did not want to replicate him. I was the man who would give her the happiness she deserved and had been denied of late.

"Perhaps it is not what she is used to, but I'm afraid it's all I can offer. I adore her. I want her to feel worshipped, like a goddess."

"She's a very lucky lady."

"I am the fortunate one to be near her and court her."

"Are you sure she is the right person for you?"

"I will have to find out for myself. Will you help me?"

Jenny instructed me on practical matters first, such as hygiene and diet. She reminded me that nobody likes to be too close to someone whose breath reeks of gin or stale food, or whose body odours are salty or muddy. She made sure I understood the importance of wearing clean clothes and having a clean body from hair to toes. She told me to use baking soda and my finger to clean my teeth, and to use a pinch of the same powder in my socks and another in my shoes to prevent bad odours. She gave me some homemade softly perfumed soap for my daily wash, instructing me how to use a cloth to wipe up twice every day, morning and night, so dirt and smells should not accumulate.

She showed me how to caress visible areas such as hands, face and hair with low whispers and soft fingertips along my face, my throat, my palms, my knuckles, and my wrists. Then she told me to do the same to her, and I imagined my mistress's soft skin responding to my touch and found myself uncontrollably aroused, but she told me to stop. She told me that if I wanted to be gentle, I had to learn to control my impulses, otherwise I would only be searching for my own selfish release, not her pleasure. She reminded me to always touch her softly, and be mindful of her mood and her needs.

The following Sunday she taught me how to kiss her lips, teasing slowly, probing softly, then deepening and pulling rhythmically, until I was breathless with excitement. I was not sure if I would ever get this far with my mistress, but I had to be prepared in case my dream came true. When I was finally allowed to release the tension of the previous Sundays, she told me I had been too clumsy and quick, and I apologized for losing control. The following weeks she taught me to be in command of my force and rhythm in order to please her, instead of myself.

"Which type of woman are you, Jenny?" I asked after my last lesson.

"I always say I'm the rough type, because most men aren't patient enough to cater for the tender types. They are in a hurry to please themselves and don't care much for caressing. They just get on with the last stage right away, then they're over quick as lightning, and get out with a grunt for a thank you."

"Is it not painful?"

"Sometimes it is. Some are big, heavy, and brutish, but they're usually over quick. They don't mean no harm, they don't think I'm a person with feelings, too. I'm just a doll to please them most of the time. Fortunately, I can pick and choose, and I don't have to accept the favours very often. As soon as my children get a proper job and can fend for themselves, I won't never have to do it again. I can pay for my own food and lodging with my honest earnings. I might even find a nice gentleman, who might want to make an honest woman of me and have me all for himself!"

She asked me if I wanted to be rough with her too, to try it, but I declined. I had learned what I needed to know. There was only one lady I would ever lie with again, and that was my mistress. I gave Jenny a present the last Sunday I saw her. It was a bone china vase with a white rose. She cried saying no one had ever given her a present before and put it on the dining table. I told her I would not visit again, because I did not want to hurt her. I feared she might become too attached. She had told me herself that once a woman surrenders voluntarily to a man, he remains in her heart forever, and she was surrendering far too willingly in our last meetings. I pray for Jenny every night and hope she will find a good man who loves her and treats her well, because she deserves to be happy.

Once she told me she had been to Thornfield Hall, many years ago. Mrs. Leah had employed her for a special occasion. I asked her if she had ever met Mrs. Rochester and she replied that there was another Mrs. Rochester at that time, a monstrous lunatic. She said it had been a creepy place full of ghosts, devils, and secrets, and that I should be careful and not trust anyone there. When I told her Eyre Hall was not like Thornfield, she said she had heard of Eyre Hall and it sounded like a similar place, because Leah had called her again nine years ago due to another appalling secret. She told me she felt very sorry for both Mrs. Rochesters, and insisted I should be very careful with Mr. Rochester, who was a very powerful and unscrupulous man. I reminded her that he was currently an invalid on his deathbed.

I stopped seeing Jenny some months ago. I live every day in the hope that I will be able to show my mistress how much I love her and compensate for her unhappy marriage

Chapter IV

Bertha's Baby

I examined Mrs. Rochester under Adele's attentive scrutiny. First, I palpated her pulse at the radial artery, in order to check for any signs of hysteria. I observed a regular rhythm and counted seventy beats, which was within the expected range. She seemed calm enough. I then proceeded to use my newly acquired binaural stethoscope, in order to listen to the internal sounds of her lungs, heart, and bowels. I applied the cylinder to the patient and connected the ivory earpieces at the end of the two flexible extremities to my ears. I heard no wheezing or abnormal sounds in the first two organs, only clear rhythmical reverberations, which clearly indicated that everything was in order. The third presented a noisier activity, which I also deemed normal for the time of day. I pronounced her quite recovered and recommended rest. When I had finished, Mrs. Rochester said she desired to speak to me privately and Adele left gracefully. I wondered what her mysterious business with me was. Surprisingly, she started asking me about my son.

"How is Harold progressing at Oxford?"

"Very well. Mrs. Carter and I are most pleased with his evolution. He is soon to finish his training as physician at Oxford, and we hope he will go to Edinburgh or London to acquire some experience before setting up his own practice in this area. Perhaps in Hay or Millcote. He is our only son, and Mrs. Carter would not like to see him settle down too far from home."

"It must please you greatly. I am sure you are proud of his achievements."

"We both feel blessed on this account."

She scrutinised me curiously and asked a strange question.

"Do you enjoy living at Ferndean, Dr. Carter?"

"Indeed we do, Mrs. Rochester. It is a most comfortable lodging."

"How long have you lodged there?"

"Mr. Rochester was kind enough to rent it to us nine years ago."

"I believe your present payment is very reasonable, is it not?"

"I have no complaints, and I hope you have no complaints regarding my loyalty to the Rochester family."

She curled her lips into a taut smile and pierced my eyes with an intimidating look. I felt uneasy. I had had little direct contact with the mistress of the house. My allegiance had been with her husband since we were children. My father was one of his most prosperous tenant farmers, so I was able to attend the same Grammar School at Millcote, as the two young Rochesters did. I remember the tragic and languid Rowland, who took after his mother, Rose Fairfax, and high spirited Edward, who was the astute old master's duplicate. I had served Edward loyally since our school days, convinced that he would inherit the estate and reward me accordingly, which he had always done. I followed Edward's suggestion and trained with the local surgeon, who was childless and close to retirement.

Mr. Rochester was a powerful ally. He possessed over a thousand acres of land from Eyre Hall to Millcote. Almost all the inhabitants were landless and had been so for centuries. Ingram Park, ten miles west of Millcote, was the nearest great estate, and there was another smaller estate, the Leas, held by the Eshtons some miles to the north. The rest of the land, including the greatest part of Millcote, was owned by the Rochesters, who rented out to tenant farmers, skilled labourers, and professionals. I myself had a three-generation leasehold on a modest two room cottage in Hay, until Mr. Rochester kindly offered my family the possibility of taking up residence in his Manor House, Ferndean, which he had used mainly as a hunting lodge until his health and Mrs. Rochester's dislike of the sport led him to relinquish its use.

"The rent you pay for Ferndean is less than a maid's salary."

She had obviously been looking into the accounts, as her husband lay agonizing. Perhaps she was shrewder than I had thought.

"Mr. Rochester has been most generous."

"At the moment, Mr. Briggs has informed me that you have a verbal agreement with Mr. Rochester."

"That is correct, madam."

"One could make a larger profit on it by increasing the rent, could one not, Mr. Carter?"

"One could, madam."

"One could also offer leaseholds or sell to new investors. There are many prosperous local mill owners, wire manufacturers, and wealthy town dwellers, not to mention Londoners, who would no doubt enjoy the prospect of a rural Manor House for the hunting season. Don't you think?"

"No doubt there would be interested candidates."

"Of course, I could also offer you a reasonably priced leasehold on Ferndean, for say, 99 years, which would safely look after your son's and grandson's future, would it not?"

"It would, indeed."

"Dr. Carter, I will speak frankly to you. I need to know..." she paused to thrust a daggered look, "to be sure..." another fierce pause, "that you will be as loyal to me and my son as you are to Mr. Rochester."

"I implore you most earnestly, madam, do not doubt my unconditional loyalty to you both."

"You will start proving your loyalty this minute, and I warn you, no more secrets!"

"You have my word."

"Tell me about Bertha's daughter."

I had known this moment would come sooner or later, but even so, I was not prepared. Drops of sweat gathered on my forehead, and slid down my temples, drenching my sideburns. I took out my crumpled kerchief and wiped my face, wondering in a desperate frenzy how much she knew. Could she know how often and in how many matters I had been useful to Mr. Rochester, and been ordered not to inform anyone, least of all his wife? What would she do if she discovered the full extent of my connivance with Edward? The greatest secret was still withheld, but for how long?

"I promised Mr. Rochester the incident would never be mentioned."

"Well, the incident, as you call it, has grown into gigantic proportions, and she is here now."

"Here, madam?"

"At the Rochester Arms. The infamous vulture Mr. Mason has brought the incident from Spanish Town, Jamaica, to meet her uncle and benefactor before he dies."

"I never trusted him."

"Did you assist the birth of the child?"

"I did, I mean I did not. The child had already been born when I arrived."

"Tell me everything you remember about the event."

"Grace Poole said she had woken to find the lunatic writhing with pain, screaming and bleeding until a baby was produced. She cut the cord, knotted it, and informed Mrs. Fairfax, who called me forthwith."

"Did you not notice she was with child?"

"I visited the patient regularly, but rarely examined her physically. Her malady was mental not physical. She was in good physical health. I had noticed she had grown heavier, but Mrs. Poole informed me that she ate voraciously, and the master ordered she be fed, if she so wished."

"Tell me about Bertha's illness."

"When Mr. Rochester returned from Jamaica, he brought her with him as his legal wife, whom we both know he had been tricked into marrying. I was not qualified to deal with severe mental derangement, so I recommended an eminent London psychiatrist. She was diagnosed with hysteria due to nymphomania, which is a type of hysteria brought on by obscene sexual deviations. Another tragic case of moral weakness leading to moral insanity, I'm afraid. Only Mrs. Fairfax and I knew of her existence at first. Then Grace Poole was employed to look after her, and although there was gossip, her presence at Thornfield was a well-kept secret.

"Her condition worsened, in spite of the medication. The hysterical and violent attacks did not cease, so she was removed to the attic to protect herself, and those around her. I urged Mr. Rochester to have her transferred to an institution, but when we visited one such place called Stonehill Retreat, you may have heard of it, it is some twenty miles from Millcote, he was adamant that she should not be removed there on any account.

"I must admit, I agreed with him. It was an infernal place at the time. They showed us a reclusion room, she would have been enclosed due to her destructive nature. There was a naked woman chained in manacles, sitting on her own excrement, and howling like a werewolf for six days a week. On the seventh day, their cells were cleaned. They were washed down with cold water and returned for another six days, and so on, for the rest of their days.

"He kept her at Thornfield out of humanity, madam. Although you saw yourself the harm she could do, you were in the house when she attacked her brother, Mr. Mason, with a knife, whilst the house was full of guests. You stayed with him while I was called and took him to my cottage, in order to cure his wounds discreetly."

She nodded in bewilderment, and I was relieved to watch her horrified expression, which meant she had believed my exaggerated narration. I had described a state asylum I had once visited in London, in my youth. I knew Stonehill was a private and expensive institution, which was much more humane in the treatment of its inmates.

If Mrs. Rochester ever even suspected that I had advised Mr. Rochester to have her secluded at Stonehill for a short spell, just eight years ago, for postnatal depression, I would no doubt have to leave the county, and it would be our ruin. I had not a penny to my name. All my finances had been invested in my son's education, the upkeep of Ferndean, which had obliged us to employ servants, and entertaining guests in order to secure our social position.

Mrs. Rochester insisted with more questions.

"When was the child born?"

"Twenty-three years ago, madam, I remember you were at Thornfield at the time, working as governess to Adele. The night she attacked Mason, she must have been enraged, because the infant had been taken away."

"Who is the father of the child?"

"I do not know. I believe nobody knows. When I informed Mr. Rochester, I solemnly promise that I never saw a man so amazed and shocked at a piece of news. There is no doubt in my mind that Mr. Rochester is not the father. Mr. Rochester was often away for months. Men regularly entered the house, the postman, the butcher, and the servants. When Mr. Rochester was at home, there were his guests and their valets. Grace Poole, as you may remember was loyal but unreliable, no doubt due to her fondness of gin. I often warned Mr. Rochester, and he had on occasions asked Mrs. Fairfax to see to a replacement, unproductively."

"What happened after the child was born?"

"Her brother, Mr. Mason, was informed forthwith. He was in London on business at the time, and he travelled to Thornfield instantly. Mr. Mason was unmarried, but surprisingly, he accorded to take the child with him to Jamaica and Mr. Rochester agreed. He hired a wet nurse from Millcote and took them both with him to Spanish Town shortly after. The child has never been mentioned to me since that day."

"Why did Mr. Rochester send money regularly for the child's upbringing?"

"I'm afraid I do not know the answer to that question, Mrs. Rochester. I presume he felt responsible for the situation, after all, she had been under his care at the time of birth."

"Indeed she had."

"Mrs. Rochester, please find it in your heart to understand the compassionate reasons behind Mr. Rochester's actions, and accept my sincere apologies if my loyalty in keeping this secret has given you cause for concern."

"No more secrets, Dr. Carter. I warn you."

"Rest assured, I will be your most humble ally from this moment on."

"Thank you, Dr. Carter. I am sure we will get along now that we understand each other. Shall we go upstairs to see how Mr. Rochester is today?"

Chapter V

Mr. Rochester

When the doctor left, Jane asked me if I was tired, or if I would like her to read to me. She looked uneasy and unusually severe. I wondered if she were unwell. She told me she had had a "peculiar" morning, unwilling to give me any further information. When I insisted, she said "later" without even attempting a smile and looked at me for some minutes with pursed lips. I knew not what to say, being weary and unwell myself, so I was silent.

Lately, since my illness, Jane had changed. She had become more distant and less inclined to spend time with me. Although she visited me every day, several times, she never stayed long, finding excuses for being somewhere else and doing something more important. She had to dispatch with Leah regarding the running of the house, or she had to help Adele with her absurd suitors, childish tantrums, or ridiculous poems and letters. On other occasions, she was discoursing with the curator or the teacher at the parish Sunday school, or worst of all, spending time at that damned filthy charity hospice she was involved in, which was taking up far too much of her time.

She would no longer allow me my marital rights, which I could understand and tolerate due to the nature of my malady. Although it had not been my fault, some unscrupulous London whore had seduced me and infected me, maliciously. I noticed late this evening she begrudged me her hand to hold and seemed moody and reproachful, which was so unlike her. I believe she is behaving most ungratefully towards an ailing husband, after all the love and lavishing I have given her in the last twenty-three years.

She held my quizzical look for some more instants, hesitated, and finally spoke in a very businesslike manner.

"I should like to read you some psalms today, Edward."

I thought it would be best to humour her. What else could I do? I supposed they would hold a key to what she wanted to say. I was trapped. Where was I to go? What was I to say? Deprived of my strength, of my youth, and of my body, I answered lamely.

"Thank you, my dearest. I would like that. But come here and sit with me and hold my hand."

"The candle is too far. I cannot see well enough. I shall sit on the chair."

She was facing me with tight jaws. I fancied that the light shone more on my face than on her book. The charcoal candle shadows flickered between us against the orange light, like dancing demons. She started reading quietly. She read twenty psalms. When she finished, she closed the sacred book and scrutinised my visage.

"I must speak to you on a delicate matter, Edward."

"Of course, my dearest." I was in no mood to speak, but I had no choice but to humour her.

"Someone called to visit you today. Is there anything you'd like to tell me about your first wife that I do not know yet?"

Cruel wench! She knows I am unwell. She would never have spoken to me thus, if I were not so feeble. In my final days, I must be helplessly tied to this bed, and to her capricious whims.

"Why do you importune me thus, Jane?"

"Why does it displease you, Edward?"

"Because I am sick and dying. Is that a good reason, Jane? Or do you want another reason?"

"Another, I'm afraid." She pronounced the words far too softly. I could tell she was enraged.

"Speak, Jane. I'm not in the mood for games."

"Mr. Mason called today."

"Mason? That devil! What did he want?"

"He wants you to meet someone."

"Never!"

"You know who the person is, then?"

She was watching me like a hawk, waiting for a reply. I thought she understood that woman and her brother were conniving sorcerers. They had conspired to ruin my life, our life together.

"She is nothing to me." I sighed.

"Are you sure?" She replied softly, almost inaudibly.

"Absolutely. There is no doubt about it, Jane. I swear..."

"Stop!" She interrupted me viciously. "Be careful what you say. There may not be time to confess on this occasion."

She cannot consider herself innocent of what happened at Thornfield. She led me mischievously. She teased me with her presence, her witty tongue, and tantalized me with her elflike, ethereal beauty. I breathed Jane Eyre, saw through her eyes, did what she wanted me to do, told her only what she wanted to hear. She did not want to know about a ghost of the past. She knew there was someone in the attic, all the servants knew, but she wasn't interested. She, too, looked the other way. I writhed in my bed. What was she thinking while she observed me so piercingly, so mercilessly? Whatever I did was for her, to be with her, to make her happy, and this was how I was to be repaid?

"Would you speak to me like this, because I am old and sick?"

"You know that is not true. I nursed you back to life after the accident, and I will nurse you now, as long as you need me."

"Come to me, Jane, you are still my angel. I have never loved anyone except you, never. Everything I have is yours. I have bequeathed everything I have to you. You will be my sole heiress until John is thirty, and even then you will retain a life interest in Eyre Hall."

"I thank you earnestly for the wonderful years we have spent together, and for all the love you gave me once, and in honour of that love, which I also professed to you, I will stay by your side to the end of your days. But you know after all that has happened, I can no longer love you as I once did, as you would like me to. Remember you stopped loving me first, Edward."

How could Jane be so heartless and indifferent to my supplications?

"I need to speak to you frankly, Edward. The matter is urgent and important. The child is in England, at the Rochester Arms. Mason has come to claim her dowry. He wants to find a husband for her. She wishes to settle down in England."

"Never!"

"And one more thing, he wants the generous donation to St. Mary's Convent to be recommenced. What were you thinking of when you told me I need not continue sending the money?"

"I didn't think it would matter after so many years. I thought she might be wed already… I thought she had died, I thought…"

"You thought… Why did you lie to me?"

"I did not lie to you. I tell you I have nothing to do with that creature! Ignore his intimidation, Jane. You were never one to shy away from a problem."

"This is not a problem. There are people involved. People I love dearly. He has threatened to speak."

"Bastard! It is a lie. He has no proof."

"But she is Bertha's daughter?"

"Yes."

"Born while you were married?"

"Yes."

"What is there to prove?"

"I tell you I am not the father."

"Perhaps you speak the truth."

"I never lied! I protected you from the truth, Jane! I wanted to protect you from her!"

"You were not successful, because she is here, breathing, walking, eating, speaking, and just two miles away from us."

"I tell you she is not my daughter!"

"But she was born while you were legally married to her mother. Surely you are then responsible. She was your wife and under your care due to her illness."

"I will not take responsibility for her lascivious nature. You don't know what she tried to do to me in Coloubri. She and her slave,

Christine, worked their heathen magic on me. They tried to destroy my soul!"

"Maybe, but as I remember, she was a prisoner under lock and key in Thornfield."

"She found her way out on occasions, as you yourself witnessed the night she tried to burn me. You told me yourself you heard her cries in the attic and saw her shadows in the corridors."

"And you all lied to me then. You told me it was Grace Poole, who happened to be her incompetent carer."

"Everybody knew, but no one dared speak. You must have known, deep down, that she was there, all along. Tell me you knew, Jane."

"I did not know you were married, or I should have left Thornfield the day I met you and fell in love."

"Jane, we were meant to be together. Don't let her come between us once more. I tell you, I promise you, I am not the father of that creature."

"Then it was a guest at your house? Someone who had easy access to her room? And permission to enter and force her?"

"I'm sure there was no force. She complied. It was in her nature."

"You must know who could have visited her in her jail. He must take responsibility for his actions."

"Frankly, I didn't care then, and I care even less now."

"The damage must be repaired. The rumour will not be spread."

"I am past caring about rumours."

"It will ruin your son's reputation."

"He has enough money not to worry about that."

"His engagement to Miss Elizabeth Harwood may be affected."

"He will find another suitable wife. He is a good catch."

"But she is Judge Harwood's daughter, and he will help him in his Parliamentary career."

"He needn't work. In fact, he shouldn't work. He is a gentleman. No one in my family has ever worked. He has land and property. He is a Rochester, we do not need to work. We have tenants, and income from the colonies, and fortune. Surely you must know that by now, Jane?"

"But he wants to work. He wants to do a service to society, to improve the quality of our lives."

"Those are the insane revolutionary ideas you have put into his head. It will do him good to forget about working in London. He belongs here, at Eyre Hall. He must manage the Rochester land and properties."

"I don't want him to ignore his ancestral heritage and obligations. He can do both. He is a very intelligent, hardworking, and capable young man."

"He will have to live with gossip and scandal, all the Rochesters have."

"You don't care when the scandal explodes, because it will no longer affect you. Think of your son, Edward. Think of me. I have endured enough gossip and pain on your behalf. Your first wife, her death, your London life and friends, your solitary visits to Ferndean and the Ingrams, now this other daughter, and God knows what else. I have a feeling there is more you must yet confess to before you are taken by our Lord."

"You exaggerate, madam."

"You are selfish, sir."

"I am tired of this conversation. I need my rest. Leave."

"As you wish, but she will dine here on All Hallows, and you will come down to dinner to meet her."

"I shall not."

"Everyone believes you are her kind benefactor and uncle."

"Leave!"

"Unless of course you tell me the man who is responsible for her existence, you will be held responsible for your actions or carelessness with your first wife's wellbeing."

"Get out, I said!"

"I will carry your burden once more, but you will carry yours, too, while you are still among us. Good morning, Edward."

"Out!"

She walked towards the door coolly and turned back to me as she pulled the handle towards her.

"Simon will bring up your lunch shortly, and I will come back to see you later. Please think about what I have told you."

The devil in her smiled, for the first time since she had entered my chamber. I thought she was different, but she's like the others, deceitful and cunning. I would never have believed that she could be so satanical. My beautiful, pure Jane. My angel. How dare she speak to me in that manner? Where is my darling? Where is the innocent, helpless, and charming little elf I fell in love with twenty-three years ago?

Our relationship has gone through many phases. We were happily married at first, as she nursed me back to health after the fire. She was my arms, my legs, my eyes, my very self extended. My eyesight improved in the only available eye left, which enabled me to go about my life in an almost autonomous manner. I also gradually recovered the strength in my limbs. In spite of the pain in my leg, causing my unbecoming limp, I could walk independently and fairly long distances. My arms regained enough strength to carry a walking stick or even a bag, if needed. I felt myself again, or almost. Jane at my side, at every second, was my greatest aid and incentive. We were in love and able to show it freely for the first time. I could hardly keep my hands away from her, chasing her around the gardens, the bedroom, or wherever we were. She told me that I should be calmer, but I only wanted to feel her and be with her every second of the day, and she acquiesced most of the time.

Our blissful honeymoon lasted longer than I had expected, but it ended the day she discovered she was with child. I thought things would improve after the child was born, but inexplicably matters worsened. After the baby's birth twenty-one years ago, she always had other, more important things to do. First it was the baby, who cried all day long. She moved to another chamber, it was impossible to sleep with its cat-like screeching, which protracted into the night. Then during the day, she was always busy with it. I pleaded for her to get a wet nurse, but she wouldn't have it. Damned stubborn witch that she was, she said it was a degrading and oppressive way to treat women. And I reminded her that it also allowed them to feed their own unfortunate offspring, and do something useful in life.

When she was pregnant again, God knows how, for little time did she spend in my bed, I was most annoyed. I was sure of the consequences. I wouldn't have it. I prayed every day that she would miscarry, and she did, the first time. After that, she returned to my bed regularly, and I understood that it had been my greatest blessing. John was no longer breast feeding and she was mine again, as she had been before. I would say even more mine than before, a lust had worked up in her, which was as unusual as it was gratifying to me. It lasted three short months until she became pregnant again.

She seemed to know, as much as I did, that a little roughness might disintegrate the creature, so she left my chamber once more for the nine months of the pregnancy. Being the witch that she was, she knew immediately the child was conceived, and refused to return to my bed, as was her duty. I realized then that she had been seducing me for an ulterior motive, another pregnancy had been her objective all the time. How stupid of me not to realize she was using me for her own benefit once more, that every time we lay together, her frenzied limbs were entwining me for the devious purpose of another son. I felt betrayed.

Another two years of deprivation was far more than I was prepared to accept. I made sure she would be suitably punished. This time she did not miscarry, however the child, a skinny, ghostly looking female creature, was stillborn. That was her punishment, and my victory. No breast feeding and no child meant she would return to my bed and entice me once more. No matter how hard she tried, she would have no more children. Her fate and theirs had been decided.

Unpredictable as the human mind is, I could not have foreseen what would ensue. How feeble women are, and how easy it is to sway their mental balance will never cease to amaze me. At first, I thought I would have to have another attic built to accommodate her madness. Fortunately, Carter advised caution and suggested it was something called "post-natal depression," and that we should be patient. Doctors will invent anything to swindle money out of gullible patients. I told him I didn't care what it was called, or what caused it, either she recovered her former self, or he could find somewhere else to hide her away. I would no longer accept mad women under my roof.

Fortunately, the good doctor came up with a small miracle called laudanum. It did the trick. She seemed to eat less, and grow more agitated at times, but she was cheerful most of the day. She even returned to my bed, much more compliant and submissively than ever before. Another profit was she rarely argued any more. In fact, she spoke little. As if her mind had clouded up, somewhat, freeing her from the inner demons, which undoubtedly came from thinking too much about what could have been, but would never be. Those were a happy two years. I made sure she was regularly purged with a vinegar solution, so if she ever was with child, nothing would come of it. Adele looked after John most of the time (Jane wouldn't have a governess anywhere near the house), and Leah took care of the running of the house, proving to be just as loyal as Mrs. Fairfax had been.

Every morning I would wake up late to the feel of her soft sinful flesh, smothered by her iniquitous hair, inebriated by her briny fruitful vine, and besotted by the spell she had cast on me. After a hearty breakfast, we would take long walks with Piper. Pilot had died due to an unfortunate fight with a fox. Once more we would spend hours just stroking each other's hair, caressing our faces, and sometimes even rolling on the damp meadows, if the weather permitted. After a light lunch, we would retire once more to our chambers and indulge in each other. Often she was too tired to respond, but she was even more tired to resist, so I was able to indulge at my leisure. She never complained that I wanted her too much, and I wanted her so much. I needed her so much.

No woman had ever loved me with such honest and disinterested devotion as Jane. I have no recollection of my mother, having died when I was in my infancy. My father attended to my elder brother, who was exactly what he expected in a son. He was tall, fair, and blue eyed like my mother, cheerful yet sober, always more docile and refined. I grew up as an ugly duckling and second best, short-tempered and dark like my father, having to suffer the humiliation of exile and marriage to a Creole heiress.

I had thought Bertha, my future wife, was English, like her brother and father. Her mother, Mrs. Annette Mason, had been clever enough to procure two English husbands for herself. Mr. Cosway, Bertha's father, was the first, and Mr. Mason, Richard's father was the second. So when I arrived in Jamaica, I learned Bertha was Richard's half-sister, his father's second wife's spawn. Richard's father had been generous enough to honour Bertha and her mother with his surname, but in spite of her two English surnames, Bertha née Cosway, later Mason, was Creole, like her mother. They were a race apart, retaining their singular half breed features and mind. In spite of their pathetic attempts to become English, their mongrel madness and beauty is passed on like a curse, to all women. My Jane was a different woman, a pure entirely English breed of serene beauty and quiet strength. I have had many women in my life, but I have never loved any other woman as I have loved Jane Eyre.

In the afternoons, after napping, she would go down to the drawing room and sit at her desk and write. She told me she was writing a book. I thought it was a playful, useless thing to do, and it only took up a few hours in the evenings. It also kept her away from John. She had been too obsessed with him. Mothers should not spend too much time with their male offspring, or they soften their minds, and their spirits become feminized, idle, and oversensitive. More writing also led to less speaking, which meant she was no longer so inclined to argue with me.

When I saw an absent look cover her visage and asked what she was thinking of, she would say she was pondering upon her book. I humoured her. One day she said she had finished it and asked me if I wanted to read it. I saw no harm in it, so I did. It was indeed a beautiful book. It was a love story, the story about her love for me.

The novel really begins with the moment we met and finishes when we marry and have our first son. I asked her to change a few things. She resisted at first, but I easily convinced her that my honourable motives should be clearly explained, lest I should come across as a heartless materialist. I reminded her that my childhood had also been harsh, and when I returned from Spanish Town to Thornfield, I was alone in the world. My family had died, my wife had gone mad. I had no one except Mrs. Fairfax, whom she guessed was my aunt, having married my mother's brother.

I reminded her that I had cared for Bertha while everyone else had abandoned her, including her own family. I suggested she clarify how I had become a better person after the accident and our reunion. The ending should be as positive as possible, showing the best of me and our marriage. She agreed, and my appreciation was right, it became very successful. Fortunately, she published under a pseudonym, James Elliot, and we were not often molested by the press. She always hated London or being in the public eye. I saw to it that most people in London knew my wife had written a very descriptive biography of me, but she was rarely willing to speak about it publicly or accompany me to London. I even led some to believe I might have been the writer myself, due to its bold and manly roughness and language. This I naturally did to protect her from curious intruders.

She wanted to write another novel about workhouses, governesses, orphans and the like, which I strongly discouraged. A certain Mr. Dickens was doing enough of that in a most vulgar way, and I did not want my wife pursuing such liberal endeavours.

In the evenings, after dinner, Adele and John would join us for a while. Jane would play the piano or draw. I would read or listen to her play, sometimes I would sing, as I had done in my youth. Later, in our chamber, I would tease her with her nightly dose of laudanum, giving her each drop individually, asking for my reward in so doing, until I was satisfied with her pleading and submission. Sometimes, if I were pleased enough, or if she begged enough, I added some more drops to ensure a good night's sleep. Others I would give her less, so that she awoke in the night, restless and disarmingly lascivious until she got everything she needed from me. She enjoyed those memorable nights far more than I did, seeming insatiable at times.

Once more, my years of happiness did not last long. Following the publication and success, she ate less, and became more irritable. I was away in London more often, dealing with publishers and critics. She obviously missed me and substituted my absence with more laudanum, unaware of how dangerous a substance it was when used carelessly. I had always been careful to supply the minimum dose, but she must have overlooked my advice.

When her cousin Mary came to visit, she was much surprised and shocked by Jane's excessive loss of weight and the cough, which seemed to accompany her all day long. Both Dr. Carter and I protested, but Mary insisted, and against my wishes took her away without her medicine. I knew the worst was to come. She would convulse, get worse, and either become a lifelong lunatic or take her life. Laudanum was a one way street. I knew that, but it was good for her, it made her a better person, and it gave her a new life. What did she have before it? Misery? Pain? Loss? The dead wimp she had given birth to visited her dreams nightly, followed her around the house during the day, calling "mummy" in the afternoons, and playing hide and seek in the evenings. She was convinced the creature was alive! She would have lost her reason without her medicine.

Carter had tried to convince me to send her to an institution, but I refused. I had already had a mad wife, and I preferred a drugged wife to a lunatic, but Mary was not in agreement. Her husband, the self-righteous clergyman, Mr. Wharton, was of the opinion that God was to be her saviour. What had God ever saved her from? If it hadn't been for me, she would be sweating in India with her mystical cousin, surrounded by little black, devilish children. No more laudanum, Mary and her husband sentenced. When I told her of my misgivings regarding Jane's future without the miraculous substance, she offered to take care of Jane, if she became permanently indisposed. On that argument, I agreed.

Jane cried bitterly, grabbing my clothes wildly, whispering in my ear that she needed my love, and begging me to take her up to our chamber for a nap. When I refused, she dropped to her knees, hugging my legs and shouting she loved me, and accusing me of killing her. It was a pitiful scene. If I could call Cronus to reverse the handles on the clock of time, and I were to return to that moment, she would not leave, because that was the last time I saw my beloved, meek, Jane.

She was brought back to me some months later. But the person who returned was not my Jane. It was another woman. A woman who had decided God had saved her and that she should repay him. She moved out of my chambers again, back with John, making him into a spineless intellectual. She spent all day looking after him, hugging him, reading to him, and pandering to him. What was left of the day was spent with Adele, reading, writing poetry, and letters. She took to attending daily services at Mr. Wood's chapel, and running a Sunday school for children who worked during the week. She also set up two parish schools, one in Hay for the local tenants' children, and another in Millcote for millworkers' children.

She insisted that John should attend Rugby, instead of the local grammar school as I had done, because she wanted him to go to Oxford. I told her that no Rochester had ever been to university, or needed to work for a living. He had the tenants and the land, what more could he possibly need? If that wasn't reason enough to infuriate me, she refused to obey me and constantly tried to convert me to her way of seeing the world, because she said it would save me. I need no saving, except from her madness! She said she had been reborn, and her role was to help fallen women, so she contacted Mr. Dickens, even visited him in London, and planned to embark on her useless hospice for poor flappers, but I put my foot down on that occasion.

Thus have been my last ten years, reader, no wonder I took to London, to the opera, the theatre, my club, my gay friends. What was I to do? My wife had taken to a world of nunnery, completely ignoring my needs. Now that I am sick in bed and in my last days, my demons are come to haunt me. My health is frail, I am no longer strong, my wife defies me, my mad Creole wife returns to haunt me yet again, and what else is in store for me? Why can I not rest in peace? Why must I always be reminded of what I wish to forget? I refuse to recollect things that should never have happened in my final moments. I want some peace! Is that too much to ask for?

Chapter VI

Daphne's Tale

That evening Miss Adele and Mrs. Rochester had dinner early, at 7:30, then Miss Adele went up to write her letters. When I returned to the dining room to withdraw the plates, my mistress asked me to sit down with her at the table, because she needed to speak to me.

"Michael, Adele has informed me that you have collaborated with her in hiding her correspondence with Mr. Greenwood." She spoke sternly.

"It is true, Mrs. Rochester. I have no excuse. I am truly sorry if my conduct has offended you. Miss Adele insisted very much that it should be kept a secret, and I know Mr. Greenwood to be a respectable London author, according to the literary magazines in the library, that is why I agreed to help her."

"You have explained your reasons, and although your motivation is genuine, I am upset with your behaviour. In the future, I would like to be able to trust you to be loyal to me, before anyone else in this household. I do not like secrets. There have been too many. Do you understand, Michael? I thought I could trust you. I need to know I can trust you." She sounded upset, and I felt devastated that she should even consider I had let her down, so I replied as quickly and earnestly as I could.

"You can trust me, madam. Please forgive me. It will never happen again. You have my word. I would never ever do anything you would not approve of, madam. Never. You saved our lives. I, we owe you everything."

She must have realized how upset I was, because her face relaxed as it melted into a warm friendly smile.

"It is difficult to know what is on your mind. You speak so little, yet I am sure you have a great deal to say."

"I don't like speaking much. I prefer listening and reading."

"And writing? Adele also told me you helped her write poems."

"That is an exaggeration, madam. I only advised to the use of certain words. My mother read the sonnets of Shakespeare and Sydney. We copied them, all of them, and read them, many by heart, so I am acquainted with the vocabulary and style."

"Do you like reading novels, too, or only poetry?"

"Although I read mainly poetry and the Bible, I also enjoy reading prose. I have read *Pilgrim's Progress,* and I enjoy reading Mr. Charles Dickens' novels. I read your novel, *Daphne,* too, madam."

"You did?"

"Adele gave me a copy to read and let me keep it. I enjoyed it very much."

"What was it about the novel that you liked?"

"I liked the way in which it was written, and the plot was cleverly disclosed. Anyone who starts reading will want to finish it, to know how it ends."

She looked at me placidly, as if she wished me to continue, so I did. I had wanted to talk to her about the novel many times.

"None of the characters are who they seem to be. For example, Daphne, the narrator, appears to be an innocent and naive young governess, but really she's the strongest character, standing by the man she loves throughout the tragic events, and helping him to pull through. Jessica, the deceased wife, whom everyone seemed to admire, was really an unstable lunatic, who was also driving her husband and daughter to insanity. She is the evil character. On the other hand, Leonard appears to be a desolate widower, but the truth is, he is glad his wife has died, although he feels guilty because of his feelings. Amy, their only daughter, who seems to hate her father and love her mother, was actually terrified of her mother and loved her unapproachable father. I liked the way their real motivations and feelings evolve gradually throughout the novel."

"Life is quite like that, don't you think? Nothing is what it first appears to be."

"It depends. In my world, most people are what they appear. I think it's in the secluded world behind the fortress-like walls of the ancient mansion where masquerades are encouraged. I'm glad the novel ends with reality and truth."

"And what is the reality and truth of the novel?"

"The truth is uncovered the day Jessica's body is discovered on the beach. The real facts regarding her life and death are disclosed. Leonard is able to tell his story, and thereby, he is freed from his guilt. Amy can understand, forgive, and bid her mother farewell. Jessica's body is buried at last, albeit in unblessed ground, and the ghost leaves the house to roam in purgatory. Daphne and Leonard are able to admit their love and are finally free to marry."

"Many critics disliked my ending. Some said it was immoral, because Leonard was absolved of covering up Jessica's suicide and concocting the funeral farce, which was an affront to the sacred sacrament. Others considered that the relationship between the governess and the master was improper, especially with a young girl in the house. Of course many critics saw the novel's strong points, some of which you have pointed out. In any case, all the fuss made me decide I would not write another novel."

She paused and turned away looking into the hearth absently, "I'm not sure Leonard was innocent anymore."

The flames danced on her contorted face.

"You could clarify that aspect with a sequel. What happened to their marriage?"

"No sequel is needed. In the last pages I explained exactly what happened after the marriage. They had two sons and lived happily ever after. Amen."

"In the real world a marriage is never an end. It is a new beginning."

"Not in this case. I'm quite sure. No sequel. No more novels. I wrote the novel at a difficult time in my life, after my daughter was stillborn. In spite of its success, it brings unpleasant memories."

Her thoughts wandered with her eyes, this time to the window fixing themselves somewhere on the leafy horizon. I was sure she would write another novel, and I had my heart set on being one of the main characters.

She signed and turned back to me, ruffling her dress, as she did when she was agitated.

"Once we have found Susan a suitable occupation, we will have to find one for you, Michael. Perhaps Adele is right, and you are wasted here at Eyre Hall. Have you thought of religious studies? Clergymen are always needed all over the country, even overseas."

"I would not like to leave Eyre Hall, ever."

"Ever is a long time, Michael. Don't you miss London? You lived there with your family and later with your sister for some years."

"London is busy and noisy. There are too many people….. I would prefer to stay in the provinces, here in the north, at Eyre Hall."

"If you are so attached to this property and this area, perhaps you could stay nearby. Mr. Wood is advancing in age and will retire within a few years. Would you like to be his apprentice?"

"I have never thought of leading a religious life, madam. I like being a valet. I could become a butler, if ever you needed one, I mean. I would certainly never work in another household."

"Your loyalty is touching, but wouldn't you like to prepare Sunday sermons, advise parishioners, console the relatives of dead, and carry out baptisms, weddings, and funerals? You could help at the Sunday school or the parish school, too. Would you like to study at Oxford? I am sure you would pass the exams."

"Not if it means leaving Eyre Hall."

"There is a big world waiting for you, Michael. We cannot keep you in this secluded corner of the globe. You are silent, what is the matter?"

"You and everyone at Eyre Hall are the only family I know. I am not ready to leave... not yet..." I stopped speaking, realising I had spoken too anxiously, but I could not bear the thought of being sent away. She looked at me probingly for some seconds before speaking.

"I would miss you, too, Michael." She was silent once more and raised her hand to my face, as she had done years ago, when we first met. Her fingers caressed my cheek, arousing my longing heart. She looked as if she had recognised someone, lowered her hand abruptly, and rubbed her skirt before walking away from me towards the casements.

"It is still raining." She spoke softly, resting her forehead on the windowpane.

I wanted to get up and follow her, but I had been paralysed by her unexpected gesture. Eventually she turned back towards me and spoke stiffly.

"We can return to this conversation regarding your future later on. There is another matter I would like to speak to you about, Michael. It pertains to your sister, Susan. Adele would like Susan to accompany her to Italy. She may already have mentioned it to you."

"She has, Mrs. Rochester. When she showed me Mr. Greenwood's letter, in which he offered to take her to Italy, Miss Adele told me she could not go alone. I myself suggested she should take Susan with her."

"You did?"

"Yes, I did. My sister is very intelligent and well read, but she herself will never have the means to travel to the continent to further her education and knowledge. I think if she accompanies Adele, it would be an ideal opportunity for her. Susan she speaks a little French and Italian. My mother had an Italian grammar book, and she made us copy the translations of Dante's *Inferno*. I knew one day Italian would be useful to us. My mother had a great belief in the Lord. She reminded us that, 'The fear of the Lord is the beginning of knowledge, fools despise wisdom and instruction.' And said that everything we learned would come in useful one day, because knowledge would turn away evil and help us understand our paths in life."

"You were fortunate to have such a wise mother, Michael. You must miss her." Her expression became softer once more, and I replied too quickly.

"I used to, before I came to Eyre Hall."

Her expression changed once more and her hand moved. I knew she wanted to touch me again. I willed her to touch me again. I imagined her fingers caressing my cheeks, but this time, I would take her hand and kiss it.

"I'm glad you are contented here, Michael."

Her gaze was fixed on mine. The candle was waning, and the flames flickered on her face, illuminating her sparkling green eyes, which softened with a caring smile. I had never been so close to her while we looked into each other's eyes. I concentrated hard on the colour, which I would be recalling all through the night.

"You have grown since the first time I saw you. I can hardly remember the young boy I met at Diana's house five years ago."

I wanted to tell her that she had changed over the last five years, too. She had become more beautiful every day. I wanted to tell her I loved her, and I did. I told her silently with all my heart, as I smiled humbly. She heard me, but broke the spell by standing up and moving away again before speaking.

"Have you spoken to Susan about going to Italy with Adele?"

"Not yet, madam. Do you think I should?"

"Perhaps you could speak to her about it first, and tomorrow morning after breakfast, ask Susan to come to the drawing room. Adele and I will discuss the matter with her. I'm sure Adele would like to leave as soon as.... when Mr. Rochester ..."

Her eyes roamed to the window once more, hiding anxious thoughts behind her creased brows. I understood she wanted to be left alone, so I thanked her and left the room.

Minutes later, while we were having dinner downstairs in the kitchen, I was called up to the front door, the young master, John, had arrived unexpectedly. Mrs. Leah was most upset, because his bedroom was not prepared, cook had to make dinner for him, and Beth had already cleared up the stove and put the food in storage. Fortunately, the master was happy to have some sandwiches and some hot broth that remained on the stove, which I served while Daisy prepared his room.

I knew if I went to my chamber I would be unable to sleep. I would lie in bed for hours listening to the wind swaying the trees, and the rain beating against the roof and gushing down the casements. So instead, I sat at my desk reading through the papers Mr. Cooper had delivered. The names were all there and the numbers in neat even handwriting, but my mind kept wandering back to his hazel eyes, his hypnotizing look, and his captivating smile. Why did I touch him? Why did I need to touch him? Why did the thought of losing him alarm me so? Why did I feel agitated and anxious? Why did I feel the earth was moving under my feet and my head swirling?

I have noticed a peculiar feeling when he is near. I find myself searching for his thoughtful, pleasant countenance while I eat, write, or read. I am both contented and at ease in the safety of his gaze, and right now, just the thought of seeing him entering the room quickens my breathing. I must be losing my reason.

My son's arrival was a most pleasant surprise, which forced me out of my disquieting thoughts. "John, it is wonderful to see you! How long will you be staying?"

"We have been given a week's break for midterm."

"That's wonderful, darling! What will you do tomorrow?"

"I would like to visit Bishop Templar tomorrow morning. I have not seen him for months."

"That's a good idea, John. The Bishop is an intelligent and honest man. He has helped you and taught you well."

"Do you like him, Mother?"

"Of course I do. I told you, his opinions on social reform gave me much interest in starting my parish school work, and he has been such a positive influence on you."

"There are rumours, and many people who speak ill of him since he left Rugby."

"Do not pay attention to them, John. They are feeble minded and spiteful. We both know he is a good man."

"He would like to visit Father before ... it is too late. Can I invite him to come for dinner this week?"

"We will be having dinner guests the day after tomorrow, on All Hallows. It would be pleasant if the Bishop came, too."

"Annette Mason and her uncle?"

My flesh shuddered on hearing her name coming from my son's lips.

"What do you know about them?"

"I met her quite by chance. I nearly crushed her with my horse while she was walking from Hay in this direction, so I took her back to the inn."

I was too shocked to speak.

"She sprained her ankle and hit her head on a stone. She told me she was waiting to be invited to Eyre Hall."

"What else did she tell you?"

"She told me Father was her uncle by his first wife's deceased brother, and she wished to meet him."

I shuddered once more, feeling the blood drain from my head.

"Don't worry, Mother, Adele told me about Father's first marriage some time ago, but she made me promise that I would never tell you I knew. She said you wanted to forget and so did Father. But that was a long time ago. Who cares about that poor madwoman now?"

I was still speechless and quite dazed. It was too cruel to be true. They had already made their first move.

"I can see you are tired, Mother. Let's talk tomorrow. I will ride out in the morning to visit Bishop Templar and stay till the evening."

"I will tell Leah to prepare the Bishop's room. Ask him to stay for a few days. It will be too late to leave after dinner."

"Of course. How is Father? Can I see him? Everyone tells me he is well, but he looks worse every time I come."

"Dr. Carter has never lied about his condition. It is irreversible. We can only endeavour to avoid as much pain as we can. Unfortunately, that is all."

"I can't bear to think of him dying."

"There will be time to grieve. Now is the time to rejoice. He is alive, at the moment. There is no point in mourning ahead of time. He will be pleased to see you, I'm sure."

"Shall I go up now?"

"Wait until tomorrow morning. He is probably sleeping now. Go to the dining room, I'm sure Michael has brought you something to eat."

He bent down to kiss me before leaving. I was exhausted physically and mentally since Mason's visit. I sat at my desk and reread the first pages of my novel. Nobody knew about my new venture, and I wanted to keep it that way until it was completed. Simon's clumsy hands dropped the coal and the wood noisily while he lit the fire, spreading the soot and wood chippings around the carpet freely.

"Need anything else, ma'am?"

"No, Simon, thank you. Please attend Mr. Rochester, he is uneasy today. Make sure he is comfortable and has everything he needs."

Simon turned to leave, tripping up on the carpet and knocking over a china vase on the sideboard, which miraculously survived the fall, before shutting the door with a loud bang. I never understood what Edward saw in this clumsy young man. Of course after Mason's visit yesterday, everything was falling into place. The name sounded familiar when I saw it on the accounts. Monthly amount due to Miss Daisy Pickering: fifty pounds. Simon had told me when he first came that he had worked for an actress with that name. I never understood, until I saw her name on the accounts, why Edward had insisted on bringing him to Eyre Hall to work as a valet. Fortunately, he is patient and resourceful with Edward, and at least now he has learned to speak, so we can understand him, and he looks a great deal cleaner.

Michael returned moments later to ask me if I needed anything before retiring. He always looked so dependable and seemed so capable. He was the only person in the house I trusted completely. I wanted to ask him to sit down and listen to my heavy load and advise me about what to do, but instead I thanked him and asked him to kindle the fire and bring me some tea. I returned to my papers once more with his voice in my mind. When he returned, I spoke to him.

"Michael, would you sit down with me for a few minutes? I would like to talk to someone, and I'm afraid everyone has retired."

"Of course, Mrs. Rochester. A problem shared is a problem halved."

He smiled and I felt myself succumb and smile back. I sighed and relaxed. How could he make me feel so at ease, just by smiling at me?

"Imagine a person you love and trust is not the person you thought he was. You had imagined he was honest, noble, and worthy of your devotion, but you discover you were mistaken. He has not told you the truth. He has kept many secrets from you. There is one serious secret. The event happened a long time ago. It was an evil, heartless deed, which this person committed."

I waited for him to speak. He took his time.

"Sometimes there is a good intention behind a lie. Some lies are meant to avoid sorrow."

"But if the purpose of the lie is to conceal an evil deed and to make a person seem better than he really is, because he wants to hide a horrendous crime against a poor child and an innocent young girl? What if the aim of the lie is to cover up treachery? Once the secret is disclosed, there is no going back. It cannot be undone or unsaid. What can be done?"

He observed me quietly for some seconds before replying, "The person who has lied will be brought to justice. For God will bring every deed into judgment, with every secret thing, whether good or evil."

"I trust that will be the case, but what of those who remain? Who will assist those who have been deceived and wronged?"

"Perhaps something can be done by another nobler person to repair the event in some way?"

"Yes, I suppose there is something that can be done to repair it to some extent, but it would be most painful."

"Sometimes we have to suffer injustice and hard times, but the Lord upholds all that fall and raises up all those that are bowed down. The person who finds it in his or her heart to repair a wrong deed, even though it may bring some discomfort, will be rewarded."

"I wish it were easier to do good and to repair this particular deception."

"It would be even more difficult for a good person, as yourself, to do the wrong thing."

I heard the fire crackling and moved my arms closer, rubbing my palms. Michael shot up, brushing past my hands, and kindled the fire. I watched him busy himself and was thankful that he was with me. He turned and smiled, and suddenly Annette was no longer a problem. I felt the security that he could solve all of my troubles, or at least that I could cope with all my strife if Michael were by my side.

"Yes, that's what I thought, too."

"Can I help with anything else, Mrs. Rochester?"

"Are you good with numbers, Michael?"

"What kind of numbers?"

"Household accounts for example."

"Sometimes I help Mrs. Leah with the bookkeeping."

"I imagined someone must help her, the accounts are much more ordered of late."

Why had I not realised he was here to help me all along? How could I have ignored his worthiness?

"I wonder if you would help me with my accounts."

"I shall try, Mrs. Rochester."

"In the last few months Mr. Rochester's illness has worsened, and he has lost all concentration and most of his reason, I'm afraid. Mr. Cooper, his agent, has been running his financial affairs for years, since before we married. In fact, I think he also worked for his father. In any case, I would prefer to supervise the accounts myself, so I have asked Mr. Cooper to bring his books, and here they are."

I pointed to various thick leather bound books piled on my desk.

"I must ask for your absolute discretion. No one has seen any of these documents, except Mr. Cooper, Mr. Rochester, and me."

"Mrs. Rochester, you can trust me."

I knew it was true. I had always known I could depend on him, and now I needed him on my side and by my side.

"I am not satisfied with the way Mr. Cooper handles the accounts. I do not doubt his honesty, but his books seemed most unclear. I have started by making a list of the monthly expenses. Do you think you could check to see if my additions are correct?"

I handed him an open book with several pages of lists of initials and amounts due. There were three separate lists. The first list included payments to specific people, the second list included general expenses of the estate, and the third were other expenses, which could not be classified under either of the previous headings.

"I have added the expenses on the three lists separately, then I have added the three totals to produce the full total expenditure, excluding the running of Eyre Hall, which is mostly supervised by Mrs. Leah and recorded in her books."

I pushed the books over to him, "When that has been finished, we will have to make a similar list with the diverse incomes."

He turned the pages slowly, looking puzzled, "This must have taken you a long time, there are hundreds of numbers."

"It has taken almost three months to order the lists and add up the total monthly amounts. Mr. Cooper manages the accounts by alphabetical order, instead of date of payment, making it very difficult to classify and oversee them in perspective. It has been excruciating to decipher the regularity of payments and the recipients. I'm dreading doing the same with the income, which is naturally a far greater amount than the expenditure." I waited while I watched him look through the pages and pass his index finger over the numbers, gauging the work to be done.

"Well, can you help me?"

"I will gladly help you in the evenings, when I finish work."

"Thank you, Michael. I will put all these books in the library, here is the key. It's the only key Mrs. Leah does not have, nobody has it, not even Adele."

He took it and put it in his pocket.

"I shall put the books in the first drawer. The key is in the small purple china vase on the mantelpiece. You may go there and work whenever you wish. Let me know how you get on. When you finish checking the payments, we shall try to ascertain and reorder the income together."

"Shall I take these books into the library now? They are very heavy."

I nodded and followed him out of the drawing room and across the entrance hall. I used my key to open the library door. It was cold and dark.

"From tomorrow, light the fireplace in here every day. I don't want you to catch cold."

We walked across to the table, where he lay the books, "I love this room. I remember you used to let me come in here to read, when I first came to Eyre Hall."

"Yes, you were such a shy little boy, so quiet, always reading and watching me."

"You were, I mean you are, very kind to me, to everyone."

We were standing so close I could feel his breath on my cheeks. The moonlight was shining on his face, and I looked up to see his glassy eyes in the dark. He looked so solid and dependable, and I felt the need again to touch his face, but I refrained.

"Thank you, Michael. Thank you for helping me and for your loyalty. It means a great deal to me. Leave the books in the drawer and please rest, it is very late."

"I may start right now."

"As you wish. Don't forget to lock the door when you leave. Good night, Michael."

I forced myself away from his side, perturbed by the feelings his presence was provoking in me. I have not shared a bed with my husband for almost six years, and in all that time, I have felt no need of comfort, as if my womb had closed up and my desire had frozen. I had become the Snow Queen of this icy castle. Recently, and quite suddenly, Michael has transformed. The quiet, insecure young boy had become a handsome and vigorous young man. His presence distracts me. I can sense he is near me without seeing or hearing him, the sound of his voice brings a smile to my lips, and when he approaches me, I tremble with excitement. His presence, no, even the thought of him, stirs something inside my very soul that I fail to fathom, but it is warm and gratifying. Yet, for all its pleasantness, it also disturbs me, because I cannot understand my feelings, as if they belonged to someone else, and they do. The snow is melting. I feel myself glow and shine, because I need him and he is with me.

Chapter VII

Jenny

Jenny's tiny room was cosy and warm. It even looked like a home. The bed was squeezed under a sloping roof, which was so low in the corner where the bedstead was, that I hit my head on the ceiling every time I got up. Jenny and the two children slept in this same bed (the only one in the room), facing the window with its thick, loosely hanging, mauve curtains. A matching cloth covered the small table in the centre of the room, and small, square cushions rested on the three wooden chairs tucked under the tabletop. Behind the table there was a tall cupboard with three plates, two glasses, a large painted dish, and a set of tea things on the shelves.

I lay on the ruffled hot sheets, clasping her cream coloured spongy arse, and imagining what it would feel like to strike it so hard my fingers would be marked on her skin for weeks. I watched her resting languidly across my chest and pulled her hair, jerking her head violently, she moaned but hardly moved. I had been nice today, for old times. Next time I would make sure I branded her. She would enjoy a good thrashing.

She smelt sweet, her movements were sinuous, and her voice soft. The black women I was used to bedding were compliant, but their skin was thicker and their smell was saltier, their movements more abrupt and their cries louder. The latter were more satiating, but the former was saucier. It was harder to find a clean white whore in Jamaica, so Jenny was a treat. Such healthy looking pink flesh, such radiant clear eyes, such defined lips and short shapely upturned nose. So satisfying to lick, knead, and smack into. I had had the pleasure of her company years ago in Jamaica, and occasionally on my visits to England, which had been few and far between in recent years, but that would be changing soon. I paid her generously and asked her if she would consider working at Eyre Hall, but she was not enthusiastic.

"I ain't never worked in a house, and I have no intention. I ain't a maid. I don't like saying 'yes, milady or milord' and 'no, milady or milord'."

"You amaze me, my dear Jenny. You do not care to serve a gentleman or a lady, but you do not object to selling your charms and saying 'yes, sir', or 'how would you like to fuck me, sir'?"

"That's only occasional and I pick and choose my customers. If I worked in a house, I would be curtseying all day, every day."

"You will earn double. Whatever Mrs. Rochester pays you, I will give you the same amount, too."

"I don't want to work there."

"Why not?"

"It's a creepy place with weird people."

"It seems to me that all houses in this country are similar. I can assure you it is more agreeable than the inn, and although this room is comfortable enough, it is cramped, dark and damp. Would you not care to live in a grand house for a change?"

She looked grave and lost in deep thought, "Is there something you are not telling me? Have you ever been there, Jenny?"

"No, ain't never been there. I was at Thornfield, as you know, but I ain't never been to the new house. It's in the same spooky place. I bet it's full of them ghosts I heard at Thornfield. They live in the tree trunks and earth caves around the house. They whisper in the night, sometimes they come out and play mischief."

"Nonsense, my dear. There are no ghosts at Eyre Hall, neither were there any at Thornfield."

"They are strange people who live there. Look at that ugly spinster who dresses and acts as if she were fifteen: sinister Leah, pining for the chilling Mr. Rochester, who thinks the house would collapse without her; Simon, who makes fools look brainy; Margaret, who quarrels with all the merchants, nobody wants to take errands there; and Mrs.

Rochester, who only wants penniless, abandoned young orphans as servants."

"You seem to know a great deal about the inhabitants of the house. How is that?"

"People talk. I hear a lot of talk at the inn."

"You must work at Eyre Hall. It is my wish."

"Why?"

"I need a friend in the house. A friend who will tell me what occurs inside."

"I don't want Nell living there. She's a very sensitive girl. She would be frightened."

"Then you will have to reassure her, won't you? Think of it this way: she is a pretty girl, so she will be safer at Eyre Hall than with you at the inn. Anyway, you have lost your job there. You will leave of your own accord, or I will ask the innkeeper to dismiss you."

"But why, Richard? Do I not please you?"

"Indeed you do. That is another reason I want you at the Hall. Now that Bertha's daughter is back home, I plan to be there often in the near future. Once you are there, you will be mine exclusively. Would you like that?"

"I like the way I live now, on my own, with my children. How do you know they need any servants, anyway?"

"I do not. We'll have to find out, won't we? Are you still friendly with Leah?"

I met Jenny twenty-three years ago, when my sister had the baby. We needed a wet nurse and Leah called Jenny, who had recently had a baby herself, then she came with me to Jamaica and stayed for over a year. She was a most pleasing companion, very obedient, never argued or contradicted me. She was perhaps a little too eager to please, and even enjoyed bedding my friends. However, I was fond of her, so I asked her to stay, but unexplainably she wanted to return to her cuckold, idiot of a husband in Millcote.

"I see Leah on occasions, but I know someone better."

"Who?"

"Susan, the parish teacher, lives at Eyre Hall with her brother, Michael, the valet. She teaches my little ones. She's a good girl, teaches my kids for free, and Mrs. Rochester is fond of her. She's at Sunday school today. We can go and see her now, if you like."

"Good idea. Clever girl. Get dressed then, let's go!"

"What's the hurry? Sunday school is open till five. I need some coats and boots for the children."

I gave the artful hussy five more pounds for the afternoon's pleasure and the children's clothes. I got a smile and a delicious velvet tongue job in return.

———❧———

My schoolroom is a little room with whitewashed walls, and a stone floor containing twelve painted chairs around a square table. There is a small uncurtained window opposite the door and a wooden clock on the wall. It is very cold most of the year, so often the children cannot remove their coats or hats. It is just after five and the children have all gone, except Betty, a little orphan who works as handmaid to Mr. Wood and has not yet finished copying from the slate. Most of them, except two new children, can read. Although, only five of them can read sufficiently to recite the Bible, three can write, and the same number can cipher. All the girls knit and a few can sew a little. They speak with many incorrect expressions, the broadest accent of the district, and all of them are poorly clad. A few of them are unmannered, but most are docile with warm hearts and a desire to learn. I was mostly content in the schoolroom, because I could see their progress. I was guiding the children on their path away from ignorant coarseness towards godliness.

It had been unusual to have Nell and Thomas at Sunday school this morning, and it was even more surprising to see Jenny collect them in a fine looking carriage, accompanied by a hideous looking, middle-aged gentleman I had never seen before. They both ran out to greet their mother, but instead of walking away, she walked back them towards the schoolroom.

"Susan, I need to speak to you. I have a problem, and if you could find it in your heart to help me, I would be most grateful, on my behalf and my children's."

"What is the matter?"

"My work at the inn is not enough for us to live. I fear for my children's wellbeing. I am easy prey to the travellers at the inn, whom I will have to please or lose my job. I don't want that kind of life for me or for my children. If I could have a proper job, for example at Eyre Hall, and if the children could stay there with me, it would solve our problems, and I could lead a more Christian life, as I would wish. I know Mrs. Rochester speaks kindly of you, she would listen to you, if you would recommend my services. Would you do that for me, Susan? I have experience cooking and cleaning at the inn, and I am prepared to work hard to improve my children's lives, as well as my own. Would you help me lead a more Christian life?"

I promised to speak to Mrs. Rochester as soon as possible, but I told Jenny I did not know if her services would be needed or when. As she left, I watched her get into the carriage with her children and the sinister looking gentleman. He looked out of the window and smiled at me. I smiled back out of politeness, but I would not like to see his large, creased face or his wicked eyes smiling at me again.

I was not sure whether it was a good idea to recommend Jenny as a maid at Eyre Hall. It would be an improvement for the children, because Mrs. Rochester would make sure they were well looked after. She would find them a suitable trade, but I was surprised at Jenny's sudden interest in working at Eyre Hall. She did not seem the type to enjoy working as a maid, and on the other hand, she was not the kind of person Mrs. Rochester employed. She had never employed adult women since I had been there. She preferred orphaned children, like me and Michael. I wondered if her mysterious friend had anything to do with her desire to work at Eyre Hall.

That night huddled in bed with Nell and Thomas, I wondered how our lives would change from that moment on. It might be advantageous for them, or it might be disastrous for all of us, if the secret was ever discovered, but of course it never would be. I was the only person who knew what had happened, and I would never reveal it.

I never thought I would live in the same house as Mrs. Rochester. It is the last place I wanted to take my children. My parents had been honest country folk, the same as their parents. My parents, grandparents, and great-grandparents had worked on a farm on the Ingram's estate, as far back as any of them could remember. I should have done the same, except I married Stan, a blacksmith by trade, who lived in Millcote, on the Rochester's Estate. He was a good, honest, hardworking man, or so I thought, and we soon had a son. I would never have imagined he would have sold me, his wife, but he did. If my father had found out, he would have killed him, but no one ever told him.

Life in the workshop in the overcrowded town was very different from the life I was used to on the farm. I had helped my mother with the chickens, cows, and in the kitchen making cheese, cream, butter, and buttermilk, which we sold to the cheesemongers. Stan's hours were spent heating iron with coal furnaces until it was soft enough to be bashed with hammers, then he'd bend and cut the metal with anvils and chisels to make gates, grilles, railings, horseshoes, and farming tools or parts for carriage wheels. Sometimes he would fix cooking utensils and furniture, too.

It was a noisy, dirty, and dangerous job. Stan's hands and arms were always grubby, gritty and black. No wonder they were called blacksmiths. Black was the colour which oozed from his pores and covered the walls of his workshop. The devilish glow from the blacksmith's forge reminded me of Hell. I hated the shop, and I hated the persistent smell of burnt metal and smoke. I wondered how I hadn't noticed the smell when we courted, but I hadn't, or I wouldn't have married him. The smell impregnated the rooms we lived in above the shop, which had belonged to his father. Stan told me he had died after an accident, when a hot steel railing had cut off his feet. But Stan's arms were large, strong, clean, and loving. They had made me feel safe and loved when we met.

When we married, he worked all day and sometimes he even continued on during the night. His skin was always sooty and his brow sweaty, while his heavy black boots covered vile smelling feet. His touch was rough and his hands coarse. I soon learnt to comply with his demands and pretend I loved him. That is what I have been doing ever since with all the men I have known.

Then I met Grace Pool and Leah. They came to Millcote looking for a wet nurse and I was breastfeeding at the time. I have often wondered how different my life would have been if I had refused to accept the job, but I did. I was alone all day anyway, because Stan was always working. I was allowed to bring my baby with me, and quite frankly, I was glad to get away from the pounding, deafening noise of the shop, and the stink and filth in our rooms.

I remember being terrified the first day I arrived at Thornfield. It was such a gloomy, ghostly, frozen shell of a place. I was asked to dress in a maid's uniform and taken up to the top floor into a windowless room hidden behind an ugly hellish tapestried door. It made my Stan's workshop seem cheerful. There was a hairy, unkempt, madwoman tied to the bed. They said she was the mother, but they didn't want her to feed the baby. Her cries were worse than the pounding in the shop. When they told me she was Mrs. Rochester, I could hardly believe it. The best thing was that when I finished, I was allowed to eat as much as I wanted, there was always roast meat and cake. Mrs. Fairfax was kind enough to even give me food to take home for Stan. They paid me well and made me promise not to tell anyone. I never did.

I was brought in every morning and taken back home in the evening, until one day Leah came with a middle aged gentleman I had never seen before. He told me he was Mrs. Rochester's brother-in-law, and he wanted to speak to my husband regarding an urgent matter. That evening, my husband sold me to Mr. Mason. Richard told him he needed to take me to Jamaica with him as wet nurse for his niece. He paid Stan a very generous sum and promised to send me back in a few months, as soon as he found another wet nurse in Jamaica.

Peter, my son, was to stay behind with his father. Stan's sister agreed to look after my baby while I was away. I stayed with Richard for eighteen months, and when I returned, my husband and my son had died of cholera. My sister-in-law and her husband were living in our rooms above the shop. The shop had been taken over by his apprentice, his cousin Stephen, and I had nowhere to go.

I suppose I could have gone back to the farm with my parents, but how was I to explain what had happened? How could I tell them I had abandoned my son and my husband, and left England? Or worse still, how could I admit that I had been sold as wet nurse and mistress to Richard Mason? In any case, I was too restless and depressed to go back to the quiet farm. Richard had given me some money, which was enough to live on for some months, while I found a means of making a living.

I had been Richard's child minder and mistress in Jamaica. When he decided to take Annette to the convent, he asked me if I wanted to return to England or stay with him. Sometimes I think I should have stayed there. It is a beautiful country with a heavenly climate, but I missed my son, and strangely my husband, who had been a kind, tender lover. Had I known they were dead, I would have stayed with Richard, in spite of his humiliations. He would offer me to please his friends, or trade my services to cover his debts, and when he was irksome, he would strike me. In compensation, he made me feel like the lady of the house. I had pretty dresses, a lovely colonial residence with native servants, and plenty of food and drink. I was never formally introduced to any other members of the English community, and he always referred to me as the baby's nurse.

When I returned to Millcote, I stayed at the George Inn while I decided what to do. I became friendly with the couple who ran it, the Earnshaws, and they offered me a job cleaning and sewing. The railway had recently been built, so many occasional travellers stayed there, and I drifted into various casual relationships with some of the guests.

One of the travellers was, Mr. Rosset, who called himself a poet. He offered to marry me and I accepted. I moved to these rooms, which he still pays for, and imagined I would soon become Mrs. Rosset. When I became pregnant, we married so people would think I was an honest woman, but he soon told me he was already married to his cousin in London. Shortly after Thomas was born, he left and never returned, but I am grateful, because everyone knows my husband left me, and that makes me more respectable. Three years later, Nell was born. I cannot know for sure who her father is, so I always tell her that he's dead.

I have fed and clothed my children on my own since they were born. Cleaning and sewing at the inn, helping in the kitchen, and occasionally exchanging favours for money. I want something better for my children. I don't want them to have to feel humiliated, cheap, or worthless. I want them to learn a useful trade and earn an honest living. That was why I asked Susan, the schoolteacher, to teach them on her free afternoon. Then I met her brother, Michael, such a quiet, sweet, boy with sturdy muscles and ambitious objectives. I would have fallen in love with him, if I had not realized he was obsessed with another woman with whom I could never compete.

Now Richard wants me to be his informant and mistress at Eyre Hall. I am terrified of meeting Mrs. Rochester face to face. I saw her once at Thornfield, walking in the orchard with Mr. Rochester and Adele. I asked Leah who she was, and she told me she was the governess. I saw how Mr. Rochester looked at her while the child played, and I realized why he kept his mad wife a secret, but they all found out in the end, when Richard told them the truth on their wedding day. I was sure Richard had returned one more time to uncover another of his brother-in-law's embarrassing secrets. I had never met Mr. Rochester, although I had breastfed both his daughters. I had lost my son by attending to his daughter, although he had inadvertently repaid the debt, and now she was returning home.

Chapter VIII

Annette's Story

My mother wrote a diary. She started writing when she was a young girl in Coloubri Estate and stopped writing when she left Saint Mary's Convent School in Spanish Town, Jamaica, before meeting and marrying my father. Thirty-one years later when I finished my studies at the same school, Sister Angela gave it to me and advised me to read it carefully, in order to forgive my mother for her madness and blasphemous death, understand her tormented life, and lead a more pious one myself.

The diary is unfinished, covering only her childhood and early youth, before she met and married Mr. Rochester, my father. It includes no mention of her married life or her years in England at Thornfield Hall. Neither does she mention Jane Eyre, the second Mrs. Rochester, the woman who poisoned my father against my mother. The detestable woman I am about to meet and will be my unwilling benefactress in my new life in England.

Three weeks ago, Uncle Richard came to see me at the convent and told me I could not remain there, because my benefactor, Mr. Rochester, had cancelled the payments. I did not understand the problem at first, because I had been working at the school as a teacher for over two years without any financial compensation. So I believed my work there was enough to cover my living costs, but my uncle insisted that it was a serious offence, and I should seek what is rightfully mine.

I was shocked to discover that my benefactor was in reality my father. Until that moment, I had believed that I had been born to

Henry Mason, my Uncle Richard's brother, who had died in an accident with my mother, shortly after I was born. My uncle told me the time had come to tell me the truth. Henry and Sybil had never existed. My uncle's only sister, Bertha Antoinette Mason, was my mother, and her husband, Mr. Edward Rochester, was my father. Miss Jane Eyre, his second wife, had refused to accept my presence in England after my mother's death, and my father was unable to oppose her wishes, so I was brought to Jamaica by my only uncle.

Now that my father is dying, she is trying to deny me all my filial rights. Unfortunately, I am not in a position to claim my inheritance, because there is no proof of my birth at Thornfield Hall twenty-three years ago. My father convinced my uncle to bribe the local government officials and register my birth in Spanish Town, Jamaica, as daughter of Henry Mason and Sybil Hyde, both recorded as deceased.

Before these events had been disclosed to me, I was perfectly happy to live a quiet and secluded life at the Convent of Saint Mary. When I first had news of my parents' real identity, I was devastated. After the initial shock, I was furious. I told my uncle I did not care for any inheritance, and I certainly did not want to travel to England to meet my father, who had rejected me for a young concubine. I even suggested I would be prepared to take Holy Orders if necessary, in order to remain within the convent walls. But Mother Superior and Uncle Richard convinced me that my father wished to die in peace, repair his sins by meeting me, endowing me with a generous dowry and maintenance in England, therefore, I should humbly accept his apologies and my rightful inheritance.

My uncle reminded me that he had saved my life, and told me the time had come to repay him for his kindness by following his advice. I was to accompany him to England and recover what was rightfully mine: a respectable allowance, a suitable English husband, and a generous dowry. I told him I was not interested in marriage or a dowry. I did not want to make the same errors my mother had made by succumbing to a frivolous life of luxury and pleasure, or being forced into a loveless marriage in a faraway land. My uncle assured me that I would not marry anyone I did not love, and he insisted that I owed it to him.

He promised me if I didn't like England he would let me return to the convent, but I suspect he will not keep his word. Mother Superior has told me I must obey him, because he is my only living relative (she has not been told that my father is alive), and she is convinced it would be most advantageous for me. She thinks England is a wonderful place to live, even though she has never been there herself, so I do not believe her, but I must obey. Once more, I am as helpless as the baby who was torn away from her mother!

The days passed, and the more I read the diary and thought about my mother and my father, the more I wanted to travel to England, meet him, and find out more about her. I wanted to see the places she saw and feel the emotions she felt. A great empty space I had been ignoring was growing in my heart and needed to be filled. I had to return to England, the unknown land where I had been born.

So here I am at last, sitting on a woollen bed, in an ancient inn, which leaks and smells of stagnant water and squalor. The sky has been steel grey since we arrived two days ago, and the sun is trapped behind the heavy cloud curtain spitting unceasingly onto the bogged land. The small wooden windows are stiff with dirt, and there are no verandahs to walk out onto. The people dress in compliance with the weather, in drab colours, their faces lack expression, and their voices lack cadence, except when they are drunk, and they shout and sing dull monotonous tunes. I would die if I had to live here. Perhaps that is what happened to my mother. I turned the pages of her diary once more while I waited for my uncle to return from his errands in Millcote. I had read it so many times I could almost recite it by heart.

I was named Annette, after my grandmother, renown as the most beautiful woman in Jamaica, according to my uncle Richard. Annette, originally from Martinique, married a prosperous English plantation owner, who lived in Jamaica, called Mr. Alexander Cosway, at a very early age. My mother, Bertha Antoinette Cosway, and her brother Pierre, were unlucky enough to have been born at a time of financial decline and severe political and social changes, which were most detrimental to their interests. All the other estate owners, except my mother's family, had abandoned the area after the emancipation of slaves.

My grandfather, Alexander Cosway, was an English plantation owner, who drank himself to death, when my mother and her brother, Pierre, were still babies, shortly before the big problems started. He left my grandmother unproductive grounds, which they could not abandon. Soon the estate was isolated at a short but currently unreachable distance from Spanish Town, especially when the roads could not be repaired, and most horses either died of starvation or at the hands of desperate owners. They were completely stranded, when my grandmother's horse was poisoned by the resentful former slaves.

My grandmother, who had left behind a Creole background of poverty in Martinique, had experienced the privilege of colonial splendour through marriage, and was naturally devastated at the thought of experiencing poverty and rejection once more. She became melancholic and withdrawn, ignoring both my mother and her ailing brother.

Their house was old and leaky, so my mother took refuge walking around the roofed terrace with an unrestrained sea view. She would look out for hours, talking aloud, as if she were imploring the sea gods for better fortune. Her father had died, her mother was neglectful, and there was no possibility of going to school, so my mother was able to run as wild as a bird in paradise.

She could not go to school or leave the estate, because the freed slaves who had left the plantation hated the whites, cursing and abusing my mother and grandmother whenever they saw them. Having no other children to play with, except her sick bed ridden brother, she took refuge in Christophine, their Negro cook, who had been one of her mother's wedding presents, and had chosen to stay on after emancipation.

For a time my mother made friends with Tia, a black girl, who was her own age. They would go to a pool in the nearby river, where they would swim and summersault in search of brightly coloured pebbles, which covered the riverbed. Then they would eat boiled green bananas and sleep under the shady trees. Years later, Tia would throw a jagged stone full of hatred at my mother's incredulous face, almost killing her, and teaching her that no one was to be trusted in their shifting world.

Other times my mother would wander around their garden, which was more beautiful and mysterious than the Garden of Eden. It was wildly overgrown from neglect. The vegetation flourished freely with a mixture of bright purples, mauves and greens, oozing sweet, intense perfume. In the evenings she would roam around the old derelict sugar works and disused water wheel, imagining what it would have been like when the machinery was working and the plantation was bustling with life. She dreamed she was the queen of a forest, thick with emerald reeds and leafy ferns, smelling of river water, sweet seaweed, and diving fish. She imagined the lizards and snakes were evil sorcerers, who retained her in captivity with the help of the insects, who were their obedient armies. She fancied knights in armour, who came from England in large boats, would save her by transporting her to a castle she had once seen in a drawing in one of the old books, which Christophine used in the kitchen as a slab to cut the bread. Other times she would stack the books and jump from one stack to another, until the top book slipped and fell open on a page with a black and white drawing of houses and people she had never seen, so they too were included in her daydreaming world of magic.

This idle and undomesticated life persisted for five years until my grandmother, thanks to her beauty and elegant dancing, remarried a wealthy English gentleman, called Mr. Jonas Mason, and their lives took a fortunate turn. Mr. Mason had brought up various properties in the West Indies. Estates were going cheaply, as a result of the slump in the sugar market and the emancipation, so he ventured to the islands in search of a profitable investment.

Mr. Mason had a son by his first marriage, my Uncle Richard, who was living in Barbados and managing his father's estates in Trinidad and Antigua. He often travelled to England on business, so they did not see him often at that time. The marriage transformed my mother's life. The house was repaired, new servants were employed, they ate beef and mutton and puddings, and they were happy for a time.

My mother did not like her stepfather at first, but she took a liking to him, when she realized he had saved them from their misery. He was a generous, kind man, with good intentions, but he did not understand our way of life in Jamaica. Mr. Mason said the natives did not want to work, so he imported workers from the East Indies, as other English landowners were doing. My grandmother knew this would rekindle the hatred and resentment towards the whites, but Mr. Mason did not understand his actions would create more conflict with the local population. Within a year my grandmother wanted to leave, due to the increasing hostility towards the white landowners. She sensed wicked deeds were brewing.

My mother also realized they were in danger, since the moment their horse had been poisoned years earlier, so she slept with a long narrow piece of wood with two nails sticking out at the end, like a shingle, by her bed, in case she needed protection. Christophine took the nails out, but let her keep the shingle, and after the West Indian workers came, she slept with the shingle in her arms. It was the only way she felt safe. Eventually, the night she would need her shingle arrived, although it was of no use, because there were so many of them. The Negroes stood outside their house, armed with torches, machetes, and sticks, rhythmically repeating foreboding chants. They set fire to her bedroom and Pierre's crib, and then the whole house was an amber blaze against the indigo sky. The only home she had ever known was burned to a cinder before her very eyes. Part of my mother died that day, the rest died in smaller parts, some in Spanish Town, and others in England. So she was almost all dead by the time she finally fell off the battlements at Thornfield, the year after I was born.

After escaping from the shock of Pierre's death and the loss of her home, my grandmother fell ill and was cared for by her widowed Aunt Cora, who nursed her back to health in Spanish Town. My mother went to see her at the institution, where she was convalescing, but my grandmother pretended not to recognize her, or perhaps she really had lost her memory. My mother wrote that there are always two deaths, 'the real one and the one people know about.' She said her mother had died her real death the night they burnt Coloubri, although they buried her some years later.

Shortly after visiting her mother for the last time, when my mother was fifteen, Mr. Mason decided she should go to a Catholic Convent School to learn some manners and discipline, or she would never be able to marry a suitable Englishman. The first day she thought she would die of suffocation. The classrooms were hot and stuffy, because the windows were too small and too high up, in order to avoid distractions. The pine benches burned her skin. The stone floor, white walls, and pine desks, confined her oppressively. She longed to return to the freedom of Coloubri, but there was nowhere to return to. She must have felt very lonely and alienated at the school. Her father was dead, her mother was unavailable, her Aunt Cora had returned to England for a year, her stepfather visited very rarely, her brother had died, Christophine was living with her son and never visited, and her beloved Coloubri no longer existed.

However, as the days passed, the convent became her refuge, and she grew to enjoy the activities. She learnt to cross-stitch colourful flowers on a pale oblong background while Mother Justine read the lives of Saints and Holy Martyrs. They bathed regularly, using scented soap under long cotton chemises, and ate buttered rolls and drank coffee for breakfast. She learnt to forget about happiness and pray five times a day, and praise at the wooden crucifixes hanging limply from the nun's waists. Christ taught her to distinguish Heaven from Hell and to pray for happiness to come to her one day. During the following eighteen months, her stepfather visited more often and brought presents, such as a locket and a bracelet. I wonder what happened to her personal belongings. I never saw anything that belonged to her, except her diary, which is a great deal, but not enough, not now that I know her so well.

The diary ends one day shortly before her seventeenth birthday. Mr. Mason came to visit her and told her she was a grown woman, and it was time for her to leave the convent and return to the real word, to a world full of laughter, dancing, and young people. She was to stay with her Aunt Cora, who had returned from England, and meet his son,

Richard, who had some friends who wanted to meet her. He promised her life would change for the better, but she remembered how he had said the same, when he married her mother, and although things had improved in some ways, they got much worse in other ways.

She had many nightmares and was apprehensive about leaving the convent, which had become a safe place for her. The world outside would be unpredictable. Her mother had gone, and Coloubri no longer existed. The diary ends with the desperate fears of a young and insecure orphan. Every time I read the final pages I shiver. I feel as if my mother were speaking to me, warning me about marriage and England. I do not know what she looked like. I watch my reflection in the rusty mirror, over the rickety chest of drawers, and wonder if I look like her, if my life will be like hers, or if my death will be like hers.

My uncle has informed me of what happened after she left the convent. However, I am aware that his knowledge is incomplete. Jonas Mason and Edward Rochester's father were old acquaintances, who connived to solve a common problem. The former wanted to marry his beautiful stepdaughter to a well bred Englishman, and Raymond Rochester wanted to marry his son to a rich heiress, so they wrote up the marriage contract. Edward was to receive 30,000 pounds and Bertha Antoinette would be married to an English gentleman of good race. My mother was seventeen years old and one of the most beautiful women in Spanish Town.

When Mr. Rochester first arrived in Jamaica, he was very pleased with the arrangement. Although, he was not so pleased when he learned she was Mr. Mason's stepdaughter. He was informed that my mother was Jonas's second wife's daughter by her previous marriage to a certain Mr. Cosway, a drunken former slave owner, whose reputation was far from respectable. He began to hear rumours about my grandmother and how she lost her property, her son, and her mind, just two years after marrying Mr. Mason. He also found out her mother was a Creole from the island of Martinique. In addition, Mr. Rochester was a very jealous man, and my mother was dazzlingly beautiful and gay. Her mother had taught her to dance, and she had an innate sense of colour and style, so she became one of the most strikingly dressed women in Spanish Town. All the men, who admired her, could not fail to envy him.

My mother's life changed radically in months. She was introduced to Jamaican society by her stepbrother, Richard, who proudly accompanied her to parties and dances. Bertha Antoinette was able to wear beautiful clothes, dance, have fun and enjoy herself. She revelled in her newly found freedom and enjoyed the attention no one had ever given her before. She imagined she was back in colourful Coloubri, the belle of the plantation. In fact, when Mr. Rochester finally arrived, she wanted to postpone the marriage on the excuse that she was too young. However, she was duly convinced that her time had come to be an English gentleman's wife. At first their marriage was happy, she was compliant and he was satisfied. He promised to take her to England, and she promised to be a faithful wife, but the problems started too soon.

According to my uncle, Mr. Rochester was greedy, selfish, moody, choleric and possessive. He hated the natives, the food, the insects and the tropical climate, and was far too attracted to the fiery and submissive native women. I suppose my parents were too young, impulsive, and inexperienced. Whatever the reason, my father soon lost interest in my mother, finding the local women more submissive and soliciting. My mother was enraged with jealousy and lost her mind. On the other hand, Mr. Rochester's life took a turn for the better, he was a fortunate man. He already possessed my mother's bountiful dowry, and months later, due to the sudden deaths of his brother and his father, he inherited his family's estate in England, where he decided they should return at once.

Unfortunately, my mother could not get used to the climate, the people, or the way of life in England, and her health worsened after I was born. When my father met Miss Jane Eyre, he locked my mother away, so nobody would know of her existence. I was transported by my uncle to Spanish Town, where I was brought up by the same nuns at the same convent as my mother.

The convent school has not changed much since my mother's days. We eat plentiful and nutritious food four times a day and wash regularly, because we have been taught that cleanliness is next to godliness. I learned to sew, embroider, paint, and play the piano. We were also taught how to cook and cleaned our rooms daily. We prayed five times a day and read the Bible in the evenings, mainly the word of Christ through the Gospels. I have been teaching the younger girls for two years. Most of them are pious and well behaved, and I enjoy teaching them music, sewing, and embroidery.

I can understand how my mother felt when she left the convent. I also feel terrified of life outside the safe walls, which have been my shelter. I have never lived anywhere else or known other people. My uncle has visited me regularly, but infrequently. On occasions, he has taken me to his estates in Jamaica. I know, because Mother Superior has informed me, that for some time his finances have diminished, so it is my duty to accompany him to England and repay him for saving my life.

Although he has refused to acknowledge me as his daughter, I am thankful to Mr. Rochester for having provided for me, and I am looking forward to meeting him before his death. Uncle Richard has told me I must be polite to Mrs. Rochester, because she will administer Mr. Rochester's inheritance. I am terrified of meeting her. Uncle Richard has told me how wicked she is, and how she captivated Mr. Rochester while he was married to my mother, so that he locked her in the attic, which led to her lunacy and death. I do not want to meet, or be polite to the person who was responsible for my mother's captivity and destruction. My uncle has told me not to worry, because he will look after me, but he never has, why should he do so now? The sisters at the convent have looked after me, but they are so far away, in another lost world, like Coloubri.

Before we left Spanish Town three weeks ago, my uncle took me to the shops and bought me suitable clothes for the occasion: colourful dresses, bonnets, capes, boots, gloves, and some pieces of jewellery. I told him not to spend so much money on me, but he reminded me it was only a loan, because I would have to pay him back, once I received my inheritance. He said I had to look rich and beautiful.

He insisted I learn to dance before coming. I cannot dance. I have never danced. I complied, although, I fear he wants to advertise me in search of a wealthy husband, an idea which I abhor. I begged Mother Superior to let me stay, but to no avail. I am truly terrified of being face to face with Jane Eyre, and I dread the day I have to marry a wealthy, English gentleman I have never even met. Since I have arrived, I have dreamt of walls caving in and burying me, and flying monsters carrying me away with their claws across a rough sea and dropping me in the ocean, where I drown. I have drowned many nights in the Wide Sargasso Sea, since I learned I was to come to England.

Incredible and terrifying things have happened to me in the last three weeks. I feel as if I were on a big fair wheel, which is spinning violently and will not let me get off. The last troubling event happened yesterday. We had arrived at the Rochester Arms the previous evening, after a ten hour coach drive from London. Yesterday morning, my uncle went to Eyre Hall to visit Mrs. Rochester. He wished to procure an invitation to visit Mr. Rochester.

Yesterday afternoon, my uncle left on another errand. I was alone at the inn, when the rain halted, or at least seemed to lessen, so I ventured out for a walk. The inn is on the outskirts of Hay, which is a small village with few shops and houses on dusty unpaved roads, much like the abandoned paths that lead to the sea in Spanish Town, where I would sometimes walk, except at home it was warm, and the air smelt fresh and crisp like the sea breeze, and the horizon was deep blue like the sea. Here the horizon is grey, the air smells of damp weeds, and the wind is cold and furious. I walked towards the moors, away from the dwellings, for a while.

The ground was hard and the road lonely. In the distance I could hear a church bell, although I could not see the belfry, which I guessed was over the hill ahead of me. My uncle had told me Eyre Hall was just a short walk away from the church. I imagined my father and Mrs. Rochester were hearing the same sound, and I wondered if they were as concerned about meeting me as I was about meeting them. Curiously, the sun, which had not appeared all day, was suddenly visible, pale and low on the distant horizon. Seconds later there was absolute silence and solitude, even the wind decided to hold its breath. The day darkened, and the white outline of the moon, which was less than full, was growing more intense. I should have returned to the inn at that moment, when the bushes and the trees were turning from green to grey, and the first stars were starting to shine. But I stayed.

I sat on a stile by the path, looking towards the place where I was born, wondering what my life would have been like if I had stayed here, when I heard the ground rumbling, as if it was going to snap. The sound became louder and louder, and in the distance I saw a great dark shadow approaching me, which seemed to have the huge head of a wild unicorn and the body of a dragon. I jumped off the stile in terror and ran back towards the safety of the inn, slipping on a sheet of ice on the causeway and sliding down to the path, hitting my head on a stone. I closed my eyes and covered my head, expecting to be either trampled on or swallowed by a monstrous beast. The rumbling stopped, and I heard an animal rear up by my side and halt seconds later.

"Who are you, and what on earth are you doing walking at night in the middle of the causeway? You could have got yourself killed! I didn't even see you!" shouted the rider.

I felt a terrible throbbing in my head and warm fluid trickle down my brow. I wiped it away with the back of my hand, but as I brought it back down, I realised my glove was covered in blood and screamed. The rider jumped off his horse and bent down to help me.

"Are you all right? Let me help you."

He tried to lift me up, but I screamed with pain.

"Does it hurt?" I nodded. "Where is the pain?"

"My ankle hurts and so does my arm, and my head."

"Excuse me, but may I see if it is broken?"

I nodded and shivered as his hands pressed my foot, feeling for broken bones. No man had ever touched me, except when I had embraced my uncle, but it was not a moment for shyness. I was injured and needed his help.

"No bones are broken, although it is already swollen and will probably swell even more tomorrow."

"Now let me look at your head." He said, as he took out a kerchief and wiped my forehead, "Don't worry, it is not a deep cut. It is no longer bleeding. May I take off your glove? It is full of blood, and you will spoil your cape." I nodded and gasped, as he slid it off and wrapped my hand in both of his.

"I'm sorry. Did I hurt you?" I shook my head."Your hand is stone cold." How could I tell him that my whole body had rippled as his fingers covered my hand?

He smiled sympathetically, "Can you try and stand up? Take my hand, I will pull you up."

I put my gloveless hand into his. "Now rest on my shoulder, and I will take you to the stile, where you can sit down." I laid my weight on his shoulder, limped, and screeched with pain.

"May I carry you?" I nodded and fell limply in his arms, feeling spoilt like a queen.

The moon was brighter now, and I could see my interlocutor's face clearly. He was a young man, not older than me, wearing an elegant fur collared riding cloak and riding boots. He was tall and strong, because he had easily lifted me onto the stile. I couldn't make out his features, but I noticed he had a perplexed look in his large dark eyes, a decisive aquiline nose, and a firm chin. He was the first Englishman I had met, except for the host at the inn, and I found him disturbingly handsome and heroic. He was like a gallant knight in shining armour, and I was the damsel in distress, lost and wounded in a foreign land.

After his initial irritation, he was now most gentle and considerate to my injuries, apologizing and cursing the lack of daylight for almost killing me. After setting me down on the stile, he wanted to satisfy his curiosity.

"Tell me, why were you running onto the pathway? You almost fell under my horse!"

"I was trying to get back to the inn. I thought you and your horse were a monster." He laughed loudly, and I felt quite silly, "I'm sorry, I didn't realize I was running onto the path."

He seemed amused. "You should have stayed on the stile. I would have galloped by and nothing would have happened." I felt a fool. He was right. I had practically run under his horse.

"May I ask you what you are doing in this solitary lane, on your own at so late an hour?" His eyes were running over my clothes, and I was glad I had worn my best crimson cloak and bonnet.

"I am staying at the Rochester Arms with my uncle."

"Indeed. Do you live in the area?"

"No. We have come to visit some relatives, and you, do you live here?"

"Yes, I do. I live just behind the hill yonder."

"Beyond that hill over there? By a church?"

"Precisely. I live at Eyre Hall."

"You do?"

"I do. Have you heard of it?"

"Yes, I have."

"Where are you from?'

"I have been living in Spanish Town, Jamaica."

"Jamaica? That's a long way to travel to visit relatives. May I ask who your relatives are?"

"Mr. Rochester is my uncle."

"Mr. Rochester is your uncle? Mr. Rochester who lives at Eyre Hall?"

"Yes, sir."

'Have you ever met him, or been to the Hall?"

"Never. That is why we have come. I believe he is unwell, and I would like to meet him before it is … too late. He has been very kind to me."

He looked puzzled, and then asked, "Have you met Mrs. Rochester, his wife?"

"I have not, but strictly speaking, she is not my aunt."

"How is that possible?"

"It is a long story, but I will be brief. My father was his first wife's brother, but he died when I was born, both my parents died when I was born." He looked quite surprised at my explanation.

"Do you know Mrs. Rochester?" I asked him warily.

He must have noticed the apprehension in my voice, because he answered very quickly and cheerfully. "I do, and I wouldn't worry about meeting her. She is one of the most wonderful people you will meet in England. She is devoted to Mr. Rochester. If you are his niece, you will be well received at Eyre Hall."

I shuddered. If only he knew.

"May I ask your name and your uncle's name?"

"My name is Annette Mason, and my uncle is Mr. Richard Mason."

"Do you live with your uncle, Miss Annette Mason?" I shivered as he mentioned my name and looked into my eyes probingly. I noticed they were not blue, but they were not dark. I guessed they were green or hazel, but there was not enough light to distinguish the exact colour. In any case, I could easily gaze at them all day long.

"No, my uncle is unmarried. I live in a convent school, where I was brought up. I am a teacher there. I mean I was, before I came to England." He smiled and looked at me intently, but who was I conversing with? "May I ask you your name?"

"My name is John Rochester." I gasped incredulously. I had met my brother! He stretched out his hand to shake mine, "Mr. Edward Rochester is my father and Mrs. Jane Rochester is my mother. Pleased to meet you, Annette." He grinned proudly from ear to ear, as he held my hand firmly, "I have no brothers or sisters, and you?"

"Pleased to meet you, John Rochester." I said, as I tore my bewildered hand away, "I am an only child, too." I lied.

"When are you going to meet my father?"

"Soon, I believe. My uncle has been to visit Mrs. Rochester this morning, and we are waiting for an invitation."

"I will be staying for a week. I live in Oxford, where I am reading law. I hope you shall be invited to visit soon."

"So do I, the inn is not so pleasant a place to stay."

"Eyre Hall is a most comfortable house. You will enjoy staying. I will tell my mother I have met you." Even the mention of her name made my blood curdle.

"Don't worry!" How could he notice my apprehension? Was my face so easy to read? "She will like you, especially when she learns you are a teacher. She is of the opinion that it is the most important occupation in the world. My advice is to talk to her about your teaching and you will win her over."

"Do you think perhaps you could help me return to the inn? My uncle may be looking for me."

"It is not too far to walk. Lean on me. I will return for my horse."

John carried me most of the way, because my sprain was still painful. When we arrived at the inn, the landlord and my uncle were worried and shocked to see me limping and dishevelled. John explained what had happened, and the landlord's daughter helped me wash and undress. I was given some hot soup and tucked into bed. When my uncle came to see how I was, he told me he was very pleased with my evening adventure. I told him how terrified I was of going to Eyre Hall, but he told me everything was progressing according to his plans, and I would soon be a very rich and respected English lady.

I was not so sure if I wanted to live in England, or be rich, or be an English lady, or marry a wealthy man. I had met the man I wanted to marry, but the marriage was impossible. Before leaving, my uncle told me John would be having dinner with us tomorrow night at the inn, but he did not yet know when we would be going to Eyre Hall. I was in turmoil, feeling a mixture of nervous expectation at the thought of seeing him again, and embarrassment due to my indecent feelings towards my brother. I had a different dream that night, I was being pursued by a giant unicorn, and John carried me away to safety on his winged horse.

Part Two: The Germs of Love

I had not intended to love him; the reader knows I had wrought hard to extirpate from my soul the germs of love there detected; and now, at the first renewed view of him, they spontaneously arrived, green and strong! He made me love him without looking at me.

Jane Eyre. Chapter 17.

Chapter IX

A Letter from the Past

Monday, 30th October 1865.

Mornings at Eyre Hall are always hectic. After a hearty breakfast of bread, eggs, cake, and plenty of tea, we are rushed off our feet until lunchtime. Beth and Daisy take hot water up to the bedrooms and bring down the chamber pots and the laundry. They sweep and dust all the halls and galleries, as well as the dining room, while cook prepares breakfast for the mistresses and bakes bread and cakes for lunch and tea. Simon takes breakfast upstairs to the master, helps him wash and dress, and lights the upstairs fires. I prepare the fires downstairs and serve breakfast in the dining room for Mrs. Rochester and Miss Adele while the girls sweep the drawing room, where my mistress sits after breakfast, writing letters or looking through the accounts books.

After serving breakfast, I sometimes help Miss Leah with her bookkeeping. Later, I take Mrs. Rochester's letters and messages to and from the schools, the church, and the hospice at Millcote. When I am in the house, I attend the front door and anything my mistress requires. If no more is needed of me, I am sometimes lucky enough to have a few minutes rest before twelve thirty, when I serve lunch for the ladies and make sure the hearths are still going strong.

On those scarce moments of quiet, I often retire to my room to read some passages from the Bible, or poetry, especially *In Memoriam* by the Queen's favourite poet, Mr. Tennyson. I also read the novels I overheard Mrs. Rochester discussing with visitors, or the ones she writes about in her letters, which I am ashamed to admit, I often read.

She writes very loving and gregarious letters to her cousins, Mary and Diana. She also writes to Miss Richards, the parish school benefactor, regarding the running of the school in Millcote. Once a month she receives a letter from Miss Brookwell, the parish Sunday school teacher, at Hay, and Mrs. O'Shea, the schoolteacher at Millcote, informing her of the children's attendance and progress. Occasionally, she receives correspondence from authors or other educated gentry regarding her novel, mostly in praise, and sometimes suggesting further instalments. She always replies politely that she is too occupied to write novels at present.

On rare occasions, she receives very formal letters from her editor in London, in which he encourages her to write another novel, and she replies, equally formally, that she has no time. I know that is not true, she *is* writing a novel. I have seen *The Orphan* written on the first page of a leather bound journal, which is kept under lock and key in her desk in the library. Within its covers she has started to write the story of a young orphan girl, who is in a workhouse, accused of stealing bread. A new inmate recognizes a chain she is wearing and informs her that her mother, who had abandoned her due to tragic circumstances, has the same chain and is looking for her daughter. It is a pleasant book, so far, but the experiences narrated are not fully accurate. It is easy to see that my mistress has never experienced a workhouse. I am glad for that, but it makes her retelling too glossy. She is more precise portraying the upper classes, as she has done in *Daphne*.

I much enjoyed the last book I had read called *Oliver Twist*, which portrayed the crude reality far more realistically. Today I was going to make a start on *David Copperfield*, also by Mr. Charles Dickens, of whom Jane speaks highly on a personal as well as on his literary capacity. She recommends his novels to her cousins, but warns them that there is some exaggeration and melodrama in his work. I must disagree with my mistress on this matter. I have lived in the workhouse and seen events and characters such as those recounted in *Oliver Twist*. I have met pick-pockets like Dodger, seen scared, battered women like Nancy, and felt abandoned and hopeless like Oliver. I have smelt the raff and refuse of the Thames and watched the young mudlarks, waded thigh-deep in the putrid, muddy river, retrieve anything that could be sold on the streets. I have heard the rumbling stomachs of the hungry children, who cried themselves to sleep. I am glad that she thinks it is an exaggeration, because it means she has fortunately not experienced nor seen such debasement and degradation.

I had just rested my head on my pillow and was about to start reading my copy of *David Copperfield*, which I had borrowed from the library, when Simon approached me sheepishly and sat by my side whispering mysteriously, "Michael, would you help me with a letter I have and needs to read?" He chewed his lower lip, winked his bulging pale eyes, and made me promise I would never reveal how he had acquired the dispatch.

"Is it not addressed to you, Simon?"

"It's not my letter. I come by it quite by chance, but it's mine. It was given to me as a payment."

"You were given a letter you can't read as a payment? For what?"

"When old Mr. Raven, landlord at the Rochester Arms, died, I helped smarten him up 'cos I worked in an undertakers, when I was in London. Then I helped Martin pack up his father's things. Lord, did he have humbug in his rooms! The bed was full of lice! I'd forgotten the dirt there is outside of Eyre Hall. This is the fanciest, cleanest place I've ever lived in. The master's a bad tempered old faggot, but the missus has such a sympathetic look. She's like an angel walking on earth, ain't she Michael? I'd serve her in Hell, if needs be. Bet you would, too!"

"I'm sure Mrs. Rochester will never be anywhere near Hell, Simon."

"True. Can't see what she ever saw in that monster of a husband, except the chink of course, what else?"

"That comment is offensive and unfair. She is our mistress and she treats us kindly, Simon. You just said so yourself. Please refrain from any impolite reference to Mrs. Rochester."

"Michael, you's a good man, but you still ain't realized it's them and us. No matter how well you speak and read, or how hard you works, or how polite they pretends to be, you'll never be anything to them. They'll never stick up for you either. We servants, we clean their scum and say yes, sir, no sir, and that's it."

I really didn't think it would be wise to argue with Simon, who is an infant intellectually. He is decent in a basic sort of way, but he always seems to get himself into trouble by being in the wrong place at the wrong time, and speaking more than he should. He has arrived home on his monthly free afternoon, more than once, beaten up after a binge drinking night. Once he had been robbed of his coat, gloves and boots, which meant he arrived in a deplorable state, dragging his bleeding feet into the kitchen. He was constantly making fun of everyone who crossed his path, including our masters, so it was a question of time before his lack of common sense and big mouth got him into big trouble. I wondered what he had meddled in this time, "You were telling me about a letter, Simon."

"Well, as I says, I was helping him with the rubbish and I seened a box, a little wooden box with encased shiny stones. Thought it might be worth a guinea at least, so I says, 'can I have this little box?' And he says 'yes'."

I looked at him incredulously. His shifty eyes and uneasy fingers persuaded me the events had not happened exactly as he was recounting them.

"Truth is the box was pretty, I thought it would make a nice present for a lass, might get me a favour, so I says 'ta and takes it without telling Martin, 'cos he says 'take anything you likes', but I thought he might not like me taking such a pretty box, so I says naught and puts it in me pocket. When I got home, I was mighty pleased. I cleaned it on the outside with the oil Beth uses for the furniture and it looks real new. Sure any girl will be tickled when I gives it to her.

"On the inside it was blue and smooth as silk. It was empty but dusty, so I takes a kitchen cloth and wipes it. The bottom was loose, so I lifts it up, and underneath there was a letter. A very long letter. Ain't no good at reading. Ain't never been to school. I can count and I can read and write me name, and some big letters I can read them, too, like I can read The Rochester Arms, that's why I know it's from the master. It's signed by Mr. Rochester, and it's got one of those fancy seals they use for letters, but I can't read a single word of what it says. Might be important, mightn't it? I know you read well, better than all the rest of us. I seened you with all those fancy books. Well, will you read it for me?"

I scanned the letter his trembling hands had thrust into mine. The date was written in Roman numerals. It was addressed to, "My Dearest Uncle", and signed by Edward Rochester. The spidery handwriting was indeed hard to read, but I was able to discern that it was a document of the utmost importance, and a very dangerous document to possess, especially by the likes of feather-brained Simon.

As I read the last lines, I slumped down on the bed, "Could you bring a candle, so I can read it more easily, Simon? There's not much light in here."

It was an overcast grey day, but the letter was not difficult to read. I needed time to think. It would have been most unwise to inform Simon of the contents.

"Well? What is it?" He insisted minutes later, nudging me with his bony elbow.

"It is a love letter to Mrs. Rochester. He is asking her to marry him." I lied.

"It's old then?"

"Yes, it must be over twenty years old."

"Go on! Read it to me, Michael."

I noticed my cheeks redden and my heart race violently. I had to think quickly and improvise. The letter was long, taking up almost a whole page, so I should ensure my rendering was not too short to lead to suspicion, even in someone as simple as Simon.

"Just a minute ... I'm trying to decipher the words ... the writing is very uneven." I said, in an effort to buy some time for my invention. What did I know about my mistress? I gathered all the scattered information in my mind, as quickly as I could. I knew that the only family she had in the world were her two cousins, Diana, Mrs. Fitzjames, the Colonel's wife, and her sister, Mary, Mrs. Wharton, the clergyman's wife. They had a brother who lived in India. I knew nothing about him. I knew she had no father or any other male relatives. Her uncle and benefactor had died, too. I also knew, from Mrs. Leah, that she had met Mr. Rochester when she had been employed as Miss Adele's governess, and of course, I knew that her maiden name was Eyre. That would have to be enough. I started reading slowly, giving myself more opportunity to elaborate a proposal.

My Dearest Jane Eyre,

This letter should be addressed to your father, but unfortunately he is deceased. It could also be addressed to your uncle, but he is likewise deceased. You possess no living relative in the world, except your cousins, Mrs. Wharton and Mrs. Fitzjames. Your personal situation makes it impossible for me to address any third party. You are now your own mistress, working for a living in my household. I therefore address this letter directly to you, in the hope that you will do me the honour of reading what I have to offer you, which is all my love and all my possessions. I sincerely hope you will forgive my forthright approach, in which I most humbly ask your permission to express my most sincere affection. With God's help, I am committed to make you the happiest woman on earth. My whole life will be devoted to this purpose, if you kindly accept this offer of marriage to your most humble servant.

Edward Rochester.

"Is that all?"

"Yes, well, there are a few lines I cannot decipher, but the message is clear. It is a petition for marriage."

"Wow, what fancy words! But why don't they come to the point and say, "I love you" or "marry me"? D'you think it's worth anything?"

"Not much. Who would want an old love letter?"

"Suppose not." He rubbed his stubbly chin first, then picked his bushy eyebrows, as if he were concocting a plan to obtain some sort of benefit from the epistle.

"Simon, it is only valuable to Mrs. Rochester. She must have mislaid it, or someone stole it from her. I'm sure she would appreciate it being returned. It has sentimental value. It's from her husband, and he is dying."

"What if I offers it to her? Do you think she might give me a tip for it?"

"You might have to answer a lot of questions, like: where did you find it? When did you find it? She may think you took it and are returning it for your benefit. Anyway, you're not guaranteed she'd give you anything for it."

"Michael, you're so clever. You think of everything. What can I do with it then?"

"I suggest you put it on her desk, so she will find it. She will no doubt be pleased to recover it. It will be your good deed for the day."

"I ain't interested in no good deeds. Good deeds never fed no one. I'll put it back in the box then and keep it for a while. You never know when it might come in handy."

I realized the letter would bring serious problems, not only to whoever owned it, but also to both Mr. and Mrs. Rochester. He was on his deathbed, but the scandal would surely affect my mistress and young Master John. I realized I needed to keep the letter and give it to her myself at the right moment.

"I wouldn't keep it on me, if I were you. What are you doing with a private letter written by your master to his mistress? It would surely get you into trouble."

"What do you suggest?"

"Get rid of it."

"You mean burn it?"

"No, don't do that. I'm sure Mrs. Rochester would like to have it. Put it on her desk, and she'll find it there. She won't know who put it there or why, but she'll be glad to recover her husband's love letter."

"Perhaps you're right. What good is an old love letter from a husband to his wife, anyways?"

"Mrs. Rochester is reading to Mr. Rochester now, but she will be coming down for lunch shortly. While she is having lunch in the dining room, go to the drawing room and put the letter on her writing desk. Make sure you draw the curtains between the two rooms, so that she does not see you. After lunch she goes back to the drawing room, sits at her desk, and writes her letters. She'll find it then and read it."

"Where shall I put it?"

"Put it in her diary, it's a large brown leather covered book, which is always on the table next to the quill and the ink pot."

He scratched his head, looking confused.

"And Simon, I wouldn't mention it to anyone. No parodies or games, or you'd have a lot of explaining to do. This letter could get you into trouble, if anyone knows you have it. Count on me to keep your secret."

"Suppose you're right."

"Let me read it one more time before Mrs. Leah comes."

"Be my guest, mate. I'm going to have some lunch. Stew smells good."

I sat on my bed and reread the distressing words.

Dearest Uncle Robert,

I know my father does not pay you well, and you know he does not treat me well. We must work together to free ourselves from his devilish claws. I am prepared to compensate you generously, if you help me get out of this inferno. I would prefer all the flee-ridden rats of London to these disgusting insects that pursue and bite English men, giving rise to a fever that makes a man loose his reason, as well as control of his limbs. Rats scuffle away when they see a man, but these murderous creatures of Satan pursue a man and drive him to a destiny, which is worse than any plague. The fever turns you into another being with no reason, no will power. They reduce a man to a zombie. I tell you, I must return to England! I am plagued by a sorceress, who has gone mad, and this place is full of lazy, useless, sweaty, natives, who cast spells and hypnotize innocent Englishmen.

My agent, Mr. Cooper, who has delivered this letter, has informed me that my brother has been taken ill. He has told me Dr. Carter says it is a deadly scourge that is eating his liver. There is no hope for him. Uncle, I beseech you, I must have news of my father's death, as soon as possible, and return to Thornfield to claim what is rightfully mine. I beseech you to assist me as you see fit, any discreet means, such as suffocation will be sufficient. He is old and weak, therefore, he will not resist. Know also that you have the compliance of both Mr. Cooper and Dr. Carter for any endeavour. Your apprentice, Mr Wood, could be easily convinced to be of assistance, if needs be, but better leave him out of it, lest he should have an attack of guilt and take it on himself to confess.

As soon as this is done (the sooner the better, or I may never return, and die in this Godforsaken hell), I will entreat to you half of my dowry. I would gladly give it all away to be rid of this inferno, but the other half will be used to take care of the mad creature, who has been thrust upon me. Destroy this letter as soon as you have understood the contents. Send a message through Mr. Cooper, when all is clear to return home.

You are a good, kind, man and may find it difficult to accomplish this task, but may I also remind you how savagely my father treated my mother, your sister, probably breaking her heart and her body into irretrievable pieces? Let this thought give you the strength you may need to help me and avenge her memory. I trust your kind wife, Mrs. Fairfax, is in good health and recovered, after her recent illness. Rest assured that neither of you will ever need anything, as long as I am Master of Thornfield.

Your nephew,
Edward Rochester.

I was not sure what should be done with the letter, yet, but I did know it should not fall into unscrupulous hands. My mistress had enough worries on her mind. I realised it was time for her to receive some good news, so I proceeded to write a letter, which she would receive, instead of her husband's murderous request.

I returned the letter to Simon and went upstairs to Adele's first floor tower room to get some paper and a pen. I knew she had gone out for her usual midmorning walk with the dogs. Her room overlooked the gardens, so I would see her return. I wrote my letter in a few brief minutes. I had written many imaginary letters to my mistress over the last three years. None had been put to paper, because I never thought I would materialize my fantasy until an hour ago. Suddenly it dawned on me that the precise moment had come, not only to write the letter, but also to deliver it to the woman I had adored in silence, since I was a boy. I reread the contents until I saw Adele approach the front door, followed by Piper, Keeper and Flossy, who were busy sniffing the limp, battered leaves along the driveway. I put the letter in my pocket and dashed down the stairs to open the door for Miss Adele.

"Nice walk, Miss Adele?"

"Quite chilly actually, Michael. I can hardly feel my hands, in spite of my mittens. Make sure all the hearths are in full swing today, it is deathly cold!"

"Yes, miss."

"What's the matter, Michael? You're breathless, and you look quite dishevelled. Mrs. Rochester will be most shocked if she sees you serving lunch like that! For God's sake, go and clean yourself up!"

"Yes, Miss Adele. At once. Will you be having lunch in the dining room with Mrs. Rochester today?"

"Yes. Something light. Jane isn't very hungry today. Bring up some bread and butter, milk and honey, some hot broth, and cold meat, preferably mutton, and some tea for me."

"I'll ask cook to prepare it immediately."

Later, when I brought up the lunch tray and set it on the table, my mistress was indeed pale and lost in her thoughts. I had imagined my declaration would cheer her up. It would let her know that someone loved her more than himself, more than anything in the world. Suddenly my chest tightened, and I couldn't breathe, perhaps my letter would not please her. Perhaps it would trouble her, even more than she already was. Perhaps she would expel me from her side, and I would never see her again. No! That would be worse than death.

"Michael? Are you alright? You look most unwell." Adele's voice was sharp and loud, as usual, unaware of anyone's feelings, except her own. She might understand me, if I could speak to her about my silent adoration, but of course I had to keep my secret. I coughed and started breathing, "I am very well, Miss Adele, just a little cold."

"But you were too warm, only a while ago. Perhaps you have a fever!" Insisted Adele with a prickly scream.

"Michael, go and rest for a while, if you are not well." My mistress's voice was absent, but soft and caring. Her heavy eyes rested on mine for a moment longer than I could bear. I wished I could embrace her and tell her she shouldn't be distressed, because I loved her and would protect her from anyone who ever tried to harm her. I wanted to tell her I would gladly die for her, because my life without her is worthless. Instead, I turned my eyes down to the table and insisted that I was in good health.

She spoke again softly, "You had a busy day yesterday. Make sure you rest after lunch, Michael."

I could hear Simon in the drawing room, fidgeting by the desk. Much as I detested the idea that he would touch her diary and her personal papers with his uncouth hands, it was the only way to recover the letter. He would leave it there for her, and I would exchange it for my love letter and keep the Master's letter myself. I heard the wood squeak under the weight of his footsteps, then the sharp snap of the door closing.

"Thank you, Mrs. Rochester, but I am well. I will go to the drawing room and make sure the fire is kindled. I'm afraid today is the chilliest day we have yet had."

I slid the curtain to one side, making sure it hung back in its place behind me. As I approached my mistress's majestic oak desk, I heard Adele's piercing voice once more reproaching my appearance. I heard my mistress answer quietly, asking Adele to stop berating me, because I had never been sick for a single day in five years. I was sure she valued my service, but I shuddered to think what she would feel after reading my letter. Simon's letter bulged in her diary. I pulled it out and replaced it with mine, sliding her husband's letter into my pocket, and walked towards the fire, poking the coals to spark up the flames.

The blood had drained from my head and chest, and descended to my heavy feet. I fell to my knees before the fire and begged God to save my mistress from pain. She deserves to be happy. She deserves to be loved. The bright orange flames glowing on my face warmed my soul. She would soon read my letter. I have opened my heart to her, it is in her hands. What will she do with it? Crumple it in her fingers? Burn it in the fire? Laugh at me for my presumptuousness? Hate me for my cheek? Cast me away for my depravation in daring to even think of her in such a way? It is true. I am not worthy of her, no one is good enough for her. How could I dare to love her? How dare I importune her? I must remove the letter. I was a fool to even imagine she would want to read its contents.

I stood up, my body warmed, my blood circulating once more, and returned to the desk to retrieve the imprudent words I had written. Too late! Adele drew the curtains with a swift sharp pull before I could complete my purpose.

"Shall we sit here and rest a few minutes, Jane? It's the warmest room in the house."

"Yes, stay with me for a while, Adele."

My mistress turned away from Adele to look at me before speaking, "You look much recovered, Michael. Are you still cold?" I nodded, unable to speak once more. I was about to leave the room, when she called me back.

"Just a minute, Michael. I would like you to run an errand for me this evening before supper."

She got up and sat at her desk, then moved her diary to one side gently to make room for some note paper. My legs felt as heavy as lead and then soft like jelly, as her hand inadvertently approached my letter. She dipped her pen in the ink bottle and scratched a brief message, blotted it, folded it over, and slid it into an envelope, which she closed with the Rochester seal.

"Please take this message to the Rochester Arms. You must deliver it personally to the person whose name is on the envelope and wait for an answer." I nodded. "And Michael, ask Mrs. Leah to come up when she has had lunch, I need to speak to her about dinner tomorrow and housekeeping arrangements. We will be having guests shortly."

My letter was still inside her diary. Unseen. Untouched. Unread. No longer in my possession, but not yet in hers. What had I done?

"Michael, what is the matter? You are quite pale once more."

I could not reply. I was paralyzed with fear and quite unable to move or utter a single word. Had I made a mistake beyond repair?

"Rest for a while before you take the message. The next few days will be very busy at Eyre Hall."

She took a step closer and deposited the envelope in my hand, which she squeezed lightly. Then she pressed her other hand against my forehead.

"Michael, your hands are cold and your face is too warm. Tell me, are you feeling unwell?"

"I told you he was unwell, Jane" accused Adele from the other side of the room, on the couch by the hearth.

I heard myself speak, "I'm sorry, Mrs. Rochester. I must have caught cold yesterday on my way to Ferndean."

"Sit by the stove in the kitchen, keep warm, and eat before you go. If you do not feel better, Simon can take the message." She took my hand with both of hers and spoke softly, making sure Adele did not hear, "It is very important, so I would prefer if *you* could do it for me, please. And do take care, Michael."

My hand was trapped in hers, and my heart was lost in her imploring eyes for the longest moment in time. When she finally released my hand, I nodded and said, "Of course, Mrs. Rochester," before leaving the room.

I leaned against the wall in the hall, too dazed to walk down to the kitchen at once. Adele's renewed admonishment rang through the walls.

"That boy is either sick or in love. Stuttering and stumbling like a schoolboy..."

I held my breath, waiting for my mistress's reply.

"Nonsense, Adele! Michael is too healthy and too sensible for either."

Chapter X

Mrs. Leah

I took my housekeeping diary and pencil and went up to the drawing room as required to plan the weeks' housekeeping with the mistress of the house. I had worked for the present Mr. Rochester since I was thirteen, almost two years before Miss Jane Eyre arrived at Thornfield Hall, as governess to Miss Adele.

I had been lucky to work for the Rochester family at Thornfield Hall. Everyone in Millcote, Hay, and the surrounding hamlets had heard of the Rochesters. They had owned most of the land in the area for at least four generations. Anyone who rented from them, hunted on their lands, or worked there, had been appointed, or at least authorized by them. I myself had been sent to work at Thornfield from Highgrove Orphanage at Millcote. The Headmaster, Mr. Brockbank, told me how lucky I was to have been chosen to work at the Rochester's Great Hall. Although I had never been aware of being chosen, and never found out how it had happened. In any case, I was happier than I had been at Highgrove. The rooms were warmer, and the food was more plentiful.

There was no mistress at Thornfield Hall, which was an obvious advantage, as mistresses are far more demanding and intrusive of their servants' work. There was a master, who was often moody and at times vociferous, but we hardly ever saw him, because he was usually away.

The work was hard, because the house was big and there were few servants, so we rarely had an afternoon off, but the conditions were pleasant enough. Mrs. Fairfax, the housekeeper, was an amiable manager, who rarely scolded and usually deemed our work had been well done. Her late husband, Mr. Robert Fairfax, who had been clergyman at Hay, had been a relative of Mr. Rochester's mother. She made no fuss of it, although to be sure, she always kept her distance from the rest of the servants, and would have dinner with the master when he was in the house. She informed me that Mr. Brockbank had told Mr. Rochester that my mother had been a hapless Irish maid who had died at childbirth.

Mrs. Fairfax was especially kind to me, from the very first day I arrived. She would often ask me to read to her due to her failing vision. She was keen on the *Book of Proverbs*, because she said they contained God given counsel to help us discern between good and evil. I presumed they were the ramblings of an old woman, yet over twenty years later, I often find myself rereading them and recalling her wise words and gentle voice, as she explained the teachings while I read to her.

I'll never forget the day I met Jane Eyre. It was the beginning of October, twenty-four years ago exactly. She was short and slight, and sickly pale. She stood insecurely in the kitchen, as if the ground might sink in under her feet, and looked quite ghostlike in her coarse, thickly woven black dress and black straw bonnet. Her hands were covered with black gloves and a muff. A black and grey woollen cloak, which seemed quite insufficient for the freezing weather she must have encountered, hung over her shoulders.

She had just arrived at Thornfield Hall after an eighteen hour coach journey from an institution for orphans in Lowood. Mrs. Fairfax had sent a coachman to collect her at the George Inn in Millcote and bring her to our household. Miss Eyre looked as frail as a porcelain plate and as hungry as a church mouse. Her round, lidded and corded wooden trunk, which resembled a shipwrecked treasure chest, easily weighed more than she did herself, clothes and all. Mrs. Fairfax must have thought, as I had, that she hadn't eaten in a week, and asked me to make her some hot negus and cut some sandwiches, no doubt to get some life into her, in case she would die of exhaustion and starvation that very night.

Miss Eyre, as we were to call her, had come to be governess to Miss Adele Varens, Mr. Rochester's 'ward', whom we all knew to be his illegitimate French daughter. Adele had arrived with her French nurse, Sophie, just a month before, in September. The spoilt little brat, who shouted in French and ran around the house dancing and singing like a drunk parrot, was flouting the peace at Thornfield. So Mrs. Fairfax, following the master's orders, and out of her own desperation, had searched in the *Northern Herald* for young ladies, who advertised as governesses. Unfortunately for my master, she found Miss Eyre, who spoke French and had good references.

We had been expecting the governess impatiently, so that morning I had prepared her chamber, a small apartment on the first storey at the back of the house, next to Mrs. Fairfax's room. She arrived late in the afternoon, ate a little, said she was fatigued after her long journey, and asked to be shown to her room. Her soft, low voice and waif-like demeanour fooled us all. We thought she would not last till the Beaver Moon. Adele was taller and fuller bodied than her new governess, and she was more vigorous and forceful. However, surprisingly, Miss Eyre made great progress with her pupil, who seemed quite tamed in conduct and refined in her manners by the time Mr. Rochester returned in January.

Miss Eyre was a strange creature, who spoke very little and spent many hours floating around the Hall like a sleepwalker. She tiptoed about, peaking behind closed doors, and there were plenty of them (I had counted over forty), wandering around the rooms and peering out of the windows, as if she were a lost soul in a cemetery. More than once I saw her climb to the third storey, raise the trapdoor of the attic, and look out over the fields and hills with a strange longing in her eyes. Then, when the master came, I realized what it was she desired, what she had desired since the first day she set eyes on the estate. She wanted Thornfield and everything in it, but she hadn't even imagined that one of its invisible occupants was far stronger willed than she was.

Thornfield was a dark vault-like house, with plenty of nooks in the sombre galleries. I was young and impressionable, and I often saw strange unearthly shadows in its shady corners, but we all knew that one of the ghosts was alive. She, too, must have heard the whispering and the laughing, or seen her shadow in the gallery, when she escaped from her room, which was far too often to remain unnoticed. Only Grace Poole had actually seen the monster face to face, but she told us enough stories to make our blood curdle. Grace was a big, strong woman, who looked after the lunatic and helped me with the sewing and ironing. Grace was usually loud and noisy due to her weakness for gin, which, being colourless, was easy to disguise as water, except for the stench in her glass and on her breath. She earned five times my wages, of course she was the only one who was strong and brave enough to look after the hideous wife Mr. Rochester had concealed in the third storey.

Miss Eyre, who would have liked to become Mrs. Rochester far sooner than discretion would have advised, always said she did not know about the madwoman in the attic. I did not dislike Miss Eyre, she was pleasant enough, but I came to the conclusion that she pretended not to know by ignoring any type of conversation or gossip on the matter. She very rarely conversed with any of the servants, except Mrs. Fairfax, who wasn't really a servant, being as she was related to the master of the house. They both had the privilege of conversing directly with the master, and sitting with him after dinner. Jane Eyre was keen to improve her station in life. Her first attempt failed most shamefully at the altar, although she finally got her own way a year later.

Two months after the marriage farce, the lunatic nearly got us all killed by setting the house on fire. She escaped from her windowless chamber in the attic, and while Grace dozed in drunken slumber, she took her keys and let herself out of her hole. She left the room with a candlestick and set fire to the drapery that covered the door of the tapestried room next to her own. Then she got down to the second floor, went into the room, which had been her rival's, and lit the curtains and the bed. Fortunately Mrs. Fairfax, who slept in the room next door, advised the master who was fast asleep. We all heard the cries and smelt the thick smoke, a mixture of cloth, furniture, wood, and stone.

As we left the building and looked up, we saw the fiend on the top floor battlements waving her arms and shouting against the flames. Mr. Rochester stood behind her on the roof. We heard him call 'Bertha!'

and we saw him approach her, and then she fell off and smashed on the footpath. We all said he had tried to save her, but the truth is that both were up on the battlements, quite alone and out of reach on a dark night. Nobody else knew what really happened up there, and only one survived. Strange that Mr. Rochester should risk his life to save her and lock her up again, wouldn't you say? But who was to worry about a dead lunatic?

Months earlier, when Mr. Rochester had walked into Mrs. Fairfax's parlour and told us he was going to marry the governess, we were thunderstruck. Mrs. Fairfax said no good could come of their wedding because 'A wife of noble character is her husband's crown, but a disgraceful wife is like decay in his bones'. And poor Mr. Rochester was decayed to the bone by his mad wife. Mrs. Fairfax told us how Mr. Rochester had followed his father's unwise instructions and married the mad woman in his youth. Unfortunately, his father did not possess the wisdom of King Solomon. The old brute had cared only for his eldest son, Rowland, and discarded young Edward as second best, sending him to Jamaica to marry a rich heiress. Master Edward's father should have told him how much better it would have been to gain wisdom than gold.

Jane Eyre finally married Mr. Rochester, and imagined she would live happily ever after. But that is not how it occurred. At first, he doted on her, pandering to all her whims and agreeing to all her proposals. She feigned reluctance at first, but soon accepted all the frills and jewels the best London shops could offer. She insisted they move away from modest Ferndean. She had inherited a great deal of money from an uncle who had passed away childless, and with her unexpected booty, she decided to build a new mansion on the Thornfield site, in time for the birth of their son.

Eyre Hall was built by one of the best architects in the country, who was responsible for rebuilding large London mansions in the new Gothic style, which included towers, cusped ceilings, and pointed arches. She had a central tower built with two wings on either side, plus an adjacent servant's quarter. It was decorated with carved mahogany furniture and fashionable buttoned upholstery. The floors were covered with the most lavish Turkish carpets, while French chandeliers hung from the ceilings, and English landscape paintings decorated the walls. Richly coloured damask fabric covered the chairs, the best oak was used to panel walls, and sterling silver dishes and ewers decorated the chambers. I witnessed how she became quite the self-righteous, smug mistress she had always said she would never be.

I know my place, and my relationship both with Jane Eyre and with Jane Rochester has always been courteous. After the fire, Mr. Rochester sent Mrs. Fairfax away with a handsome and well-deserved annuity. I accompanied her for a time, but her heart was weak, and she died shortly after. When the new building, Eyre Hall, was finished, I was working as upper chamber maid in a grand hotel in Millcote. Mr. And Mrs. Rochester asked me if I would like to be their new housekeeper. I was offered an exceptionally good salary and a superior position, so I accepted. I always imagined that she wanted me back there, because I had witnessed her rise in the world, and I would continue to confirm who she had been and who she had become. It was a fair deal, we both improved our station.

At first the marriage was happy, but then came the miscarriages, the stillborn baby, her illness, her charity work, her novel, his trips to London, the other women, and the rift, which had always existed, grew even wider. She did not seem to mind her husband's new pursuits, because she was too busy with her own ambitions, which knew no limits. She wanted to be the mistress of a great house, and she wanted her son to be the greatest Rochester of all. She certainly seemed to be on the right track. Unfortunately, Mr. Rochester's imminent death and Mr. Mason's arrival could prove to be setbacks to her great plan.

Last night she informed me of the exceptional and surprising arrangements for the following days. We were having a full house with many unexpected guests. In the first place, Mr. William Greenwood, the famous London poet and Miss Adele's latest suitor, would be staying in the Green Room. He was not the first gentleman to court her and visit Eyre Hall, but he was the first in several years, and the first to be invited to stay overnight. So I supposed there were more chances of success on this occasion.

It was proving very difficult to marry Miss Adele. In addition to her immature character and spoilt upbringing, she had no social standing and no money of her own. Mrs. Rochester was very fond of her, and Miss Adele repaid her generosity by helping and supporting her while John was a child, through her miscarriages, and especially through her mysterious illness. Her dowry would no doubt be generous, but she had little else to offer, and her childbearing years were almost over. She had become an eccentric spinster, who spent most of her days walking the dogs, reading romantic novels, and writing poems and letters in her solitary tower.

The next guest, Bishop Templar, who had been John's headmaster and mentor at Rugby, would be staying in the Blue Room. Mrs. Rochester wanted to make it very clear that John had invited him, but I was sure it had been at his own request. He was a widower, and according to local gossip, he was living with his housekeeper in intimacy. It was my guess, knowing of Mr. Rochester's deteriorating health, he was interested in paying his respects to the future widow, in case she was looking for a new husband.

Mrs. Rochester was a young and wealthy lady, who had become well-known for her social concerns and her novel. I doubted she would remain a widow more than the required year's mourning. Bishop Templar was an ambitious man. It was rumoured that he would become Archbishop of Canterbury, and he shared her charitable and educational concerns, so they were well suited.

However, the most extraordinary visitors of all were Mr. Mason, Mr. Rochester's first wife's brother, and Miss Annette Mason, Mr. Mason's niece, both from Spanish Town, Jamaica, who would be staying in the adjacent Golden Rooms, which we used for our special guests. I knew of the Masons' existence from my days at Thornfield. Mr. Mason had visited his sister at the old mansion and interrupted Miss Eyre's first marriage attempt by reminding Mr. Rochester what we all knew too well. I had never seen him again after that day. He did not even attend his sister's funeral. Mr. Rochester had said he would shoot him, if he ever had him within reach again. He must have taken the threat seriously, because he did not appear, although we heard he was in

England at the time. Mrs. Rochester should have been buried at a crossroad and staked to prevent her soul haunting the living. But instead, she was buried near midnight, at the corner of the churchyard by the wall, in an unmarked grave. Mr. Wood pronounced some words, because he was a good and just man. He should have insisted on an impalement, which would have put an end to her curse.

The lunatic's spirit has returned. Simon told us he overheard Mr. Mason tell Mrs. Rochester that the child, Annette Mason, was Bertha's. I did not tell Simon, or anyone else, but I remember the day Grace Poole ran out in horror, screaming that the devil's child had been born on the third storey. Dr. Carter arrived forthwith, and we employed a wet nurse until Richard Mason took the creature back to Jamaica, where it belonged. It was never seen, heard of, or talked of again, until this very morning.

Mrs. Rochester wanted to make sure the domestic arrangements for the following days were to her liking.

"Leah, have you thought of the menu for tomorrow night?"

"May I suggest asparagus soup and broiled salmon for the first course; pheasant casserole, green vegetables for the second course; roast goose, grilled mushrooms for the third course; and port wine jelly, apple pie, and custard for dessert. Finally some ices, wafers, biscuits, tea, coffee, Madeira wine and brandy."

"That's an excellent choice, Leah, as always. Please see to it that cook has everything she needs. Will you need any extra staff?"

"We can manage for one evening. It is more time consuming to teach them, once they've been taught, it's time for them to leave."

"Bear in mind, we will be having four extra guests from tomorrow, and although Bishop Templar and Mr. Greenwood may be leaving soon, my cousins, Mrs. Wharton and Mrs. Fitzjames, will be coming next week with their husbands to stay for at least a week. I suggest you call the George Inn and ask them to send you some extra maids for the chambers and to help cook."

"In that case, I will make the arrangements at once. Is that all, Mrs. Rochester?"

"Just one more thing, Leah. No girls under the age of thirteen, and employ orphans and poorer girls who attend the Sunday school, preferably."

"Of course, madam."

After deciding on the menu and extra staff, she told me Michael would be occupied doing her urgent errands and insisted I should not to keep him busy with too many household chores, except those related directly to her, such as breakfasts and lunches, and of course her dinner.

She is becoming too protective of her pets, Michael and Susan, who both worship her as their magnanimous saviour. Michael is far too clever to remain a servant for much longer. He reads and writes as well as the masters. He is better at bookkeeping than I am, and far too attractive for his own good. His sister is almost as praiseworthy. I am suspicious of their intentions. Now that Mr. Rochester is dying and Mrs. Rochester will be mistress on her own, the ground is moving under Eyre Hall.

Chapter XI

Michael's Letter

I was not the least bit hungry, so I asked Simon to bring up bread and tea. The tea was warming, and the bread was dry and thick to swallow, but I made myself eat some, lest I should fall ill. Dr. Carter was most insistent that I should eat at least four square meals a day, so I would try my best. I would not be of much help to anyone if I were unwell.

John had gone to Thornby, a small hamlet beyond Hay, to a small secluded cottage, where Bishop Templar had moved with his housekeeper, in an attempt to avoid the gossip in Millcote. Adele had retired to her Tower Room to rewrite her letter to Mr. Greenwood, and Michael was on his errand to the inn, so I was left with the strangeness of dining alone with careless Simon noisily rattling the cutlery and crockery.

After eating, I pulled the curtain and headed to my desk and the comforting privacy of my pen and diary, grateful for the silence and the solitude, at last. As I opened the book, I noticed there was a folded piece of paper inside, which I did not recall having inserted. I pulled it out softly, and for some unknown reason, I imagined it was a precious gift. I unfolded it delicately, as if it would disintegrate in my fingers.

It was a letter addressed to "My Dearest Mistress". I looked down to the end of the page, but it was not signed. An anonymous letter? Who could have put it here, in my diary? Michael's troubled eyes, as I had given him the note after lunch came to my mind, and my heart fluttered.

My Dearest Mistress,

My hand trembles as I write this letter. I humbly entreat you to consider it a token of my eternal loyalty and adoration. I can no longer wait in silence while I watch you suffer unjustly. You are not alone. The place I most cherish is by your side or better still, in your shadow. I offer myself to you in humble and loyal service for the rest of my days. For you alone, I live, I hope, and pray. I will do anything to alleviate your distress and contribute to your contentment. You alone shall be my mistress. My only wish is to remain as close to you as I should be allowed.

I await a sign, even the very smallest token, that you are not displeased with these words and will allow me to obey you. Your most faithful and dedicated servant, who must remain unnamed, because he has no name save yours, no hands save yours, no lips save yours, no life save that which you will grant by accepting his service.

Your eternal and unconditional subject.

I breathed in on reading the first line and held my breath to the end of the letter while my eyes followed the words on the page. When I finished, I breathed out, and my eyes swelled with tears. I wiped them away with my fingers and reread the letter twice more, forcing myself to breathe as I did so. Simon burst in, as untimely as can be expected of him, and asked, rather taken aback, if I was all right, and I told him I was well. Then he looked down at the letter still in my hands and asked, "Good news, madam?" with a smile that was much too bright for Simon. For once, I was relieved that he could neither read nor write.

"Indeed it is, Simon. Good news for a change."

He smiled slyly and surprised me by saying, "Glad to hear that, madam!" before leaving the room.

My thoughts turned back to Michael. If anyone suspected how he felt, I would have to dismiss him, and the thought of being without him filled me with a heavy void. His silent, vigilant shadow protected me, like an invisible shield throughout the day, while his penetrating yet tender gaze has been sending me beams of love to warm my empty heart for years. I sighed and felt a terrifying vibration in my very soul, as I realized I loved him too, and I had loved him for a long time, too long to remember when I had not felt trapped in his devoted eyes.

The first time I saw him, he was so quiet and withdrawn. He sat with his sister in the coach, facing me with a lost look throughout the journey. I remember smiling and asking him if he was well, and he nodded. Every time I tried to speak to him, he nodded and Susan spoke for him. When he first came to Eyre Hall, he seemed confused and bewildered. Leah said he would not eat or speak unless his sister was with him. Simon said he worked hard and learned the chores with ease, but complained that the new boy was too silent. I told them to be patient, but Leah was not prone to civility with children and Simon was too uncouth to care, so I spoke to Michael myself. I asked him if he was happy, or if he would prefer to be somewhere else. He told me he had never lived in such a beautiful, warm and comfortable house. I asked him why he didn't speak to anyone at the house, and he answered that at the workhouse he had never spoken to the other men, who were rough and violent, for fear of being picked on. It was obvious to me he lived in fear of himself and of others. I told him he should make an effort to speak to everyone, because not to do so would be considered rude. His big eyes stared at me, as he promised he would make an effort to be more civil.

I knew he liked reading, so I took him to the library and told him he could take and read any book he wanted, on condition that he made an effort to speak to everyone who crossed his path in the house. He looked confused, and said he would have nothing to say to any of them. He had obviously spent the past two years in the workhouse avoiding people, and rejecting any type of spoken or physical contact with anyone, except his sister. He had retreated into a lonely shell, which he filled with books and his own reverie.

I understood exactly how he felt. It is how I had felt after my miscarriages, and especially after my daughter was stillborn. He needed help, and I wanted to set free the soul behind the armour, so I told him to come to the library every day after lunch. I started instructing him about basic greetings: good morning, afternoon, evening and night with a smile to everyone he crossed during the day. Then I moved on to explain other polite forms of expression, enquiring about people's health and well-being, or the weather. I informed him when asked a question, he should answer using sentences, not nodding or uttering monosyllabic words. I also told him he should go out on his free afternoon, because there were many things in life that were not learnt in books.

I reminded him that there were wonderful and interesting people in the world, and he would learn many things from them. Months later he had improved greatly. He was brisk and friendly and often smiled. I felt proud, because I knew I had contributed to his change of character. I promoted him to my personal valet and Adele's while Simon was to deal more especially with Edward, whose condition was worsening by days.

Surprisingly, we had spoken very little of late, but he was always there, watching over me while I ate, poking the fire when I was at my desk, and doing all my errands uncomplainingly, however miserable the weather was. He was sturdy and loyal, like the trees in the orchard. Life without him would be as if all the trees were cut down. Unbearable. I had to make sure he understood how dangerous the situation was for both of us, but how would I do it? I was too tired to think any more, so I rested my head on my arms. Eight words came to my mind, as I relinquished my reckless thoughts to Morpheus; *Wild nights, wild nights, were I with thee...*

<hr />

I returned very late that evening, after delivering the message to Mr. Mason, and went into the drawing room to tell my mistress that his reply was affirmative. The candle on her desk was almost wasted, the oil lamps on the table had been extinguished, and only a few burning coals remained in the hearth. Her head lay on the desk. She was asleep, and my letter was folded in her hand. She must have read it! I dared not wake her, so I closed the door quietly and went up to Adele's study, on the first floor tower, to tell her that my mistress should be taken up to bed.

"Michael, I'm glad you came! I have just finished writing the letter to Mr. Greenwood. Can I read it to you?"

"Miss Adele, I came to tell you that Mrs. Rochester has fallen asleep on her desk. Perhaps you should wake her up and bring her upstairs. It is very late."

"Indeed it is! You look pretty dishevelled and exhausted yourself! Where have you been?"

"Mrs. Rochester sent me to the Arms on an errand."

"An errand? At this time of night?"

"She said it was urgent."

"Who was the errand for?"

"I don't know if I'm authorized to say, Miss Adele."

"What do you mean, Michael?"

"Mrs. Rochester was most upset when she found out I had helped you hide Mr. Greenwood's letters…"

"For God's sake, Michael, don't be ridiculous!"

"She accused me of disloyalty, Miss Adele."

"She was probably jealous, because you helped me. She wants you all to herself! Tell me about the errand!"

"I'm afraid I can't."

"Then I'll have to tell Jane you read her letters, and you take paper and ink from my desk… don't deny it. I've seen you do it!"

"Please, Miss Adele, don't do that. Mrs. Rochester would be most upset."

"Don't fret, Michael. Of course I won't tell her!"

"Thank you, Miss Adele."

"Michael, she's way beyond your bounds. True, she's been fond of you since she brought you here, when you were a boy, but don't be misled. I'm sure you're clever enough not to confuse fondness or pity with … other feelings, aren't you?"

"Yes, Miss Adele."

"So, tell me about the errand."

"It was for Mr. Mason, the gentleman who called this morning."

"Mason! He's no gentleman! What's he doing here? Why didn't Jane tell me about his visit? What does he want? Do you know, Michael?"

"No, Miss Adele. I only know she received a note from him saying he would like to call this morning."

"And what did the note you took this afternoon say? Don't tell me you didn't read it, because I know did!"

"She asked him for dinner tomorrow, at Eyre Hall, and he agreed."

"I don't believe it!"

"And she asked him to stay here at Eyre Hall, as her guest, with his niece."

"His niece!"

"Is there a problem, Miss Adele?"

"There's a terrible problem, Michael. Terrible. He is Mr. Rochester's first wife's brother. He and his father tricked Mr. Rochester into marrying her for her dowry, but they didn't tell him she was mad! He's worse than the devil. Mon Dieu! And he'll be staying under this roof with us! I can't believe she has invited him to stay. I know nothing of a niece. He had no other siblings, as far as I know, except Bertha, Mr. Rochester's first wife. Did you see her? How old is she?"

"She is a young lady. I would say Susan's age."

"This is terrible news, Michael, and on Monsieur Rochester's deathbed. And John here for the weekend! I can't believe he's doing this… Michael, promise me, not a word to anyone, there will be enough gossip as it is."

"Of course. May I ask if there is anything I can do to help?"

"Look after her, Michael. Look after her, but don't create any problems. When I'm away, and John's away, and Mr. Rochester is no longer with us, she will be quite alone. Stand by her."

"Michael? Adele?" We turned to see Jane standing at the threshold with an inquisitive look on her face.

"Jane, I asked Michael to come up, because I want him to take my letter to the post office at the crack of dawn." She handed me her letter.

"Good God, Adele. Michael has been worked off his feet today, and more is in store tomorrow, I cannot believe you want him to go to Millcote at dawn, just to take your letter..."

"Don't be angry, Jane, it is important for me."

"I don't mind, Mrs. Rochester. I will be back before breakfast."

"Did you get an answer to my message, Michael?"

"Yes, madam. Mr. Mason said he will dine tomorrow with his niece."

"Very well." She sighed, as if the weight of Eyre Hall had fallen on her shoulders, and turned to Adele, "I need to speak to you."

I said good night, thinking my presence was no longer required and turned to leave.

"Michael, please stay. You are the only person in this house, except Adele, I can trust. Please sit down, both of you."

I closed the door and dragged two more armchairs by the fireplace.

"Terrible things have been made known to me today. I have learnt matters I would never have wanted to know. I wish I could ignore them, or fly away like a bird, and forget about them. But I can't. I have a son. He must never know what I am about to disclose to you both now. Adele, bring your Bible and lay it down on the table in front of us. Both of you put your right hand on it and swear that nothing I say will be spoken outside these walls."

We did as she asked.

"Mr. Rochester was the love of my life. The man I would gladly have died for. I would have given him everything I had, including my heart and my soul. Perhaps that was my sin. I should never have loved him so completely and offered my soul, because that belongs only to our Lord. Everything I had and my very self was his. I use the past tense purposefully, because matters have changed, and for some time this love has waned like a worn out candle. The reasons are private. Suffice it to let you know, he no longer merits the unlimited loyalty I offered him. I still owe him my wifely fidelity, but he has committed devilish deeds against me and other people, which I am not in a position to mention to you at this moment. I must ask you to take my word for it. I must also let you know, I have forgiven him absolutely, although it is not my place to absolve him. He must answer for his deeds, very soon, to heavenly justice. I know not where his soul will finally rest after death. The deeds he has committed are unjustifiable.

"The gentleman who visited me this morning was Mr. Richard Mason, my husband's brother-in-law by his first marriage. He has asked to be invited to stay at Eyre Hall with his niece, Annette Mason. I must let you know that this niece belongs to a non-existent sister. Richard had only one sister, step-sister, Bertha. This child was born to Bertha while she lived at Thornfield, while I was there, and you too, Adele."

"No!" Adele cried. "Ce n'est pas possible! I don't believe it! She was an animal! A mad monster! How could she have a child! I never saw any child!"

"The first Mrs. Rochester was insane. She was locked in the attic at Thornfield Hall for her own safety. Twenty-three years ago, she gave birth to a child."

"Then Monsieur is the father? Mon Dieu! Mon Dieu!"

"Mr. Rochester is responsible, because she was legally married to him and under his care, when the child was born, however, he has promised me that he is not the father, and I believe him. Dr. Carter has confirmed the events. We do not know who violated the lunatic or how. Grace Poole, her carer, and Mrs. Fairfax, the housekeeper, are no longer with us."

"Why has Mr. Mason come? What does he want, Jane?"

"Mr. Mason has demanded maintenance and a dowry for Miss Mason, who wishes to live in England. She is to be presented and treated as Miss Annette Mason, Mr. Rochester's niece. She will be presented to society, in order to provide her with a suitable husband. I have to agree…"

"No!" Adele jumped up from the armchair in protest.

"… as I did with you, my dearest Adele."

Jane got up and walked towards her with tears in her eyes as Adele spoke, "Jane, you are my guardian angel. You took me out of that horrible boarding school, where Monsieur sent me after you left, and you have looked after me ever since. You have been more than a mother to me, more than a sister, or a best friend, but I cannot accept her. Her mother was a lunatic, and we don't even know who her father is!"

"Adele, she will be coming here tomorrow. I ask you to accept her as I accepted you, with respect and humility. It is not Miss Mason's fault that her mother was violated, or that her mother's husband did not take care of his wife, as he should have. You must accept her, Adele, for me. Please, will you try?"

"I will try and be polite for you, Jane. But this is not fair. You do not deserve this."

"Do not worry about me, Adele. God has always taken care of me. He has always helped me, when I needed it, and this occasion will be no exception."

"Mrs. Rochester, there is something you should know," I interrupted.

"Tell me, Michael."

"When I went to the inn to take your message, Master John was there having dinner with Mr. Mason and his niece."

"How so? Does Mason know John?" Adele screamed in disbelief.

"John told me he met Miss Mason and Mr. Mason quite by chance the day he arrived, but I did not know he would be seeing her again today. What were they discussing, Michael?"

"They were eating roast pork and drinking mead. They seemed to be speaking amiably, but I did not hear their conversation."

"Strange things are happening, and we do not know how things will turn out. We must be patient and vigilant. Sleep now, Adele. Tomorrow will be a long day. We must prepare for All Hallows."

⁕

I followed Michael down the gallery, as he lit the way with a candle. I observed him carefully for the first time and saw a man, instead of the young boy I had brought home five years ago. His hands were strong and firm, his chest tall and slim, his shoulders wide, and his head stood firmly and proudly ahead of me.

"Michael, please follow me to the library," I whispered, and he nodded. On our way down the staircase we came across Leah on the landing, dressed in her night gown with a candle in her hand and fury in her eyes.

"What is happening tonight? The fires are lit and the candles are still burning. Michael, where have you been all evening?"

"Leah, I'm sorry if we woke you. Michael has been to the inn to take a message. Adele was not well. She is agitated, and we have been up to the tower to calm her down. Now I have asked Michael to light the fire in the library. I must write some letters at once. Please ask Simon to put out the fires and the candles."

"Yes, Mrs. Rochester."

"Has John returned?"

"Not yet, madam."

"Please ask Simon to stay up until he comes in, in case he needs anything."

"Of course. Good night, Mrs. Rochester."

Leah looked enraged, but I had too many other things to think about. We walked into the library and I locked the door. The fire was burning, and there were two candles on the mantelpiece.

"Michael, please draw the curtains and kindle the fire."

I sat on the armchair and watched him, trying to remember the little boy I had seen at Diana's house, but there was another person bending down over the hearth. A man I had just met, although I had known him for years. He finished and stood before me, looking very solemn.

"Michael, whatever made you write that letter, today of all days?"

"I'm sorry, Mrs. Rochester. I did not mean to upset you."

"You did not upset me. It is the most beautiful letter I have ever received, but it was very daring of you to write it. It could have got you into a great deal of trouble. You left it on my desk all day. Fortunately for you, Simon can hardly read, and Leah, Beth and Christy seldom enter the drawing room. I shudder to think of the consequences if it had been found, but I am more grateful for the feelings expressed therein than for any possessions displayed in this room."

He knelt down in front of my armchair and looked up at me nervously. I bent down and held his face in my hands. Such a beautiful lost boy... "What am I going to do about you?"

"You were so upset today, and when I saw you had fainted yesterday, you seemed so lonely and sad, I just wanted you to know that … that you are not alone."

"Thank you for that, but you may be mistaking your feelings, Michael. What you feel for me is gratitude and concern."

"Yes, I feel gratitude, concern, admiration, and… love."

His words brought a lump to my throat. Nobody had spoken to me so tenderly for such a long time. I suddenly felt warm, soft, safe, and speechless. He looked up to my face, longingly, "May I touch you, mistress?"

"We can't do this, Michael. It is not right, and I don't want to hurt you."

"May I touch your hair?" he whispered, probing into my eyes.

"My hair?" I trembled.

"When I first saw you, you were looking out of a window, and the sun's rays were dancing on your hair. It was plaited, wound into a bun, and looked soft and shiny. I have looked at your hair every day since then, longing for the day I would be able to touch it."

Disturbingly, nothing else mattered. The most important thing in the world was to feel his fingers on my hair.

"May I?" he insisted, and I felt myself relax and yield. I do not know what possessed me, but I heard myself say, "You may." I closed my eyes, as he swiped the tips of his fingers along the centre parting at the front of my head and stroked my face.

"May I take out your hair pins?" I nodded, and he moved to my side, still kneeling beside me. I felt his hands softly fondling my hair, pulling out the pins, and combing my tresses with his fingers, until my head became light, and my weighty thoughts evaporated, drifting far away. I realized how long I had lacked love and affection, and how much I missed feeling desired. The dogs barking and the sound of my son's voice shook me out of my reverie. When I opened my eyes he was so close to me, I could feel his heart beating. I tore myself away, out of his spell, and managed to speak, "Michael, we must be very careful. Nobody must know how you feel. I need you by my side, but you cannot stay if your feelings are noticed. Do you understand?"

He nodded. I tied my hair in a knot at the nape of my neck, and he handed me back my hair pins, which I reinserted clumsily, unable to remove my attention from his penetrating gaze. Drawn again like a magnet, I cupped his face in my hands, brushed my lips against his cheek, and whispered in his ear, "Please, Michael, do not look at me like that when anyone else is watching." I forced myself to break away and flew out of the room.

⚬——∿⚬↝——⚬

The chamber I shared with Simon was silent and dark. The full moon was wrapped in a stormy cloud, and the candles had been extinguished. Simon's head was covered up to his eyes with the woollen blanket. I knelt by my bed and said my prayers before taking off my clothes and lying on the bed, feeling too warm and excited to sleep. Minutes later, a muffled voice emerged from underneath the heavy bedclothes.

"Michael, you was right about the letter."

"Right about what, Simon?"

"I seen her read it. She cried and all."

I sighed at the thought of Simon watching her shedding a single tear.

"Are you sure?"

"She did so. I asked her if it was good news, and she says, 'Indeed it is, Simon. Good news for a change.' She smiled and wiped a tear from her eye. Reckon it made her day."

"You think so?"

"I do. Perhaps she loves the old toad after all. What do you think?"

"I think she loves the man who wrote the letter."

"Me, too."

I wished Simon hadn't told me. I'd never be able to sleep, now that I was sure she had the same feelings for me. She confided in me, and she needed me. I knew my place was by her side forever. Her hair had been as soft as I had imagined it would, her face compliant and longing, her silky skin and shimmering eyes begged for my touch. Her lips had brushed my cheek, like a feather, but I could still feel the tingle. I smiled in the knowledge that she would be mine, at last.

Chapter XII

A Ghost at Eyre Hall

Tuesday, 31st October 1865.

I was scrubbing my chamber after breakfast, when Mrs. Leah came in to tell me Mrs. Rochester and Miss Adele wished to speak to me in the drawing room. Michael told me he advised Miss Adele to take me with her to Italy, and I was most excited at the prospect. I had never even imagined I would ever travel abroad, so to travel to Italy was like a dream come true. I had admired Rome as the greatest civilization of the classical world. My mother had told us all about the Christianized pagans, who spread the word of the Lord to the rest of civilization, including our Celtic ancestors. She had also told us about the rebirth of the classical world in Florence and how Shakespeare had set many of his greatest plays in that inspiring land.

When Mrs. Rochester called me into the drawing room, she asked me if I would like to accompany Miss Adele to Italy, and I agreed immediately. I had already discussed it with Michael, who urged me to accept. I would miss my brother and Eyre Hall, but I knew my mother would be proud of me living and working in Italy, the land of our forefathers since Brutus escaped from Troy and founded Britain. I also thought it would be the most convenient moment to recommend Jenny's services.

"Mrs. Rochester, do you remember I asked permission to teach two young children on Sunday afternoons?"

"Yes, is there a problem?"

"The children have made great progress in learning to read and write. I was wondering if there might be a job for them and their mother at Eyre Hall. She is a widow, and they are in dire straits."

"Boys or girls?"

"The girl, Nell, is nine, and the boy, Thomas, is twelve."

"The girl is too young to work. She should be at school. Why is she not at school?"

"She's working as a scarecrow."

"How on earth does someone work as a scarecrow?"

"She's too little and too skinny to do proper work. As a scarecrow, she has to stand in the fields and make sure the birds don't eat the seeds."

"You mean she stands in the middle of a field in the rain, snow, and sleet, all day?" I nodded.

"How can her mother allow it?"

"They needed an apothecary and medicines for the little girl. She is a widow with a very low salary and a precarious job."

"Where does she work?"

"At the inn, mostly."

"Is she an honest woman?"

"Yes, madam. Michael has been teaching her to read."

"Has he?"

"Yes, while I teach the children."

"I will tell Michael to instruct Dr Carter to see the girl. Meanwhile, give her these shillings for food."

She took the shiny coins out of a drawer in her desk and put them in my hands.

"Thank you, madam."

"I will see the three of them. Perhaps we can find their mother a job at Eyre Hall."

I thanked her and left.

Minutes after Susan left, I rang for some tea, but before Michael had time to return, we heard alarming voices upstairs. We rushed to the door to see what had happened and heard Simon thumping down the staircase shouting, 'A ghost!' and 'I seen a ghost!'

His lengthy, sinewy legs stretching down three steps at a time, blaring as if he were possessed by the devil, was a ridiculous sight.

"Mrs. Rochester, it's Mr. Rochester. He's most agitated, screaming there's someone in his room!" He barged into the drawing room, panting and distraught.

"Simon, for goodness sake, what's the matter? Has anything happened to Mr. Rochester?"

"It's the master. He's speaking in another tongue, like he's possessed by a spirit. His voice is loud and deep, as if he was in a tunnel. He keeps saying there's a ghost in the room. It's a woman, who wants to take him to hell with her. Then he says there's a girl that wants to tear his heart out and feed it to the dogs. He's knocked over the candles, because he wants to burn the house to hell. He spat on the Bible, and told me to get out, or he would kill me. He's gone mad, but I believe it's the ghost that drove him to it!"

"Simon, Mr. Rochester is unwell. Please calm down. You must help him, not run away from him."

"I'm afraid of ghosts! I'm sure I seen them in the room, like a body covered in a white cape with black claws and wings and everything ...."

"Mon Dieu, Jane. What can we do? Perhaps it is Bertha?"

"It is no such thing. The ghosts disappeared when Thornfield was burnt down. There are no ghosts at Eyre Hall." I replied calmly, trying to make sense of all the tumult.

Simon continued with his incoherent ramblings, "Mrs. Rochester, today is All Hallows Eve. It's when the door opens for the dead to return to speak to the living. They bring us messages.... Perhaps they've come to warn us! Or to take him away!"

"Simon, stop at once! Do not be dramatic! Go down to the kitchen and have some tea, and for goodness sake calm down!" I was most annoyed with his childish hysterics. I turned to Adele, "Come, Adele, let's go upstairs."

"Mon Dieu, Jane! I am terrified of ghosts. I can't go with you, Jane. C'est impossible!"

"Adele? What is wrong with you?"

"I can't. Please forgive me, Jane." She complained childishly.

Fortunately Michael appeared in the hallway with the tea tray, "Shall I accompany you, madam?" He volunteered.

"You're not frightened of ghosts, Michael?"

"It is not the dead we must fear, but those who are alive."

"Well said. Thank God there's someone who is sensible here to help me. Leave the tray in the drawing room for Adele, take a candle, and lead the way up the stairs to Mr. Rochester's room."

I followed Michael up the dark staircase. As we reached the landing, I stiffened at the sound of Edward's ghoulish cries. We stopped at the top of the stairs and looked down the arched gallery, which led to Edward's chamber. For a moment I thought there might really be a ghost in the room, a demon that might have come to take possession of his soul. I held on to Michael's arm.

"Don't be afraid. There is only one ghost, and he is with the Father and the Son. There is nothing to fear here, except an ailing human being."

I knew he was right, but I was terrified of facing Edward in his delirious condition.

"I'm afraid he might be violent. I can hear him throwing things around the room. Please be careful, Michael."

We walked on until we reached the closed door. There was now silence behind it. Michael turned the knob and opened the door slowly. We were greeted by the sickening stench of dirt and decay, and absolute stillness. I held my breath. Michael pushed the door until we could see the whole room. It was dark, but the glowing embers and the candle Michael was holding revealed a ruffled bed in the centre of the room. The chamber pot had been overturned, and there were clothes scattered on the floor, tangled with cushions and a broken vase. Michael moved the candle to the left, and we saw Edward standing in front of the looking glass, whispering at his reflection. I gasped, and he turned towards us.

"You!" He shouted. "You called her back. You and your witchcraft. It was you all along! You brought me damnation! You bewitched my horse and spread the ice on the causeway! Away with you! Return to the devil, where you came from!"

He was pointing at me and running towards the door with his arms outstretched and his hands grasping the air like claws. I gasped. Michael thrust the candle into my hand, stopped him in his path, pulled down his arms, and pushed him onto the bed.

"Mr. Rochester, you must go back to bed. You are unwell. Dr. Carter will be here soon. Please rest."

"You! Lucifer! Get out of my house! She brought you here to kill me! You have come to kill me!"

"Mr. Rochester, please be calm, nobody has come to harm you. We have come to help you."

"Get out of my house! And take her with you! The angel of the bottomless pit is here! The onslaught of Apollyon has begun! Who will drive out the locusts?"

"Mr. Rochester, I am Michael, the valet. I am here to assist you. Is there anything I can bring you?"

"You have come! The Archangel has been sent to save me from the stings of the scorpions! They have bitten me! Look! Look at my arms! Get the creatures off my face and out of my eyes!"

"Mr. Rochester, I will remove them at once, but you must return to your bed."

Edward clumsily climbed the bedsteps with Michael's help and started crying like a child, "Help me." He repeated time and time again. I was horrified and sickened by the sound of his cries, the sight of his ashen face, and the smell, which seeped from his pores. He was but a decaying shell, fighting a losing battle against the angel of death.

"Where is his medicine?" Michael asked.

I looked in his cabinet, where Dr. Carter kept the laudanum and mercury. I shook the bottle, squeezed some drops into a glass of water, and gave it to Michael. Edward drank it obediently and soon started to breathe more rhythmically. We both stood by the bed silently, waiting for the medicine to take its affect. At last, my husband looked at me and smiled.

"Jane, you have come. Thank you, my darling angel. Thank you for coming to see this poor, dying sinner."

I forced a smile, but in truth, I was still quite terrified of the tormented man lying on the bed.

"I want to confess, my love. I need to confess a terrible sin I have committed against you."

"Don't worry, Edward. Whatever it is, I forgive you. Rest now."

"I must tell you, or she will come back. She will be waiting for me, when I have exhaled my last breath. She will not forgive me, if you do not listen and forgive me."

"Speak if you must." I deemed it quite unnecessary to hear a confession of what I already knew.

"Only you. No one else must know." He looked at Michael, who answered coolly, "Not even your Archangel, sir?"

"Especially not my Archangel. He will punish me. I must tell you, Jane, and you must keep my secret and forgive me. Then it will be forgotten."

I turned to Michael, expressing my fear of being alone with him.

"It is my last wish. I am calm at present. I will not harm you. I am as weak as a child, as a little baby, a little baby girl, a beautiful little baby, Jane. For God's sake, you must forgive me!"

He started to cry and looked helpless enough, but I was still apprehensive, and I did not want to hear any more confessions. Michael gently pulled my arm, and we moved away from the bed into the darkness of the arched doorway, where Edward could neither see nor hear us.

"Mrs. Rochester," whispered Michael, "perhaps you should stay and listen to him."

"I don't want to hear any more. I don't want to know of any more betrayals, and I am afraid of his reactions."

"He is sedated and feeble at present. He will not harm you."

"You don't understand. I don't want to listen to any more confessions."

"Forgive him. Forgive us our sins, for we also forgive every one that is indebted to us."

"How dare you quote the Lord's Prayer to me? How dare you ask me to forgive him? You don't know how he has behaved!"

"I know you do not deserve to suffer the burden of hate."

"And lead us not into temptation, but deliver us from ...."

He placed the tips of his fingers on my lips, and I felt them swell and burn at his touch.

"My feelings are not evil. My mission is to serve you." He removed his fingers from my dazed lips and added, "Listen to him."

Edward's quivering voice interrupted us, "Jane, are you there, my love?"

Michael moved towards the door, "Excuse me, Mrs. Rochester. Call me if you need me. I will not be far away."

Michael walked out and faded from my view along the gallery, and I returned reluctantly to my husband. I thought I had heard all of his offences, but I was wrong. Edward confessed to the gravest sin any man could perpetrate against his wife. What I was about to hear was much worse than Annette's conception, or his recurring unfaithfulness. I would have preferred it if he had admitted to ten more illegitimate children, but what he had to confess was infinitely worse than any crime I could have imagined.

Chapter XIII

Stillborn

"Jane, last night I saw a ghost."

"You did no such thing, Edward."

"I tell you there is a ghost in this house."

"The ghosts burnt down with Thornfield. We rebuilt the house without gables or an attic. There are no ghosts here."

"She is haunting me. I hear her in my dreams. I see her pointing at me, when I wake. I feel her touching my arm and whispering in my ear. She is beautiful with long blonde hair, a vaporous white satin dress and white furry wings."

"You have described an angel, Edward, not a ghost. Why are you afraid of an angel?"

"Perhaps it is the angel of death, who has come to prey on me?"

"Think of her as a pleasant ghost, who has come to lead you to the gates of Heaven."

"You are not listening to me, Jane. I told you. She has not come to favour me. She wishes to take me to the gates of Hell, where I shall forever burn."

"Why should she want to do that?"

"Because I harmed her while she was alive."

"Nonsense, you have never harmed a little girl. She is a good spirit, who will help you in your hardest moment."

"Jane, I must confess, and only your absolution can save me. You must promise to forgive me for what I am about to tell you."

"I cannot absolve you or anyone else. If you like, I can call Mr. Wood, or Bishop Templar, if you prefer."

"Yes, Mr. Wood, he will absolve all of my sins, but what good is that to me now? Bishop Templar, what is he to me? No, Jane, it is you, who must forgive me."

"Edward, I have told you a hundred times, I forgive you for everything, for your short temper, your relationship with Blanche, your flirts in London, your illegitimate children, and your dark past before we met. Is there anything else to forgive?"

"There is something else, Jane. I have done you wrong. I have done you a terrible wrong, but you must understand me and find it in your heart to forgive me."

"I am tired of being your conscience. If there is no solution, and it is a further unknown treachery, you must face the consequences of your actions on your own. I would prefer to remain ignorant of any further wrongdoings."

"Perhaps that would be best, but I cannot sleep, I cannot live, and neither can I die, if I do not confess and receive your forgiveness. Jane, you must help me carry my burden once more, but I guarantee that this time there will be some benefit in it for you. You will suffer greatly at first, but when I am gone, believe me it will fill your life with reward, hope and purpose."

"You have intrigued me. Proceed."

"So precise, so Jane-like. Please don't hate me, Jane."

I remembered Michael's words, "I do not wish to carry the burden of hate."

"Forgive me, my dearest Jane. You are the love of my life. I once asked for your forgiveness, and you gave it to me. Can you forgive me a second and a third time? You were a passionate, righteous woman. I had expected you to shed tears, reproach me my misdeeds, and accuse me angrily. Why didn't you forcefully make me behave? You became passive once more, and you let me go. Why? Did you stop loving me? Did you lose patience? Interest? You stopped conversing with me. You left me while you were at my side! I had to find consolation elsewhere, because you refused my kisses! You shrank from me in disgust! I am a passionate man, and you were ice and rock to me once more. I failed you, and I am sorry. If you find it in your heart to forgive me, you will allow me to die in peace."

"I cannot forgive you before you speak. What must you tell me?"

"You are cruel, but I will be brave. Your daughter did not die at birth."

"Our daughter? Our daughter born nine years ago?" I gasped incredulously.

"I loved you more than anyone! But you were constantly abandoning me. First with John, when you refused a wet nurse. You became distant and cold towards me."

"I was feeding my son, our son. You should have been proud of him and of my dedication to him."

"It was not pleasant to see you suckling a baby all day, and you left my bedchamber!"

"You asked me to leave, because the baby disturbed your sleep!"

"It should have been in the nursery with a wet nurse. That is what is fitting. It was unbearable listening to it crying all night! You only attended to the child. You stopped loving me!"

"But I loved you more than ever, because you had given me a son, in your image, to love, to nourish, to bring up to love his father, as he does. Did you not understand that?"

"A man cannot love a tiny, whining, little creature, a thing he cannot hold or even touch, a feeble delicate jelly of a thing…"

"But John adores you!"

"And I love him, too, now that he is a man. He has grown out of the baby he was into the man he is. I don't even remember him as a baby, and neither does he. What does it matter what happened when he was a tiny thing? Who remembers?"

"Childhood is an essential phase in a person's life. A person's upbringing is crucial. Children need to be taught, loved, and educated, because an adult is the sum of all his actions and experiences, both those remembered and those which are hidden in his memory. A person is more than his clothes, his appearance, his titles, or his family history. A person is the sum of those who have loved him and known him, of everything he has seen, heard, learnt, and experienced."

"Those fancy modern ideas ruined our marriage. You selfishly became concerned with other people's children and neglected your duties to me."

"You stopped loving me long before I became involved in the parish schools."

"Of course I did, because you only wanted to be pregnant again. The first time you miscarried I was grateful, then you recovered and returned to my bedchamber, but your purpose was to entice me into another conception. I thought you would miscarry again, but you didn't. I knew you would abandon me again, if you had another child. I couldn't lose you. I did it for you, because I loved you more than anything in the world."

"What happened to her?"

"I told Carter to dispose of her. I never asked how or where. First she haunted you, and now she's haunting me. You must forgive me, Jane."

"I dreamt she was alive for months. I still see her in my dreams, but I dare not mention it to anyone, lest they should consider me insane. I have seen her small, slight frame, and her golden hair, like my mother's. She is alive! How can I forgive you for taking her away from me?"

"She is gone. Yet, I must ask you to forgive me, Jane, because I never deserved your purity, your love, your innocence. Forgive me for the greatest sin I have ever committed against anyone, even against God, and I have committed so many sins… Forgive me for estranging you from your only daughter. I tell you I could not bear to let her stay. She would have taken you away from me, and I could not lose you again. Can you forgive me for that? My greatest sin has been that I loved you too much. I lost you anyway, in the end. The separation only postponed the loss. I lost you, Jane. How did I lose you, if I loved you more than my own life? Jane, speak to me, please. Do not leave me in such agony."

His monstrous words cut into my heart. I could not utter a single word. My head was throbbing violently, and my eyes stung with the brine of hate. I heard a deafening roar in my burning ears, as if a wave of blood were to explode and seep out. The room dimmed and blackened once more. I must be unwell, fainting again like a debutante.

I never suspected he could have been so heartless. How could I have been so blind? I should have realised when he tried to trick me into a bigamous marriage, when I was an innocent young girl. Later, when the rouse failed, did he not wish to make me his concubine? Has he not been unfaithful and discourteous to me in the last seven years? Parading mistresses and flaunting his money with rascals in London. Yet, all those insults seemed insignificant now.

"No, Edward, I will not forgive you this time. I am not a nineteen-year-old naive and penniless young orphan any more. Call Mr. Wood, no doubt he will acquiesce, and you will easily buy your absolution. Do not look for any consolation in my words. This time you have excelled yourself, what you have done is diabolical and unforgivable."

"Please, Jane. I am damned, if you don't forgive me!"

"I cannot forgive you, but I will keep your monstrous secret for John's sake. He must never know who his father really was, in case he should be burdened by the idea of expiating your sins, which are your own and nobody else's."

I hoped he would never ever find peace after dying. I wished his soul would roam the underworld until the end of time. I walked unsteadily to his medicine cabinet before leaving the chamber, ignoring his agonizing calls.

Mrs. Rochester left the room and stumbled along the gallery. I rushed to her side, asking her how she was.

"Not very well, I'm afraid." She looked bewildered and added, "Michael, make sure the room is cleaned. It smells disgusting, and see to it that Dr. Carter visits Mr. Rochester this evening."

"I'll see to it at once, Mrs. Rochester."

"I would like to see Dr. Carter in the library, when he has finished."

"Of course. Is there anything else I can do for you?"

"No, thank you. I'm going to my room to rest. I'm not feeling very well." Her voice was oddly slurred.

"Shall I bring you something to eat or drink?"

"No, thank you. I just need to rest for an hour or so."

"But you haven't eaten since…"

"Michael, I cannot fight against all of you. Stop arguing with me, and please do as I said."

She moved on, leaning unsteadily along the wall.

"Please, let me help you, Mrs. Rochester."

She looked at me with bleary eyes. I put my arm around her waist and escorted her along the gallery to the steps leading up to her room in the third floor tower. When we reached the tapered staircase, I realized it was too narrow for both of us.

"May I carry you up?"

She nodded and I took her slight frame in my arms and carried her easily up to her room, pushed the door behind me, and put her feet on the floor. She felt like clay in my hands, as she rested her head on my chest and her hands on my shoulders while she cried softly. I spoke into her hair.

"Was his confession that terrible?"

"Michael, it was more than terrible. It was so appalling, I want to die."

"You can't die. You mustn't speak like that. We need you. I need you, John needs you, Adele needs you. The children at your parish schools need you. You can't give up."

"He has killed me. I tell you, I want to die."

Her words made me hate him more than anyone in the world. I would have sunk his skull with my bare hands that minute for making her suffer unjustly.

"Come, you need to rest." I whispered, as I walked her over to the bed and rested her head on the pillow, "If you were my wife, I would worship you every minute of the day."

"I'd like that." Her dazed eyes turned up to mine provocatively. She was behaving most unlike herself. I supposed it was the shocking confession she must have heard.

"Jane Rochester must die, just as Bertha Rochester did. He'll drive us both to our deaths. Will you help me die? Would you let me die?"

"I would kill him first."

"Let me die with you." She held my hand, drawing me nearer.

"You must rest." I whispered hoarsely, pulling away.

"Let me die and I will be free. Kill Mrs. Rochester, Michael. Kill her. She is a very unhappy woman."

"Rest, Mrs. Rochester." I whispered, as I stroked her hair. She closed her eyes and moaned, "I am not quite myself, Michael. I'm afraid I took some of Mr. Rochester's drops."

"How many?"

"Just two, I think. I should be recovered in an hour or two."

"I will call Adele to come and stay with you."

"He promised me he would love me and cherish me, but his promises didn't last very long. Are you lying to me, too?"

I sat for a while watching her smooth face. Her eyes were closed and her breast heaved rhythmically in deep slumber, so I spoke without reserve, caressing her hair.

"I am not like him. I love you. No one will ever love you like I do."

As I stood up to leave, she turned over, put her face down onto the pillow, and mumbled, "I love you, too, Michael."

It took all of my willpower to open the door and walk away from her room, but I was sure I would return soon.

Chapter XIV

All Hallows Eve

Eyre Hall isn't the biggest house I have worked in, but it is the cleanest and most well organized. Mrs. Leah has a schedule, which is hardly ever moved, unless a very special occasion occurs. We are worked off our feet, but I don't mind, because our rooms are warm, comfortable, and we eat the same food as the masters. Mrs. Rochester insists on that. I'm sure she's the best mistress in all of England. Mrs. Rochester is very caring, she always says to me, "Good morning, Beth, do not neglect Sunday school or the Sunday service." She often gives us a threepenny bit, when she sees us in church on Sunday morning, and we often have Sunday afternoon off. I have been in much worse households.

On All Hallows Eve, I got up at 5:30, like I did every day, took the water up to the bedrooms and brought down the clothes for laundering. Then I had some breakfast and went up again to bring down the chamber pots, empty them, and take them back up again while the masters were having breakfast, and I made the beds and cleaned the rooms. After that, I came down to finish laundering while Simon saw to the upstairs fires and Mr. Rochester, who was his special responsibility. Then I helped cook with the lunch, which was served between 12 and 12:30. Miss Leah, cook, Christy, and me had some lunch while Michael was upstairs serving lunch to Miss Adele and Mrs. Rochester, and Simon was attending Mr. Rochester.

After the men had lunch, Christy and I cleaned all the breakfast and lunch dishes and the whole of the cook's kitchen. We sometimes had a break before tea was taken up and the beds were made again after afternoon naps. Then we helped cook with dinner and finished the laundry and the ironing. Christy polished the wooden floors and brushed the carpets downstairs on alternate weekdays, the other weekdays she did the same in the bedrooms and Miss Adele's study. The silver was polished on Fridays and the windows done on Saturdays.

According to Miss Leah, today was a special day, it was All Hallows Eve, and so our routine was less hectic and more fun. Tomorrow we were allowed to get up half an hour later, because tonight we could stay up later, too. After taking the hot water up to the bedrooms, instead of polishing and brushing, I was to help cook bake the soul cakes for the soulers who came souling at sunset. We gave them the cakes and food in return for prayers for the dead.

It was fun helping cook, who never let me near the oven any other day. She told me to cream the butter and sugar together until it was fluffy and pale, then I beat in the eggs, one at a time. She said I wasn't to stop until my wrist ached. I watched cook while she added the flour, spices, currants, and raisins to make a soft dough. After that, she let me help her shape small flat cakes and make a cross on top with a knife. We cooked at least eight batches of fifteen cakes. It took us over two hours! But the smell was so delicious, I was sorry when we finished.

After our late lunch, it was almost dark, because heavy black clouds covered the sky. Cook said a thunderstorm was approaching, and Mrs. Leah said we could have some free time, because Mrs. Rochester would be having dinner alone, as Miss Adele and Master John were going to a Hallows Eve dinner at the Rochester Arms. Simon suggested we should tell stories of ghosts in preparation for their coming in the evening, and we all agreed. He started by telling us about the ghost he had seen this morning in Mr. Rochester's bedroom. His was the simplest and shortest story, but he was such a good storyteller, we were all mesmerized by his tale.

"I was closing the master's curtains and collecting the dinner tray, when the strange events happened. The master's eyes were bloodshot and wide open. He was possessed by a spirit. He pushed the bedclothes away, stood up and started speaking. His voice became low and powerful and strange words in another tongue, like a chant or a prayer, started coming out of his mouth. When I spoke to him he ignored me, as if he didn't hear me or see me. He walked straight to the mirror. I was quite surprised, because he hasn't walked in months. He stood in front of it and continued speaking, as if he were conversing with someone. Then it happened, I looked into the mirror and I saw something, which was not his reflection. I saw something monstrous shining from the mirror, and the whole room lit up, as if lightning had struck."

When he finished he looked at Michael, "You went into the room next with the mistress. Tell us what you saw, Michael. Did you see the ghost?"

"I saw a man who is sick and dying. He was standing in front of the mirror with a candle in his hand, saying he had to burn himself to purge his sins before he died."

We all gasped to at the imagine of the master in such a guise.

"Go on! What did you see in the mirror?" screeched Christy.

"Mirrors are where spirits hide during the daytime to come out at night with the stars." Sentenced Simon with authority.

"There was nothing in the mirror, save his own reflection, the reflection of a withered, sick, and remorseful shadow of a man." Added Michael.

We gasped again, this time with horror at the idea of our solemn and respected master in such a pitiful situation.

"I don't think it is your place to speak of your master in such undignified terms." Sentenced Mrs. Leah most gravely.

"It is what I saw, what we both saw, Mrs. Rochester and I."

Mrs. Leah shot a daggered look at Michael, "I am the only person here who knew the master when he was a younger man in good health, and I can assure you that he was a great man. It pains me deeply to see him in his current condition."

We all noticed she said the last words with tears in her eyes and sorrow in her heart. I thought it was unusual in Leah. I never thought she would have those feelings for men, but perhaps she did, too. I couldn't understand how anyone could speak kindly of Mr. Rochester anyway, he was usually grumpy, almost always short tempered, and never had a kind word for any of us.

Leah and Michael were staring at each other harshly, as if they wanted to have a big argument. We all knew Leah did not like Michael. I always thought it was because he was so good looking and manly, and she didn't think much of virile men, or it could be because he and Susan were the mistress's pets. Leah was well-mannered with them, but they always kept their distance. I was surprised at Michael's reaction, too, because I had never in five years seen Michael stare so furiously at anyone. He surprised us again by speaking riddles.

"It is a wise man who repents when the kingdom of Heaven is at hand, because after death comes judgment. Sinners will go away into eternal punishment while the righteous into eternal life."

"Whoever believes in me, though he die, yet shall he live, and everyone who lives and believes in me shall never die. Mr. Rochester's presence will remain in all our hearts, especially his wife's, after death. His presence will never leave Eyre Hall." Leah replied with another riddle.

I did not understand what they were saying, but I did realize they were coming close to having an argument, although I wasn't sure about what. Anyway, to change the subject, I volunteered to continue with another ghost story. I told the story my grandfather used to tell us on Hallows Eve.

"My grandfather always told us a chair and a plate of food must be left at the table for the recently departed. He said it was because they would protect us from the demons that stalk humans on the last day of October every year.

"This is a true story that happened to someone he knew and loved dearly, a man who forgot to set out the chair and cake for his good wife. She had taken her own life, so her spirit was condemned to be a living dead until she was freed by the ring. This spirit came down on All Souls Eve from a mysterious faraway island, where she lived all alone, since she had fallen into an eternal sleep, unable to live with the dead or with the living. Her husband was still in the world of the living, sitting by the fire in his home, praying for all the souls with his daughters and granddaughters.

"A stray dog, more a werewolf than a dog, passed their front door, peered in through the window, savage it was, but so terrified it could not bark. A howling wind pushed open the door, and a poor little girl dressed in white, like an angel, appeared in the doorway out of a mysterious cloud. 'I have come for the ring,' she said. 'You must give me the ring, or tonight I must take one of the dwellers in this house.' His daughters were terrified at the unearthly being.

'Close the door,' said the old man, crouching by the fire. 'We have no ring! Pull the curtains and let us pray.'

"His daughter said, 'I have the ring. Mother came to my room last night, and she gave it to me.' But no one heard her."

"She said to her daughter, 'Here it is.'"

"She said to her father, 'Here it is.'"

"She said to her sister, 'Here it is.'"

"Still no one heard her. She touched their shoulders, and they felt nothing. The door sprang open once more, the curtains were torn by a sudden gust of wind, and the wolf howled and jumped through the wall, turning into a dragon spitting fire out of his mouth. No one knows what happened, because the next morning, all the women appeared lifeless in their beds. The angel wept. The ring was on the table. She took it away to try and save another soul the following year."

When I finished, Mrs. Leah volunteered to tell the third ghost story. Mrs. Leah isn't a bad housekeeper. She's sometimes short tempered and moody. Like spinsters usually are, but she doesn't interfere in our work, as long as things are done, she doesn't complain. She doesn't ever shout at any of us, not even Christy. She doesn't like men, I noticed that soon enough. She likes to watch us get dressed in the mornings, and she likes to bathe us on Saturday evenings. Says it's to make sure we're good and clean, but I know she likes running her fingers round our tits and fannies.

I reckon there ain't no harm in it. I don't mind, and neither does Christy. I had to put up with a lot more prodding from my brothers when I was at home, before our parents died. We all slept in the same bed. I was the oldest. When they were little, they wouldn't stop until I showed them all I had down there, and they had a good poke. That was at first, then they got older, found out what the adults did, and they wouldn't stop till I let them get inside me. There were three of them and they were rough, so I never fought or complained. I had seen what happened to my mum, when she said no to my dad. You can't say no to men, or they beat you up and get their own way anyway.

Mrs. Leah was much softer and kinder, because she never wanted to hurt us. She just liked to tickle us and rub us softly till we swooned, and we swooned nicely. Susan didn't like our baths, so she had her bath on her own, when we finished.

Mrs. Leah started her story.

"This happened in the time my mother's mother was serving in a prosperous household below the moors. The story, the true story, was told to her by the housekeeper, who had first-hand knowledge of the events. It was towards the end of October and a very wealthy gentleman from the south of England, Mr. Woodstone, was travelling to an inn in the north for peace and recuperation. On his way there befell a terrible snowstorm, and he was forced to stop at a remote Manor House. The occupants were an angry looking landlord and two young servants.

"He was allowed to stay and reluctantly shown to an old run down bedchamber, which had obviously not been used in years. It was furnished with an unhinged bookcase with few books with faded bindings and yellowing pages; a single, solitary four-poster bed; a worm-ridden bedside table, and an unstable chair, perched in front of the chimney opposite the open fireplace.

"The walls were simply whitewashed, but on a closer examination, he saw that some words had been scratched on either side of the shattered casements. He was able to distinguish the word "Catherine," whom he guessed had been the former inhabitant. That night, when he fell asleep, he had a terrible nightmare in which ghosts in black cloaks followed him mercilessly across the white windy moors. When he opened his eyes, he saw a woman knocking fiercely at the window, trying to enter. She was dressed in a long, white garment and had long, dark hair and a beautiful face with tears running down from her terrified eyes.

"He screamed and the other occupants arrived. The owner, Mr. Clifford, was most distressed and asked the traveller to sleep in his own chamber, saying he would spend the night at the window, lest the ghost should return. He said he had been waiting for the ghost to come for many years since her tragic death, because they had not been able to say goodbye, so she was unable to enter the next world. The next morning, when the traveller returned to his room to recover his clothes, Mr. Clifford was found dead by the window. He looked up to the wall where he had seen Catherine's name and beside it someone had added a heart with an arrow and the word Clifford beside it. I called the servants, and they acknowledged she had returned to take him away with her. At last, they would be together forever."

When she finished, Christy asked why their love was impossible, and she wanted to know the rest of the story.

"The rest of the story is not important," said Miss Leah with great authority. "It is an important lesson in life," she added, looking straight at Michael once more. "Intrigued by his strange words and unable to sleep, he asked Mr. Clifford's servants if they knew the story of their master's love, and it so happened, they did. However, this is not a ghost story for Halloween nights. It is a true story, which may help us reflect on our place in the world."

I found it odd how she kept looking at Michael, as if she were speaking to him, because he always seemed to be exactly in his place. He always used fine words and had those fine manners. I must be missing something. I should remember to ask Simon afterwards if there was any gossip I should know about.

Michael was very popular with the girls at Millcote, but I only ever saw him getting friendly with one of them. It surprised me, he could have had any of them, but he preferred the widowed Jenny Rosset. She was older than the rest, but a mighty good-looking woman, and very sparse with her favours. She wouldn't have naught to do with the young lads, probably thought they was too young and too skint.

After her husband died, she was in dire straits at times, had two little ones to look after, too. Once she told me Michael was teaching her to read. What a waste of time I says to her, with all his reading, he's still a valet. Don't need to read to be a servant, so what's the point in making all the effort. Mrs. Rochester, she tells me off every week for not going to Sunday school, says that's what I get Sunday afternoons off for. I prefer to go and meet my friends in Hay, or Millcote, if I can get a ride. I don't want to waste time learning to read and sew. I want to be a cook when I'm older. I love cooking.

Next it was Christy's turn. She told the story of the Gytrash, an ancient legend her grandmother once told her about a huge, wild dog, half spirit and half animal that roams the moors at night in search of human prey. He is especially keen on stalking solitary travellers on lonely roads on stormy nights.

"So this tale is about one such traveller, an uncle of mine, who was on his way home on foot after a visit to my father, his brother. He heard footsteps, as if an animal were creeping up behind him and started running, the animal ran too, and my uncle tripped over a stone and fell to the ground. Nobody knows what happened, but the next morning they found him lying on the ground. They thought he was dead, but he was breathing, so they carried him home and he never spoke again. His spirit had gone. He never ate, drank, or spoke until he died ten days later without even blinking his eyes in all that time. My father said the terror had killed him, and my mother said the Gytrash had taken his soul."

After telling the stories, the sun had set completely. We lit all the candles, and I helped cook prepare the cakes for the soulers. We put them on trays to be taken out to the back door. Cook said we should also leave some around the house for the souls who might come during the night. Leah frightened us all by saying that all the candles and fires should remain lit all night, so the souls could find their way around the house.

Simon went up to accompany Dr. Carter on his daily visit to Mr. Rochester, and Michael went up to kindle all the hearths and replace the waning candles. Leah said she was tired and retired to her parlour.

156

The rest of us stayed up late eating soul cakes, drinking cook's brandy, and telling more ghost stories in the hope of seeing something bloodcurdling to talk about the next day.

Strange things happened at Eyre Hall that evening. Later that night, Simon said Mrs. Rochester had seen a ghost in the library, and Dr. Carter, who was with her, had rushed out of the house, pale as death, mumbling something about devils in the room. After that, Leah spent the night walking around the downstairs rooms, saying something was going to happen that night.

Then Miss Adele and Master John arrived, making so much noise they would have frightened the souls away. Leah came down quite distraught and bolted her parlour door, the rest fell asleep, but I had drunk so much brandy, I was feeling too excited to sleep, so I went upstairs with the last wick of a candle and saw plenty of strange things.

The library door was open and I saw two black silhouettes, one was like a ghost with a cloak and the other was a tall man, they were both walking up the stairs. The man was carrying a heavy bag and they went into to Mrs. Rochester's room. I was terrified, but walked up the stairs, in case Mrs. Rochester needed my help. I heard whispering and saw lights flickering under her door.

Thanks to the brandy, I managed to find the courage to knock on her door and ask her if she needed help. Miss Adele opened the door, quite startled to see me, and told me to go to bed immediately. She accused me of being drunk and said she would tell the mistress in the morning, who would no doubt fire me, if I didn't go down to bed at once. I insisted I had seen a ghost, but she slapped me hard, and told me to get out. I started crying and suddenly Michael appeared.

He said he had come up when he had heard the noise. He took me downstairs and told me not to cry, because he would frighten the ghost away. I had never been so close to Michael before. My legs were trembling, and his hands were holding me firmly, as we walked down the stairs. He smelt sweet, like the mistress's perfume. I told him I was afraid, because I had seen a ghost in the library, and he held me in his arms for a while in the kitchen, then he kissed my cheek, where Miss

Adele had hit me, and told me to go to bed, or the ghosts might return. So I did. I dreamed I was in his arms all night.

Chapter XV

Kidnapped

I was walking down the stairs after my evening visit to Mr. Rochester, who was more agitated than usual. His condition had worsened greatly in the last week. His mind had deteriorated even faster than his putrid body, and I feared the worst in the coming days. Simon approached me in the hall, and I was surprised that he was not carrying my hat, cape, and walking stick.

"Good evening, Dr. Carter, Mrs. Rochester would like to speak to you in the library."

"In the library?" I had always been received in the drawing room, and anyway, I was anxious to get home for my dinner. I opened my pocket watch, "It's rather late. Is Mrs. Rochester unwell, Simon?"

"She don't look too well to me." He mumbled, as he ushered me into the library.

The room was sombre, and the air was indeed full of rage. She was sitting at the desk, facing the door as we entered. The curtains were drawn, the fireplace had been reduced to glowing embers, and only a small candle on the desk lit her visage, which was stern and redder than the flames. She got up and approached us with firm steps.

"Thank you, Simon. We are not to be disturbed, under any circumstances. Do you understand?" The servant nodded and left.

Mrs. Rochester locked the door and tucked the key in her dress pocket. She had the look of a tigress on her unusually flushed face. I trembled, as she turned towards me and raised her hand high above her head, and slapped it down on my face, so hard that she knocked me onto the floor. My head hit the mantel first on my way down and then landed on the hearth rug. She stood beside me, put both hands on the mantelpiece, and kicked my side with her boots until I begged her to stop. When I tried to get up, she pressed her foot firmly on my chest shouting, "Don't you dare move, you disgusting toad!"

Then she took the fire stoker and poked my thigh, after thrusting it into the embers. I screamed and heard Simon's voice on the other side of the door asking if everything was all right.

She ignored him and continued her insults and insane attack with the stoker. Moments later, I heard Michael's voice behind the door, "Mrs. Rochester, open the door please, it's Michael."

The madness left her eyes for a moment. She dropped the stoker and walked to the door. I heard Michael's voice insisting, "Mrs. Rochester, let me help you."

I dared not turn my head, which I was protecting from her blows with my arms. I heard the shuffle of her dress as she took out the key, then the metallic click as it turned in the keyhole, then footsteps, and the key turned on the lock once more. At last someone would help me. I heard the valet ask her what had happened, and I shouted for help.

"Michael, help me. She's gone mad!"

"He killed my daughter! He killed my daughter!" She repeated it time and time again. Edward must have confessed in a final moment of remorse. I was lost! My reputation, my leasehold, all would vanish!

"I want to kill him, Michael! I shall kill him!"

I sat up, shaken by the words and blurry eyed, I saw the strangest sight.

She was sobbing, her head resting on his chest while the valet was stroking her hair and saying, "It's all right. I'm here now. I'll do it."

I screamed for help once more, convinced they were going to kill me. Michael bent down and grabbed my lapels. I closed my eyes in a state of shock, he pulled me up and threw me into the armchair.

"Michael, I had a stillborn daughter, that's what they told me, Edward and Carter, nine years ago. Today, my husband confessed on his deathbed that the baby girl had come to take him away, and she was haunting him, because he had ordered her death. They murdered her! They lied to me. They told me she was dead, and they took her away from me. How could they do that to her? To me? Why did they do such a horrendous thing?"

"You have some questions to answer before I kill you, Dr. Carter," warned Michael, grabbing my lapels once again and pushing me further into the armchair.

"Wait! Let me explain. Mr. Rochester did not want any more children, especially not a baby girl. That was the only motive. He asked me to dispose of the child, and I did." This time it was the valet who punched my face so hard that my ears started ringing. I cried out for dear life, "You'll never find her if you kill me!"

"You murdered my daughter!" She picked up the poker once more, and I shouted before she thrust it into my stomach.

"I did no such thing. Your daughter is alive!" I pleaded.

"What! Don't you dare lie to me again!" The stoker was in the air above my head, waiting to land. I put my arms up in defence.

"I didn't kill her! I couldn't do it, although he asked me to." I sobbed, and her arms dropped to her side. "She was such a pretty little girl," I added.

"Michael, my daughter is alive!" The stoker fell to the floor, and she turned to the valet, taking his hands and looking fervently at him.

He turned to me, "Tell us what happened, Dr. Carter."

There was an unnatural familiarity between them. How dare she defy all the laws of decency and decorum, and maintain intimacy with a valet while her husband lay on his deathbed?

"Speak!" She shouted with fire in her eyes.

"I took her home for a few days, but of course we couldn't keep her, she couldn't be found anywhere nearby. Mr. Rochester would have found out and ruined my life. My wife has a sister, who lives in London, and told her there was a great demand for babies, so she took her there."

"My daughter is with your sister-in-law?"

"No, she could not keep her either. She passed her on to another family, I believe."

"You believe?" Shouted Michael, pulling my lapels once more.

"I don't know who she gave her to. I never asked, and we never talked about it again. We have not seen her for some years, but she will know where the girl is."

"I must find her, Michael."

She was completely mad, looking at him as if he, a simple valet, could help her find her daughter.

"What is her name and address?" Bullied the impudent valet once again.

"Mrs. Banks, 64, Sudbourne Road, Brixton, London."

"You had better be telling the truth, or it will be your last lie, do you understand?" He towered over me, frightening me to death. He was twice my size and three times younger and stronger. He grabbed my silk scarf, this time almost choking me to death and lifted me into the chair by the desk.

"Is that the truth?"

"I promise, no, I swear it is on my life, on my own son's life. He made me do it. You know what an evil man he can be, Mrs. Rochester."

"Mrs. Rochester, it would be a good idea if Dr. Carter wrote a letter to his sister, informing her of your visit and enquiries."

"Of course, Michael, good idea."

She handed me her quill and ink, took a piece of writing paper from the drawer, and spread it out in front of me. "Start writing to my dictation."

"I need my spectacles, madam. They must have fallen on the floor, when you knocked me over."

Michael bent down, feeling the rug with his hands until he found them, and gave them to me, "Write!" Ordered Mrs. Rochester, "Dearest whatever you call her…"

"Dearest Emily."

"Dearest Emily, You will remember the infant, the baby girl, I …" She started crying and moved back to the mantelpiece, where Michael was standing, and threw herself disgustingly on his chest again.

"Michael, I can't speak. I can't breathe, help me. I'm going to faint…"

I stood up, but he told me to sit down. He carried her to the armchair and held her head down between her knees and said, "Breathe slowly, you'll be all right in a few minutes." He took a glass and some brandy and handed it to her, she drank and coughed. He handed me another glass, which I drank thirstily. When he asked her if she was feeling better, she nodded bleary-eyed and he asked, "Would you like me to dictate the letter to Dr. Carter?" She nodded and he continued.

"You will remember the baby girl you were entreated in, do you remember the exact date? Month and year?"

"May, 1856."

" …the baby girl you were entreated in May 1856 by my wife to find a suitable family? I must now ask you to reveal the identity and address of the person the child was given to. Her mother, Mrs. Rochester, has great interest in knowing the whereabouts of the child, and you must assist her in every way possible. It is of utmost importance to my integrity, your sister's, and your nephew's that you should give her all the necessary information she may require to find her daughter. Now sign it."

When I had signed, he took it to Mrs. Rochester to read, and asked her with great callousness, "What shall we do with him now? I could kill him, if you want me to." I was terrified by their savage violence, and disgusted by their illicit partnership.

"You're both mad! You will never get away with it!"

"I think we will," he answered coolly. "I came into the room, caught you attempting to violate Mrs. Rochester, my mistress, and I killed you. It would be that simple, Dr. Carter."

I realized they were serious and they were right. Everyone would believe her. The event would bring dishonour to my wife and my son. They would have to leave Ferndean in disgrace. I threw myself at her feet on my knees and begged.

"Madam, forgive me. Remember, I did not kill your daughter. She is alive, thanks to me. I disobeyed Mr. Rochester. I will be loyal to you, for the rest of my days. Please, Mrs. Rochester, find it in your heart to forgive this miserable sinner."

"He is more useful alive than dead, don't you think, Michael?" They looked at each other with disgusting closeness once more. He smiled and said, "If you say so, mistress." And I was horrified to see the look of the beast with two backs on their faces.

She turned to me, "You may live, Carter. Is there anything else I should know? Any other secrets of Mr. Rochester's?" Michael shot a piercing look. How did he know? How could he know? What did he know? She realized my hesitation meant there was another dark secret.

"It was a long time ago. Mr. Rochester was in Jamaica, after his first marriage. He was most discontent in that distant devilishly hot climate. I received instructions from Mr. Rochester, by means of his agent, Mr. Cooper, to clear the way for his return to Thornfield. Mr. Rochester's brother, Rowland, fell ill and well, he died with some assistance. Mr. Rochester has always been very generous and very kind to me and my family. I have always served him well. We all have."

"I no longer care about my husband or his misdeeds. They are on his conscience, and he will have to make his peace with our creator very soon. As I told you this morning, I am only concerned with my son's expectations. He has a great future ahead of him. I will not have my son's name tarnished in any way. He is not responsible for his father's actions. I will go to any length to protect him, because he is called to great deeds. None of these family secrets must ever affect his good name, whatever it takes. He is a good man, and he will be a great man."

"I agree, absolutely. My lips are sealed. I will be loyal to you and your son. May I ask about the leasehold you promised me yesterday morning?"

"I keep my promises, Dr. Carter, but I warn you, you will not lie to me again, or you will not live to enjoy your leasehold. Ferndean and everyone in it will be burned to a cinder. Do you understand?"

"You have my word and my loyalty."

"Well, you can start proving where your loyalty lies right now."

"What can I do for you, madam?"

"Mr. Rochester is suffering. He has been suffering a disgusting illness for months. I think it is time to put an end to his torment, do you agree?"

"Of course, madam. I will…"

"I don't want to know the details. Just do it as quickly and painlessly as possible. Now get out of my house."

She unlocked the door and I could not get out fast enough. Simon asked me if I was all right and gave me my accessories. He said I looked as if I had seen a ghost. I told him I had seen a most devilish ghost and rushed out sweating profusely all the way home, in spite of the frosty night.

⁓

Chapter XVI

Helen

When Dr. Carter left I told Simon to retire, because he was no longer needed, locked the door again, and ran back to Michael, putting my arms around him as tears rushed down my cheeks.

"Michael, thank you. What would I do without you?"

"May I embrace you?"

"Yes, you may. Hold me and never let me go."

Michael was like a rock by my side. He had been there all the time, watching over me for the last five years, and I had never realized until yesterday how much I needed him. Michael, who would serve me unconditionally, unquestioningly. Michael, who understood what I needed before I even knew myself.

"I think I'll have another brandy." I sat down by the fireplace on the hearth rug as he filled my glass, then I asked him to sit by my side. I felt the heat of the fire on my face, and the warmth of the brandy in my chest. I moved in front of him and let the weight of my body fall back on his chest. He nuzzled my hair with his nose.

"I love the scent and smoothness of your hair. It's like velvet."

He put his arms around me, and I relaxed at last, closing my eyes, trying to imagine my daughter's countenance. I had seen her face so many times in my dreams, when I thought she was dead, now that I knew she was alive, her features became even more vivid. She was small and thin with large green eyes, wavy blond hair and a lovely smile with little dimples in her cheeks. Her silent shadow had accompanied me every day, now I was sure she was a happy child. I would be able to find her, thanks to Michael, because Dr. Carter would never have felt intimidated enough by me on my own.

"Would you really have killed him, Michael?"

"I will do anything you ask me to do. Anything."

He stroked my hair once again before asking me, "Did you really want to kill him?"

"For a moment I did. When I thought he had killed my daughter. When I thought of a little girl who is alone in the world, perhaps with people who do not love her... Nine years without my daughter, Michael. All these years thinking she was dead. Feeling guilty and distressed for her death. Yes, I really wanted to kill him."

"He deserved to die. What he did is unforgiveable."

"Have you ever killed a man?"

"Many years ago."

"What happened?"

"You would not want to know. I had a hard two years while Susan and I were orphans, alone in the world, at the workhouse in London, with no home and nowhere to go, until you took us in."

"Poor Michael and Susan. Defenceless. Perhaps my poor little girl is alone…"

"Perhaps she is with a good family, who wanted to have a child." He tightened his grip, as if to reassure me that she was well.

"I wish to God you're right, but I have to find her. She is my daughter, my little girl, and they tore her away from me."

"We should give her a name. We can't just call her little girl. She needs a name."

"Yes, she does. I was going to call her Helen. Helen was my best friend at Lowood, an institution for orphans, where I lived from the age of eight to eighteen."

"Were you an orphan, too?"

"Yes, I was. My parents died when I was a child and my aunt, Mrs. Reed, took me in, but she hated me, and so did my cousins. When I was eight, they sent me away to an institution called Lowood, which was an ominous place in a foggy, damp valley. We were half starved. The little ones were severely neglected, so many of the children were frequently ill. Bouts of typhus spread swiftly in the crowded schoolrooms and dormitories, and the seminary was often turned into a hospital.

"Miraculously I survived and trained to be a teacher. I taught there for two years before applying to work at Thornfield, as a governess to Adele. Then I met Mr. Rochester, whom I thought was unmarried, until our wedding day, when Mr. Mason, Bertha's half-brother, prevented our marriage at the altar by revealing that my husband was already married. Of course, after her existence was disclosed, I had to leave Thornfield. I went to Morton, where I met three wonderful people: my cousins Mary, Diana, and Saint John Rivers. Diana became Mrs. Fitzjames, and that's how I met you."

"Tell me about Helen."

"Helen Burns was a silent child, who was usually absorbed in the companionship of a book, which she loved reading quietly by the glare of the embers. She came from a town on the Scottish border. She was the kindest, sweetest person I ever met. I never heard her complain, even when she was beaten with a rod by Mrs Scratchet, a vicious teacher, who seemed to enjoy inflicting pain on the weaker girls. Helen never spoke ill of anyone and always saw the best side of all people and events. She was gifted with the ability to see positive qualities in people, which were invisible to anybody else's eyes."

"Where is she now?"

"When we were still children, Helen became ill with consumption, and I was no longer allowed to see her or speak to her, but I disobeyed the rules and crept into the seminary, where she was taken. She was wrapped in a dark blanket, which exuded a deathly smell of camphor and burnt vinegar, but I did not care. I nestled close to her, and we wrapped each other with our arms. Even as she was dying, she was resigned to her fate. I remember she told me she was happy, and I should not grieve when she died, because she knew she was dying, she said that by dying she would escape sufferings. She said, "I believe. I have faith: I am going to God.""

"She died in my arms one night. She was buried in Brocklebridge churchyard without a headstone or any other mark, but I remembered the exact place. Fifteen years after her death, when my baby died, I returned. The spot was covered by a grassy mound, and I had a grey marble tablet inscribed with the word 'Resurgam' erected there."

"You said you left Thornfield and met your cousins, so when did you return?"

"My cousin Saint John Rivers proposed to me. He wanted to be a missionary in India and decided I would be the perfect missionary's wife, but I did not accept. I did not love him, and I did not feel any calling to venture into a life of sacrifice in India. I heard that Bertha had burned down Thornfield and killed herself, so I returned to the Rochester Estate, in search of Edward. He was living in Ferndean, maimed and disfigured, but alive. He had lost his eyesight and the use of his left arm. We married and I nursed him back to health. Well, Michael, that's my life before I married Mr. Rochester. I think I'll have some more brandy."

He refilled my glass and returned to my side, strumming my head with his fingers once more.

"He sounds like a terrifying person."

"Not the Edward I met twenty-three years ago. I loved him dearly. He was an adoring husband, at first. We had some wonderful years together, until my daughter... Helen was born and taken away from me. Everything changed then. I wanted more children and he did not. I became very melancholic and I wrote my novel. He was bored at Eyre Hall, with me, with young John. I became involved in the local Sunday school and the parish school. I suppose we gradually stopped loving each other and started leading separate lives. Now I realize what kind of a person he was, from the beginning. I don't understand how I could have loved him so much and been so blind."

We were both silent for a long time, listening to the crackling of the furious hearth. I could feel his breath on my hair, and the flames glowing on my face. I wished the moment of peace and warmth would last forever. At last Michael spoke, "What shall we do about Helen?"

"I don't know yet. I shall think of something soon. First, I need to sort out matters at Eyre Hall. I need your help tomorrow, Michael. I cannot wait for Carter to act quickly. I cannot remain here a moment longer. I have to go to London and start looking for Helen, as soon as possible, and I cannot leave while Edward is in his final moments. After tomorrow's dinner, while we are in the drawing room, go up to his room and give him some more medicine. It will be a relief for him and for all of us, and he will feel nothing. He wanted to kill a little baby girl, he does not deserve a peaceful death. When it is done, come down to the drawing room. I will be with the guests, ask me if I would like the library fire to be put out, and wait for me there. Could you do that for me?"

"I told you, I would do anything you asked me to do."

I was feeling light headed, warm and sleepy, and it felt so good to lie in his arms and speak to him. Everything that had happened was so far away and hazy.

"After the week's wake and the funeral, we will go to London to find Helen."

I must have fallen asleep. When I woke up, I was cradled in his arms, and he was stroking my hair, which was hanging loosely over my shoulders. "May I kiss you, mistress?" He whispered, lowering his face to mine. I must have said, "You may," because I remember feeling the softness and warmth of his lips on mine, but the rest of what happened that night is a blur. I woke the next morning in my bedroom with the sun in my face, feeling rested and renewed. I turned to find Adele sleeping placidly by my side.

Chapter XVII

Merriment at the Rochester Arms

Mr. Mason had invited me to join him and Annette for dinner at the Rochester Arms in Hay, and I asked Adele if she would like to accompany me. Adele seldom leaves the house, now that my father is bedridden, and guests are infrequent, so I was sure the dinner would be an amusing interlude for her. Mr. Raven frequently organizes entertaining banquets on merry occasions, like this evening's All Hallows Eve dinner, as his father, old Mr. Raven used to.

Adele has always been like a devoted older sister. I love her dearly, and I am overjoyed for her contentment. I wish her to be happy, marry, and perhaps even have a family, although my mother will be very lonely at Eyre Hall once she has left. Adele has told me all about Mr. Greenwood, her new suitor from London, who will be arriving the following evening. She is planning to travel with him to Italy to an encounter with her long lost mother.

Life at Eyre Hall is no doubt dull for merry Adele. My mother is very distracted of late, worried no doubt about my father's health and immersed in her occupations running the Estate, as well as her absorbing charity work. I often wonder what will become of her, once father was no longer with us. Her life has been so devoted to him, especially in these last few years. I am worried that she will become an eccentric recluse, although I will make sure that never happens, because I will always look after her.

Adele is apprehensive, although excited, about meeting her mother at last, but even happier at the prospect of leaving Eyre Hall for a time and becoming Mr. Greenwood's travel companion. I am glad that I shall be finishing my studies next June, so I will return home and help my mother with the running of the Estate. She wants me to embark on a political career, but I am not sure if that is what I want to do.

I would like to travel to the United States and be acquainted with the new land and its courageous people first hand. I would also like to visit our prosperous colonies in the West Indies, although my father always told me it was a devilish place, I am sure he is exaggerating. I am also keen to visit Europe, although again, my father has warned me against fickle European women. I knew he had a disastrous experience with his first Caribbean wife, who was Mr. Mason's sister and Annette's aunt. Adele's French mother had also betrayed him, and he had had a succession of capricious and disloyal women until he was fortunate enough to meet my mother and find peace and stability at last.

I long for London society, where I would meet avant-garde artists and poets, like William Morris, Alfred Tennyson or Gabriel Rossetti, although mother would prefer me to frequent social reformers and politicians, like Bishop Templar and Lord Shaftsbury. However, I am not called to being a philanthropist, like my mother, who willingly offers her time and money to needy orphans. I'm afraid I'm a traditional Rochester, like my father. I want to enjoy the privileges I have inherited. I fear I have not been called to repair the world's injustices, as my mother would wish.

Joseph took us to the inn in our best carriage and waited there with us while we enjoyed the most magical night of the year, the night in which we witness the weakening of the barrier between this world and the other, where the dead and supernatural beings abide. I hoped to be able to get to know a supernatural being I had just met, the stunning and enigmatic woman who had suddenly burst into my life. Since the first day I had seen her strewed on the causeway below my horse, I had felt captivated by her watery eyes. I had never seen such a remarkable looking lady in England. I imagined she took after her aunt, my father's first wife, and I understood how he must have been spellbound by her striking looks.

I had dreamt about her black almond shaped eyes shining like smoky quartz, and I longed to caress her flawless olive skin and kiss her dense creamy lips. I had never met a Jamaican woman, and I wondered if they were as compliant as I had been told, even though they were Creoles with English blood. I might follow my father's footsteps, but I would not commit his same mistakes. Even so, I was looking forward to looking into her face once more, just to see if she stirred the same feelings a second time.

The evening was as dazzling as I had expected. We were given a table in the corner, away from the boisterous villagers, with generous helpings of roast duck and plenty of red wine from France. I had hoped to dance with Annette, and so, have the perfect excuse to hold her hand and even squeeze her waist, but in spite of her uncle's insistence, she refused, due to her sprained ankle. Fortunately, after dinner, Mr. Mason convinced Adele to dance with him and listen to the ghost stories being told, so we were allowed to converse at our secluded table.

I realized that Annette was not the gay, undemanding type of woman I had imagined from her youth and beauty, on the contrary, she was well-read and modest, much like many of the English girls I had met. Of course she was nothing like my fiancée, Elizabeth Harwood. Elizabeth was an English rose, whose transparent skin, coral cheeks, and lips were more exquisite than any of Gainsborough's celebrated portraits. Elizabeth is beautiful, demure, and sweet, nothing like her ambitious and ruthless father, one of the most feared judges at the Inns of Court, where he would like me to be apprenticed, when I finished at Christ Church.

I love Elizabeth, because my mother adores her, and because her father, Judge Haywood, is determined that I should be his son-in-law. Elizabeth is distant and shy, and although she insists that her greatest wish is to be by my side every day of her life, she does not exhibit any passion when she is near me. I suspect she thinks I am a good catch. I'm an only son, who will inherit a large and prosperous Estate, and she is also aware that our marriage would be very beneficial to me.

I said I love Elizabeth, and I do, but I am not *in* love with her, and now, I am absolutely sure I never have been, and I never will be. I have known it since I met her, but I was sure of it two days ago. I have no doubt that there will never be any passion in our marriage, although we will probably be contented and prosperous. I am sure now that I have never been in love before, because I had never experienced such overwhelming feelings towards a woman, until a few days ago when I met Miss Annette Mason.

Annette has a wild, feral beauty I had never encountered. I was on my way back to Eyre Hall, near Hay, when I beheld a magnificent apparition in the middle of the grey wilderness. She was lying on the causeway, wrapped in a crimson cape while a thick mane of unruly black hair was set free, as her crimson bonnet bounced onto the rocky ground. I unsaddled my horse and rushed to her side, and I realized she was quite real and dreadfully hurt. She sat on the ground crying, as a trickle of blood slid down her bruised forehead, complaining of a sprained ankle, painful arm, and aching head.

My first impression had been extraordinary, but as I carried her away from the causeway onto a stile, I was stunned by her beautiful face and perfect contour. I had no idea who such an exotic and beautiful creature could be. Fortunately, I discovered that although we were related, there was no blood relationship, so my feelings were not indecent.

Yesterday, on my way back from my visit to Bishop Templar, I decided to stop by the Rochester Arms, in the hope of another chance meeting with Annette. Fortunaltely, she was dining with her uncle, who beckoned me to sit with them. I needed little persuasion to join them and find out more about the mysterious dark beauty. So far, I have discovered that her name is Annette Mason, and she has come all the way from Jamaica to pay her last respects to my father, who has been her generous benefactor since she was a child. Her parents died when she was an infant, and she was brought up in a convent school, where she is now a music teacher. She was staying with her uncle at the Rochester Arms, waiting for an invitation to Eyre Hall.

At a surprisingly late hour, while we were still eating, Michael delivered a message from my mother, which Mr. Mason, read and replied to immediately. I offered Michael a glass of ale, which he declined with the excuse my mother had insisted he should return with the answer to her message at once. I appreciated Michael, on duty all day, so obsessed with my mother's wellbeing, like a sentinel. It reassured me that he was always so efficiently and faithfully by her side, especially now that my father was so ill.

The news Michael brought could not be better. We would all be dining together once more at Eyre Hall the day after tomorrow, All Hallows. Annette and her uncle would be staying as guests for some days. I was so besotted by her that the news was music to my ears. I was determined that she should be my mistress, as soon as possible. I had to have her in my arms, and I imagined it would not be a difficult feat while she was staying at my house. Tonight I had to let her know how I felt and find out if she felt the same. Mr. Mason had insisted I return today to celebrate All Hallow's Eve with his niece, and I had naturally accepted the invitation, once more.

Mr. Raven had prepared a great feast. Everyone was eating, drinking, dancing and singing while a group of musicians played delightful songs with the aid of the German flute, an English guitar, a whistle, and a hammered dulcimer. There were at least a dozen spit-roast hogs and plenty of ale and rum for everyone.

After eating the meat, we ordered a Halloween cake. Adele suggested we cut a piece for mother and take it back to her. Each piece of cake had a button with a message for the coming year. Adele found a blue button, which meant she would be making a journey. Annette received a yellow button, meaning she would be coming into money. I discovered a white button, signifying I was to get married in the coming year. Mr. Mason got the worst one, I'm afraid. He got the black button, which predestined him to remain a solitary bachelor.

Mason naturally dismissed it with a huff as a heathen superstition, but the rest of us were very pleased with our buttons. My mother's uneaten piece obviously hid the red button, meaning she would find her true love in the coming year. I wondered nostalgically if my demanding, short-tempered father had been the love of her life, and whether she would remarry after his death. I adored my father, but my mother was too young, beautiful and marvellous to live an isolated existence at Eyre Hall for the rest of her days.

I asked Annette to accompany me for a walk around the inn to observe the other divination practices taking place, which she had never heard of in Spanish Town. I reminded her that fortune-telling was practiced on this magical night to peep into the year ahead. Most young people were interested in marriage divination. So as we wandered around, we saw groups of young boys apple bobbing while girls ate and peeled apples in front of a mirror by candlelight, in the hope of getting a glimpse of their future husband.

Other groups were telling stories about ghosts and witches, who visited the earth on this night to bring messages to the living. Annette told me many of the native people in Jamaica were very superstitious and carried out black magic and witchcraft by casting spells on naive people, usually involving chants and animal sacrifice. She did not look favourably on these practices and was surprised that English people should believe in such things. I told her it was like a childish game for us.

Annette told me about how she missed the beauty of her country, the purple red skies at sunset and sunrise, and the fury of the wind in the autumn. She remembered the closeness of the moon with its dazzling moonshine and the millions of stars that covered the skies like a glittering dome. She explained how the plants are brightly coloured and smell sweeter than honey, and how the sun shines brightly every day, melting away the cold and sadness.

She asked me if I had ever visited her island, and I promised to do so, as soon as I could. She described her colonial mansion with ample verandahs all around the house overlooking the ocean. When I told her it sounded like paradise to me, she said that was what my father had said. I did not want to displease her, so I smiled, although I was surprised by her words. My father had always spoken very negatively about her country, calling it "the hellish West Indies", but I was determined to travel there sooner than later. Annette had already convinced me of its beauty.

I told her about my mother's plans for my future, and she told me I was lucky to have a mother who loved me and cared about my expectations. She congratulated me on my engagement, but I hastened to let her know how I felt about her. She looked surprised, even shocked, saying that we were related and should not even think about a romantic attachment. Although she added that she would like to be my friend, because she liked my company. That was enough for the moment. I apologized, not wishing to contradict her. I knew she liked me, and I would have plenty of time to seduce her while she was at Eyre Hall.

When Adele and I left the inn, on our way home, she told me she was very annoyed with me for leaving her alone with Mr. Mason for such a long time. She thought he was a most tedious companion. I apologized and promised to make it up to her by being especially amiable to Mr. Greenwood.

When we arrived, Simon opened the door and asked us if we wanted anything from the kitchen. We told him we had eaten enough food for a week and went straight up to bed. As we passed the library, Michael appeared in the hall and told us that my mother had fallen asleep. He offered to carry her up to her bedroom, mentioning that she had had an upsetting argument with Dr. Carter regarding my father's health, so Adele offered to spend the night in her bedroom, lest she should have a nightmare.

I had noticed my mother behaving somewhat strangely since I had returned. She looked absent and lost in her own worries. My head was spinning from the noise, the rum, and the exhilarating evening I had spent with Annette. But the sight of Michael carrying my mother upstairs, with her arms and legs hanging limply around her pale day dress, and her auburn hair dangling loosely off her shoulders almost swiping the stairs, surprised me for its beauty. They were like two characters in a fairy tale acting out the final scene. Michael held her firmly and climbed the stairs nimbly, his eyes bursting with devotion, while Adele scolded them both for being up so late. I suspected, even in my dazed stupor, that Michael was in love with my mother. Although the idea did not displease me, I pushed it away from my thoughts as absurd. It was Annette's visage that would haunt me all night long.

Chapter XVIII

All Hallows

Wednesday, 1st November 1865.

The morning after All Hallows Eve, we all overslept and woke up to Leah's angry screams, reminding us that it was not a holiday. Christy pulled my arm and dragged me out of bed while Leah's voice rang from the kitchen, threatening to throw me out of Eyre Hall if I wasn't dressed in two minutes. I flew out of my room, apologized, and begged for some breakfast first, because my stomach was rumbling and my head still spinning. Leah agreed grudgingly, but when cook said she had a headache, too, she started scolding us again for drinking like convicts.

Leah was right, I felt so bad, I vowed never to drink again. I blushed when I saw Michael leave his room and head for the stairs to the first floor. I said good morning to him, and he smiled back and said, "Good morning, Beth, feeling better?" Christy asked what had happened and Michael answered, "She thought she saw a ghost upstairs, but fortunately I heard her scream in the gallery and brought her down."

"What were you doing upstairs, Michael?" snapped Leah.

"I was on the first floor, kindling the fires. You ordered them to be kindled all night, Mrs. Leah." He answered coolly, so coolly it seemed he was being cheeky.

The air was thick between them, as if a storm was building up. I was glad Christy broke the tense silence.

"Well," she shrieked, "did you see a ghost, Beth? Tell us about it!"

I remembered Miss Adele's words and lied.

"I thought I saw a ghost in the library. It went out of the room and climbed up the stairs."

"What was it like? Did you speak to it?" Christy insisted.

"It was black and wearing a cloak. It did not speak and neither did I. I was dead scared. I just followed it up the stairs."

"How brave of you!"

"Anyway, it wasn't a ghost. It was Miss Adele. I saw her in the gallery. Then Michael heard me scream and came upstairs, too. Then we came down to the kitchen."

"Did you see the ghost, Michael?"

"There are no ghosts at Eyre Hall, Christy." He answered flatly.

"What about the soul cakes we put out for the spirits? I wonder if they have eaten any?"

"You'll soon find out," said Leah. "Now everyone to work! Today will be the busiest day of your lives. We have seven for dinner and four extra guests staying overnight, so shake your legs!"

<hr />

Beth came into my chamber, stealthily pouring some water into the silver ewer on the toilet table and leaving some clean towels on the stand.

"Beth, I'll be having breakfast early today. Tell Michael to be in the dining room in half an hour."

"It's seven o'clock, Mrs. Rochester. Michael is still lighting the fires and clearing the soul cakes." She said surprised.

"Tell him to hurry up, then. I'm very hungry, and I have many matters to attend today."

When she left I woke Adele, asking her why she was in my bed.

"Jane, we were so worried about you. When we came back from the inn, Simon told us you had a terrible argument with Dr. Carter. Michael told us you were feeling unwell and had fallen asleep in the library. He carried you upstairs, and I undressed you and put you to bed. I thought it would be best to spend the night with you, in case you got worse.

Jane, we are so worried about you. You have so many things on your mind. Let me help you, please, Jane."

"But you are helping me, Adele. Please, don't worry. I am all right."

"What was the argument with Dr. Carter about?"

"I don't think he's doing his best with Edward. He isn't getting better, so we argued and I was upset. But don't worry, Adele. Remember, Mr. Greenwood is coming today. You will meet him at last!"

"Yes, and there's still so much to do!"

"How was your visit to the inn with John? How did you find Annette Mason?"

"We had fun! Annette est tellement jolie! And very lively! She wore a beautiful red velvet dress with black long puff sleeves and stand collar and a braid bun at the nape of her neck with the most exquisite shell comb. She was mostly quiet and shy while Mr. Mason told us about their plantation and life in Jamaica. After dinner, we all drank rum!"

"Rum?"

"Yes, Mr. Mason said everyone in Jamaica drinks rum, even the ladies. I tried some, too."

"Adele, for goodness sake, it's what sailors drink!"

"It was brown cane sugar rum!"

"I don't think I need to hear any more."

"Mr. Mason was very courteous to both of us. He is more pleasant than I had imagined."

"The rum no doubt!"

"I was as polite as possible to Annette, as I promised, and John got on very well with her. She is very beautiful, perhaps too beautiful for her own good."

"Indeed. I shall make my own judgment, when I meet her tonight."

"We brought you a present from the Arms."

"What present?"

"A piece of Halloween cake."

"Halloween cake? I have never heard of it."

"Mr. Raven brought us a Halloween cake, and Mr. Mason cut it up into five slices, one for each of us; for John, Annette, Mr. Mason, and myself, and he insisted we bring you back a piece, too."

I poured in the warm water Beth had left in the jug, into the basin, and washed my hands and face.

"Sit at your dressing table and let me brush your hair, Jane. It was in a terrible mess yesterday, but I didn't comb it, because I didn't want to wake you up. Let me do it now."

"What's so special about the piece of cake?"

"It is part of a Halloween game. It has a message for you."

I moved to my dresser and let Adele comb my hair.

"Could you twirl my hair into a bun at the back of my head?"

"At the back of your head? Won't you catch cold at the nape of your neck?"

"At the back of my head, Adele. What's the message?"

"You'll have to eat it first. It could be love, money, marriage, a journey, or the worst of all, a solitary spinster's life."

"Have you all eaten yours?"

"Yes, we have. We all know what our future holds."

I was not interested in superstitious games, and in any case, I wasn't very sure I wanted to know what was in store.

"Adele, gently please, you are pulling my hair!"

"Sorry, Jane, but your hair is such a mess. I couldn't find half of your hair pins yesterday. You looked as if you'd pulled them out after a nightmare!"

"Well, I didn't have a nightmare. I slept very well."

"Michael found you asleep in the library again."

"I was tired." I smiled, "Adele, stop talking and hurry up. I'm hungry." I was impatient to see Michael.

I slid on my silk undervest, then my high necked and long sleeved combination, "Adele, help me with the laces and hooks."

"Don't fuss so! Why are you in such a hurry?"

"Bring me my yellow petticoat, it's in the closet."

Adele helped me pull it over my head.

"Turn around, this one has some more laces at the back. Don't you want to know, Jane?"

"Now the corset, the beige one I wore yesterday. Know what?"

"Don't you want to know what's in store?"

"It's only a game, Adele. I don't believe in superstition."

"Jane, do you remember what happened to your shoes?"

"My shoes?"

"Yes, your shoes and your stockings. You were not wearing them last night when I undressed you."

"Was I not?"

"You were wearing no stockings and no boots."

"That's quite impossible. Are you sure?"

"Quite sure."

"I vaguely remember taking them off."

"In the library?"

"Yes, my feet were itching, so I took them off." I flushed. I had no idea where I had left them. "They must be in the library. I'll wear my laced ankle boots today."

I slid them on, recalling how he had taken my shoes off last night. "May I touch you, mistress?" He had asked me sensuously and I had said, "You may," and asked him what he wanted to touch, and he said he wanted to touch my feet. "Why?" I asked, and he answered, "Because no one has seen or touched them before." How could he know that?

We were sitting on the floor by the fire, they fit me loosely, so it was easy to unfasten them and pull them off. How could I have done that? And my stockings? I don't remember taking them off, but I must have.

We were alone in the dark library. The embers hardly glowed and the candles had died out, but he must have caught a glimpse of my legs. The memory makes my pulse race. He stroked my ankle, the soles of my feet and my toes, pressing softly with his fingers. I remember asking him if he had done it before.

"Never," he answered. "But my mother used to rub my feet and my sister's with rosemary oil, when we had a cough, before going to bed, and we always stopped coughing and slept well afterwards."

"What a good idea." I answered. "Next time I'd like you to use some oils."

Next time? Had I lost my mind? I slapped my cheek to check I was not dreaming, but Adele's screech brought me back to the present.

"Jane, what's the matter?"

"I need some air. Open the window!"

"Are you going to faint again? Go back to bed and rest!"

"I am not going to faint. You've tied the corset too tight, can you loosen it?"

"Jane, you are acting very strangely this morning. Please be careful. You're too good and too vulnerable. Be careful. He isn't…"

"Stop at once! I will not be sermonized!"

"Jane, I don't want you to be upset or hurt…"

"Forgive me for shouting at you my dear." I hugged her with all my strength. I knew she wanted to help, but I also knew nobody would understand my feelings. "Now, help me with the crinoline. I'm famished!"

The two flights of stairs down to the ground floor from my top floor tower chamber had never seemed so long. The red carpets were richer and deeper than ever, and the balustrade felt smooth as I swept down the stairs and pulled open the dark oak door to an empty dining room. I pushed open the casements, poked my head out to a clear blue sky, and breathed in the sweet smell of freshly cut grass. The light breeze twirled the laurel leaves, and the sound of sparrows singing tickled my ears. I closed my eyes and smiled. November felt like May. May I? May moon at Eyre Hall, May, the month my daughter was born. May. May I?

"Good morning, Mrs. Rochester. Here is your tea. What will you have for breakfast today?"

I turned my face back into the dining room, "Good morning, Michael. Come here! Look, what a beautiful day!"

He stood beside me, "May I?" He said wickedly.

"You may, my dearest." I replied, as I held his hand. It was so real, so warm and firm, "But only until Adele comes down."

"Did you sleep well, mistress?"

"Yes, very well. I have recovered my daughter, and I have you. I don't need anything else at all."

I pulled his hand up to my mouth and brushed my lips over his bruised knuckles, pushing away the memory of Carter's battered and terrified face.

"I don't remember how I got into my bed last night and woke up with Adele this morning. Tell me what happened, Michael."

"You were exhausted after your fight with Dr. Carter, so you sat by the fire and fell asleep."

"In your arms, by the fireplace?"

"Yes, mistress." He turned my hand over and his lips caressed my palms, sending ripples along my arm.

"That's the last thing I remember."

"The last thing? Are you sure?" He smiled wickedly again.

"I dreamt you kissed me."

"It wasn't a dream. I asked for permission, and then I kissed you."

"Did anything else happen?"

"I asked for permission to touch your feet."

"And I agreed?"

"You did."

"And then I fell asleep?"

"You did."

"How did I get to my room?"

"I carried you up."

"I'm afraid you are making a habit of carrying me to my room."

"Adele asked me to. I told her you had fallen asleep in the library."

"Please be strong, my dearest, do what I asked you to do yesterday, and remember we must be very, very careful. Adele will not betray me, but I think she suspects."

"Dr. Carter?"

"Carter will not speak. He has been bought, and anyway, he is frightened out of his wits. Do not worry about him. It is the rest of the household that concerns me. I may have to be distant with you in the presence of others. Trust me, until after the funeral, just one more week. Everything will change after that."

"Shall I close the window? You may catch cold."

"It is such a beautiful day! It smells so delicious! I think I shall have some eggs, cake, and tea for breakfast. I'm terribly hungry."

He turned to leave, trying to pull away his hand from mine, but I tightened my hold.

"Stay here and share this moment with me a little longer."

"I can hear Adele coming down the staircase. Please sit down and let me close the window."

I sat at the table and poured out some tea humming Vivaldi's Autumn.

"It's freezing in here! Michael, did you open the window? Are you quite mad?"

He smiled and locked it back into place, "Sorry, Miss Adele, I was just checking the latch. I thought it might be rusty, but it's all right. What can I bring you for breakfast?"

"I'll have whatever Jane's having. Oh and bring up her piece of Halloween cake we brought back from the Arms last night. It's a single slice with thick white icing."

When he left, Adele turned to me maliciously, "Michael is acting very strangely lately."

"I hadn't noticed, in what way?"

"He's unusually distant with me. I asked him to help me write to Mr. Greenwood, and he told me he was too busy. He is always too busy for me now. It's because you told him off for helping me hide Mr. Greenwood's correspondence, I'm sure of it."

"He probably is too busy, Adele."

"He might be upset, because I'm taking his sister to Italy. They have never been apart for a single day. Do you think he will dare to try and stop her coming with me?"

"Of course not."

"How do you know?"

"I know, because I asked him, and he told me he thought it would be good for Susan to be able to travel abroad."

"Perhaps he lied, not to displease you."

"Michael is not a liar, Adele. I trust him."

I realized too late that I had spoken too passionately. She stared at me in disbelief and spoke spitefully.

"Yes, he's a good boy, younger than John, isn't he?"

It suddenly dawned on me that I was smitten by a boy who was my son's age. I felt disgusted at myself. What was I doing? There was no possible future in our relationship. He was half my age and a valet. I couldn't allow the scandal to affect my son.

Michael came in with the tray full of food, and Adele insisted on humiliating me cruelly, "Michael, how much younger are you than John?"

"I'm afraid I do not know how old Master John is, Miss Adele."

"He is twenty-one, is he not, Jane? He will not be twenty-two until spring. Am I right, Jane?"

I nodded, unable to bring myself to utter a single word.

"How old are you, Michael?"

"I will be twenty-two in December, Miss Adele."

He served the eggs on our plates, laid a plate with the Halloween cake on the table to my right, and stood behind us while we ate.

"See, Jane, he's just a few months older than John. There's your Halloween cake." She pushed it towards me smugly, "Well, eat up, Jane, you said you were hungry. Look for your message in the cake."

"I'm not hungry anymore." I pushed my plate away with disgust, "Michael, take it back to the kitchen for someone else to eat."

"Cook will be most disappointed, Mrs. Rochester. She would like you to eat a hearty breakfast."

"Thank you, Michael, I agree. Jane, you must eat the cake we brought you! If you don't, it will bring you bad luck for the year ahead!"

I had a knot in my chest, which was making its way up to my throat, "I can't." I whispered, devastated.

"Mrs. Rochester, would you like me to take your breakfast into the library? I lit the fire earlier this morning. Perhaps you would like to have breakfast by the fireplace, it is a little cold in the dining room today."

"Yes, perhaps I would. Do you mind, Adele?"

"Not at all. John will be down soon. Have breakfast in the library, if you prefer it, but please, Jane, do eat it all, won't you?"

I nodded and followed Michael into the library. He pushed the armchair nearer to the fireplace and wheeled over a table with the breakfast tray. I sat down, suddenly saddened.

"Mrs. Rochester."

"Please leave, Michael."

I could not bear to look at him. He was twenty-one, barely a few months older than my son. What on earth did I think I was doing?

He knelt beside me, "Please, may I?"

I shook my head, as tears slid down my cheeks, but he insisted, "Age does not matter. It is not important."

"It is, Michael. You are too young to understand. I am forty-two years old! Almost double your age! What was I thinking of? This is madness, Michael. We must stop!"

"It does not matter how old you are, or how old I am. What matters is that you can trust me with your life, and I will help you find your daughter. You know I am right."

I did know he was right. I needed him. He was the only person in the house who was completely loyal to me, and I could not imagine a single day in my life without him.

"May I touch you?"

I surrendered and instantly his thumbs swiped my tears away, as his face approached mine. His breath caressed my ear, and I was lost under his spell once more.

"Let me love you, my mistress." He whispered, and I was enwrapped in the melody of his words.

"How do you do this to me? I am mesmerized."

"I love you." He whispered, as he kissed my neck.

"Michael, I feel quite dizzy, and I can't think when you do this to me. I can hardly breathe."

He moved away. "Then I shall leave and you shall eat. I shall see you at lunch, unless you need me before then."

"Come back to poke the fire in an hour. I miss you, when I do not see you. But just poke the fire. Don't you "May I" me anymore this morning. I need my wits about me."

We heard a knock on the door as he stood up to leave. I asked who it was and John stepped in. They greeted each other amiably at the threshold, and my heart stopped for a moment. I held my breath at the sight of the two men I most loved in the world together. I wasn't prepared to lose either of them. An unexpected sigh escaped from my tight chest, reminding me it was an impossible dream that would never last. My son should never know what a monster his father had been, or how recklessly his mother was behaving at this very moment.

Chapter XIX

The Red Button

"Good morning, Mother. I came to see how you were."

"I'm very well, John."

"Have you eaten breakfast yet?"

"I'm about to do so. Would you like to join me?"

"I just ate with Adele, but I'll stay while you eat. Try your cake first, there's a prize in it!"

I started eating the piece of cake, searching inside for the prophetic token.

"How is Father?"

"Not very well, I'm afraid. We have to prepare for the worst to happen, John. Your father is very ill. He's not getting better. There may not be much time left."

"It saddens me to hear such bad news, but if his pain cannot be mitigated, I do not wish him to suffer any further. I will accept God's will."

"You are very brave, John. Your father has had a good life, shortened by his unfortunate pursuit of inappropriate women. Make sure you learn from his mistakes."

"I will, Mother. How are you feeling? You fell asleep in the library yesterday, after a disagreement with Dr. Carter. Adele was so worried, she insisted on sleeping with you. Will you be all right for the dinner party this evening?"

"Don't worry about me, John, I'm perfectly well. I'm looking forward to this evening's dinner."

"Bishop Templar will be very pleased to see you again. He thinks the world of you. I also feel a great respect for him. He was a splendid teacher and headmaster. He helped me greatly in my formative years. Adele's Mr. Greenwood has also read your novel and is impatient to meet you. Adele says he said it's the best novel to have been written outside of London."

"Mr. Greenwood is most kind and generous in his appreciation of my work."

"Don't be modest, Mother. We are all waiting for you to write another novel, or a sequel. We all wonder what happened to Daphne and Leonard."

"There is nothing to wonder about. They married, had a family, and lived happily ever after."

"Mother, we both know that only happens in fairy tales and Penny Dreadful stories."

"There is no sequel. Why does everyone want me to write a sequel? The end is the end."

"Will you write another novel then? It's rather exciting to have a mother, who is a famous novelist."

"I suppose one day I will write another novel, if everyone insists, but not yet."

"You will also be meeting Annette Mason. She is looking forward to meeting you, too, Mother."

"Indeed."

"Mr. Mason has told me you were kind enough to allow her to meet my father, her uncle by my father's first marriage."

"It was a reasonable petition. Annette is not to blame for her parents' misfortunes. Your father has been generous to her, as he was with his first wife, who unfortunately was unwell, although he looked after her until her unfortunate death. Your father is a good man, although he has sometimes made unwise choices, especially regarding women."

"Except in your case, Mother. Thank God he met you."

"Fortunately for me, he was much wiser when I met him. Fortunately for you, you are making the right choices. Elizabeth

Harwood is a wonderful young lady; attractive, kind, intelligent, well-bred, with a wonderful family, and she loves you, John. You are a fortunate man, never take her for granted, or forget how privileged you are. A woman like that will not cross your path more than once."

"I know you are right, Mother, but…"

"But what, John?"

"But I sometimes think I'm too young to be engaged. I would like to travel… to meet people…"

"But you will travel, once you have finished your studies and are married to Elizabeth, you will be a Member of Parliament. Mr. Crowley will be retiring in a couple of years, and the seat will be yours. You know the voting for Members of Parliament is public, everyone will vote for you, when the time comes. Judge Harwood is an acquaintance of Lord Shaftsbury, who is doing so much to improve the lives of all English children by not allowing them to work under the age of thirteen, or for longer than ten hours a day. He supports the Ragged Schools and the Sunday schools for the poor children. He needs good, honest young men on his side, and I know you will be one of them."

"I would like to travel, and see the world first, before I settle down."

"If you want to travel, you could be Ambassador or Governor…There are British Government offices all over the world."

"I have no experience…"

"With time, hard work and patience, and your wife and family's position, you will be a great politician, John. You will be Lord Rochester, the first peer in the Rochester family. You have the perfect combination, John, your father's nerve and energy and my patience and temperance, plus an excellent education and good connections."

"You have everything planned, Mother. Sometimes I feel it's a heavy weight on my shoulders, and I don't know if I will be able to live up to it."

"You will, John, never doubt it. You will be a great Englishman. You will serve your country, making it a better place for all Englishmen."

"I wish I could believe it were so easy."

"I never said it would be easy, but it will be a great honour for you and all your descendents."

"Perhaps you are right, Mother."

"Mothers are always right, John. And remember mothers are always there to help and support their children through thick and thin."

"And if I should fall in love with someone else?"

"Someone else? What do you mean?"

He stood up and moved around the room nervously, finally stopping behind my armchair.

"I may have fallen in love... I'm not sure, Mother. You see, now I know I have never been in love, with anyone. Elizabeth is charming, but the sight of her does not make my pulse race. What I feel now, may be love, but I'm not sure either. I'm confused."

"Have you met someone recently, who has made you feel this way?"

"I'm not sure what it is that I feel."

"Who is it?"

"Someone who has made me think I may not be ready to marry Elizabeth."

"But you are engaged to Elizabeth, and we are all so fond of her. What will become of her future, if you do not marry her? Who will ever accept a rebuffed fiancée? You will ruin her life. I forbid you to do it!"

He moved back to my side.

"Mother! Would you prefer me to marry someone I do not love with all my heart?"

"John, you are very young and impulsive. In a lifetime commitment to a person there are many factors to be considered, which are as important as love. Romantic love is ephemeral, it is strong and powerful, but it will not last. Two people who are to spend their lives together must have like minds, similar interests, needs, concerns, aspirations, background..."

"Are you sure, Mother? How was your marriage to my father?"

"We were like minds and souls, albeit from very different backgrounds. His father had not advised him well, and he had a selfish, rather reckless youth, until he met me. His love for me changed him, for a while. Unfortunately, the change was only temporary. He wanted an eternal bride and a lifelong honeymoon. But life isn't like that. I became a mother, a writer, a social campaigner, and he did not love the Jane that was not utterly and completely devoted to him. I suppose we stopped loving each other as we had before.

"Your father is anchored in another waning generation. A generation in which landed gentlemen either command armies at war, or attend interminable dinner parties and frequent the London Season and the hunting season. A selfish generation, unconcerned with the plight of the poor or the underprivileged. A generation who never dreamed of studying at university or working for a living, because they owned enough land and servants to have anything they wanted without the slightest effort.

"John, you belong to another more modern generation of men, who are interested in knowledge, value the results of hard work, and desire to make the world a better place with less injustice. You are the first generation of Rochesters to study at Rugby, to graduate at Oxford, to desire to work away from the land, and contribute to the improvement of your countrymen, instead of using their labour and spoiling their dreams. John, I am so proud of you."

"Mother, you expect too much of me. I wish I had had brothers or sisters to share the responsibility you would thrust on me."

"I tried so hard to have more children, John, and you can be sure that I would have been just as demanding with all of them, as I am with you. You have had all the privilege and love for yourself. It is your duty to repay your country and your God for what has so generously been bestowed on you. You will love Elizabeth. She will be a good wife. She understands you, and she shares your same ambitions."

"And yours?"

"Yes, and mine. I am ambitious for you to do good, to invest your time, finance, effort, and all the gifts that have been bestowed on you in making our Empire the greatest, most advanced, and most Christian civilization that has ever been known."

"I'm not as strong or self-assured as you are."

"It is a question of time. You will understand when the moment comes."

"I have experienced the rush of love, and I don't want to live without it. What can I do?"

I thought of my feelings for Michael and realized I was in a similar predicament to my son's.

"My advice is to think cool headedly. You are not to be married for some years yet, so for the moment you can have both worlds, with discretion and respect. Once you are married, you must honour your wife and family above all things."

"I'm sure you are right, as always, Mother."

"What are you going to do after... when Father ... ? You are still so young..."

"Perhaps I'll write another novel, who knows? Of course I shall continue with my social work."

Michael returned to clear the breakfast plates and kindle the fire. I had always been fond of Michael, but I had never really noticed him before. I had taken his continuous presence for granted, as if he were part of my house. Michael, always so well groomed with his turned up collar and cravat, crisp white shirt, and a pleasant smile on his face. I recognized the buttons on his dark waistcoat, which I had once seen almost bursting on my husband's stocky chest. I noticed how much better it fitted tall, sleek Michael.

From the moment I had felt the lust in his look and melted under the desire in his touch, he became real. I had discovered his eyes were honey coloured with a dark hazel rim around the iris, and there was a darker speck on his left eye, touching his pupil. He smelled of morning dew, and his voice embraced me like the summer sun. My eyes followed him inevitably, like two lost kittens. I yielded inexplicably to his charms, because he made me feel safe and contented. Was this the love my son was experiencing? Could it be an older, married woman like myself? I shuddered guiltily.

"Michael, I'll be having lunch in my room at 12, some cold meat, bread, and milk."

"Cook has some fine looking peaches. Would you like one?"

"Yes, I'd like a peach." How could he always know what I wanted?

John stood up and turned to leave. I stood up to see him to the door.

"Mother, I promised to have lunch with Bishop Templar and then bring him to Eyre Hall for dinner. You've finished your cake. What did you find?"

"A button." I held it up for him to see. It was a large red button with two little holes in the centre. He took it from me, examining it closely.

"It means you will meet your true love." I shot a look at Michael, who was standing by the door, his eyes fixed on me, and I blushed like a sixteen-year-old. I turned to my son and spoke quickly, "What nonsense!"

"Mother, you are so beautiful," he hugged and kissed me. "Everyone loves you!" Suddenly he turned to Michael and said, "Don't you think she is the most beautiful woman in the county, Michael?"

I spoke quickly before he could even attempt an answer.

"What was your fortune, John?"

"I'm getting married. Adele is making a journey, and Annette will be coming into money. Mr. Mason got the worst one, I'm afraid he's going to remain a bachelor. I hope yours comes true, Mother. I really do. You deserve to be happy."

He hugged me once more, kissing both cheeks.

"Thank you, darling. John, just one question before you go, is she married?"

"No!" he chuckled, "Of course not!"

"Thank God." I sighed.

"What are you thinking of?" He walked to the door grinning and turned.

"By the way, Mother, on my way back, I'll also be picking up Mr. Mason and Miss Annette Mason at the inn and bringing them home for dinner tonight."

I noticed he emphasized the word Miss. The protective walls I had built around my son began to fracture. My angel was being lured away from the heaven I had built, and Lucifer was trying to slip through the cracks. My breath cut sharply into my chest. *She* was much worse than a dozen married women chasing after him.

"What time will you arrive?"

"We'll be here before 6, in plenty of time for dinner."

"Will you ask Leah to show them to their rooms? Dinner will be at eight sharp. I expect everyone to be in the dining room by then. You will help Simon bring your father down. He will meet Miss Annette Mason and sit with us for the first course, then you will take him up again, he needs to rest."

"Don't worry, Mother, it will be all right. They will be courteous and pleasant guests."

He turned to leave and walked to the door, holding my button in the air.

"Do you want your button?"

"Of course I do."

He turned to Michael, "On second thought, I think Michael will make better use of it than you." And put it in his hand before leaving the room.

"Well," I asked Michael, "what do you think of Miss Mason?"

"She's very striking, Mrs. Rochester."

"Striking?"

"Exotic looking, long dark curly hair, large brown eyes, and colourful clothes."

"Anything else?" I couldn't believe Michael was also attracted by the infernal creature.

"She looked very gay in John's company."

"I've heard enough!" I turned away, irritated by the thought of her with my son.

"I forgot the most important thing. She is …. pardon me, but she is …. most unrefined and coarse."

I surprised myself by laughing out loud, when I realized he had been teasing me all along.

"That's a relief!" I said, turning back to him, and we held each other's smiles for some seconds, and suddenly the girl seemed insignificant. I realized I must be in love with this marvellous boy, who was able to make me feel contentment while my world was crumbling around me.

"What is she really like?"

"She reminds me of Shakespeare's Dark Lady. She is dark, like a Spaniard with large dull black eyes and heavy eyelids, dun skin and long coarse hair, like black wires. Her lips are pale and her cheeks quite flat, and she has a sharp voice with a strange accent when she speaks."

"You don't find her attractive?"

"Absolutely not. I am in love with a lady who has lively green eyes, pale cream skin, rosy round cheeks, smooth wavy auburn hair, and soft coral lips."

"Really?"

"And her voice is like music to my ears."

He walked towards me and I started trembling, anticipating the magic words, which made my head spin to elation.

"May I?" He whispered.

"You may." I whispered back.

"You are the most beautiful woman I have ever laid eyes on, mistress."

His fingers swept over my cheeks, down to my jaw line, and across my throat. His lips drew nearer to mine and he whispered, "May I kiss you?"

I tilted my head back and stretched on tiptoe to receive his embrace and whispered, "Yes, Michael, kiss me."

His arms locked around my waist. I was deliciously trapped in a fragment of a frieze he had sculpted in my mind, oblivious to anything except his skin. He broke the spell by reminding me that the door was open, and I landed back down to my hearth rug. When I recovered my breath and my senses, I told Michael how I felt.

"They can't be intimate. What is it he sees in her?"

"She is very unlike Miss Haywood."

"Precisely! Elizabeth is fair, blue-eyed, and extremely refined."

"He has been attracted to the exact opposite type of person. Perhaps he is not ready to settle down and be married yet. Is it a cry for freedom?"

"He did mention he was feeling pressured into taking responsibilities. Perhaps I'm pushing him too hard... or too fast, but he will have to carry out his duty soon. I don't want him to waste his youth, like his father did."

"Annette has intelligent and generous eyes. I do not think she is a malevolent person, like her uncle."

"Very perceptive of you, Michael, but even so, I think I will be able to handle Mr. Mason. I know what he wants. But she is a mystery and must be kept away from my son at all costs. There is a slight possibility, it is only very slight, but I will not take any risks. They may be related. But I can't think about that now. We will cross that bridge when we come to it."

"May I keep your button as a token?" He held it up to me, and I wondered why John had given it to him in the first place.

"Of course," I pressed it in his palm, closed his hand, and wrapped both my hands around his. "You have my heart in your hands, look after it well."

"With my life."

Part Three: Like a Dream

'Is it true,' she said, 'that England is like a dream? Because one of my friends who married an Englishman wrote and told me so. She said this place London is like a cold dark dream sometimes. I want to wake up.'

'Well,' I answered annoyed, 'that is precisely how your beautiful island seems to me, quite unreal and like a dream.'

'But how can rivers and mountains and the sea be unreal?'

'And how can millions of people, their houses and their streets be unreal?'

'More easily,' she said, 'much more easily. Yes a big city must be like a dream.'

'No, this is unreal and like a dream,' I thought.

Wide Sargasso Sea by Jean Rhys (1966, page 24). Conversation between Bertha Mason and Edward Rochester in Jamaica, just before their marriage.

".... Everything in life seems unreal."
"Except me: I am substantial enough—touch me."
"You, sir, are the most phantom-like of all: you are a mere dream."
He held out his hand, laughing. "Is that a dream?" said he, placing it close to my eyes. He had a rounded, muscular, and vigorous hand, as well as a long, strong arm.
"Yes; though I touch it, it is a dream," said I, as I put it down from before my face.

Jane Eyre, Chapter XXV. Conversation between Jane Eyre and Edward Rochester in Thornfield Hall the night before their first interrupted marriage.

Chapter XX

Annette's Dream

After lunch, my uncle instructed me to pack my trunks, because we would be moving to Eyre Hall that very evening. I was told to put on my best dress for dinner, as I would be meeting both Mr. and Mrs. Rochester. My uncle reassured me not to worry, because I had already met Adele and John, and they would be my allies during my stay.

For months I had been anticipating what I would feel on my arrival in England. I had imagined an idyllic green land with clear blue skies and sturdy stone castles settled by sophisticated pale skinned people. I prayed to God that it would not be my vault as it had been my mother's. She too had imagined she would walk into a green and pleasant land, but instead found a satanic garret as a home and an unhallowed plot as her grave.

John had reassured me that Eyre Hall was a comfortable oasis in the middle of the inhospitable moorlands. He thought the world of his parents, especially his mother, who had been responsible for my mother's death, although he was naturally unaware of this detail. The fact he would be there with me, and seemed to be on my side, reassured me, although I knew I could never trust a Rochester.

My uncle instructed me to be polite and affectionate with Mr. Rochester, although Mrs. Rochester would be my benefactress from then on. He seemed to think she would be agreeable to both of us, and reminded me I should keep an open mind regarding my future, following her instructions in order to procure a suitable husband. When I reminded him how she had manipulated her husband, my father, to destroy my mother and steal her generous dowry, he told me it had happened a long time ago, and I should learn to forgive her.

The speed at which Mrs. Rochester had evolved from sorceress to accomplice shocked me, however, I had no choice but to follow my uncle's instructions. Since my departure from the convent, I was alone in the world, and moreover, I now found myself alone in an unknown country. Everything I owned had been given to me by Mr. Rochester or Mr. Mason. I had no money or possibility of earning any of my own accord. I was even more of a pawn than my mother had been. My worst enemy had to procure my board, lodging, dowry, and a husband. I was inescapably trapped.

John collected us in his cab at the inn, as the day was beginning to fade. Bishop Templar, whom he introduced as his headmaster and mentor, was already inside. The Bishop was a large round shaped man with puffy red cheeks and plenty of curly grey hair. His eyes slit and shone, as he smiled warmly, making me feel comfortable at once. My uncle and I sat facing them for the short ride. I watched them in dead silence while they spoke affably about trivial matters, such as the weather.

John hit the cast iron lion-head doorknocker energetically, and the sturdy valet I had seen delivering a note to my uncle, pulled open the heavy door. I looked around in awe at the mahogany-panelled hall and shimmering chandeliers. Feeling as vulnerable as a feather in the wind, I forced a smile while the servants lined up to greet us. My hand was trembling as the housekeeper, who John introduced as Mrs. Leah, wished me a good evening. Her piercing black eyes terrified me. I was sure I had seen her before in a nightmare. I turned to my uncle, who smiled stiffly as he shook her hand. The rest of the servants bowed as John introduced them jovially, then he turned to the housekeeper, "Leah, don't bother to show us up, just tell me where they'll be staying."

"Mrs. Rochester has instructed me to accompany all the guests to their rooms and make sure everything is to their liking, Master John," was her curt reply.

John smiled and relinquished the job of guide to the zealous housekeeper, "Very well, Leah, by all means do us the honours."

I followed her up the staircase, floating over the soft crimson carpet, and along the glossy darkness of the long galleries leading to our chambers. I was entranced by the brass adornments, cut glass candleholders, and gilt framed portraits. The house vibrated with wealth. It was almost ostentatious, but not quite. I looked up to the third floor, wondering if there was an attic, like the one at Thornfield, and shivered. My uncle held my arm and led me on.

Bishop Templar was allocated the Blue Room on the left wing of the first floor, next to Mr. Rochester's room. We were invited to look inside. Pale blue curtains, picture frames, and bedcovers lit the dark room, which overlooked the laurel orchard to the west of the house, above the dining room and the drawing room. We walked back towards the stairs and along to the end of the gallery in the east wing, where we were shown to the adjacent Golden Rooms, which Mrs. Leah told us were used for special guests. They were beautiful rooms with mustard curtains and bedcovers adorned with gilded ornamentation. Large bay windows overlooked the east wing and the hills, which blocked our view of neighbouring Hay.

I drew the curtains, the moon was large and shone brightly. I watched the hills, imagining a town full of busy people beyond, people who lived in their homes with their brothers and sisters and knew who their parents were. My uncle told Mrs. Leah he would like to have some Madeira wine in the drawing room before dinner and disappeared with her down the gallery, leaving me alone with John, who slipped into my chamber closing the door behind him. I felt trapped once more.

"John, please open the door. We can't be alone together!"

"Why not?"

"Because we can't."

"Are you afraid of me?"

"Of course not."

"You are. You are afraid of me. Why?"

"I am not afraid of you."

"Do you think I might want to kiss you?"

"No, of course not."

"Well, you're wrong. I do want to kiss you."

"John!"

"I've wanted to kiss you, since the first day I saw you."

"Please don't come any closer."

"I've wanted to be alone with you and tell you how I feel."

"John, we are related, please don't talk like that!"

"We are not blood relations."

"John, I warn you, I will scream."

"Just one kiss, and then I'll leave."

"What do you take me for?"

"A very beautiful woman."

I wanted to scream, but instead I froze. He came closer and held out his right hand, asking for mine, which I gave him. He drew it to his lips, then held out his left hand, asking for mine once more, and kissed it, too.

"Has anyone kissed you before?" He whispered, as he pulled me closer.

"Never," I confessed.

"Good, then you'll never forget this kiss, and neither will I." He added, enclosing me in his arms, gathering me to his breast, and pressing his lips on mine, "You are so lovely, Annette."

He pulled me onto the bed. "Let me kiss you once more."

I made no effort to pull away, drawn as I was like a wave to the sea, and he grazed his lips against mine, once more, softly teasing at first, then insisting on deepening the kiss. I allowed him to enter my heart, because I knew he was the only man I ever wanted to kiss again. Although I also knew he was the only man I should never kiss again. There was nothing I could do to stop him, or to stop myself. Perhaps I should have tried harder to keep him away, but I didn't seem to have the slightest control over my body or my life. My present and my future were in other people's hands. Was I just a puppet? Could I decide where to go and what to do? Clearly, No. So I let him decide for me until we heard a knock on the door and sat up abruptly.

"Who is it?" He asked irritably.

"Beth, Master John," was the anxious reply.

"We better let her in," he said, as he pulled me up. "Come in, Beth."

Seconds later a young maid stood at the threshold with a blank expression.

"Master John, Mrs. Leah has asked me to come and see if Miss Annette needs any help getting dressed."

They both looked at me expecting a reply, but once more I did not know what to say, so John finally spoke, "Thank you, Beth, but Miss Annette does not need any help."

When she left the room, he turned back to me and smiled, "You could have told her to stay, but you didn't. Why didn't you tell her to stay and help you?"

"I don't know. I was confused. I didn't know what to say. No one has ever helped me dress." I mumbled.

"You wanted me to stay, didn't you?" He smiled triumphantly.

"I don't know what I want anymore."

"Let me decide, then. Let me kiss you again."

I let him kiss me, because my mind was in a dream. Everything that had happened, since I had arrived in England, was unreal. I had stepped into a fairy tale and met a prince, who would look after me forever and ever in his magic castle. I would not have to think or worry about anything ever again. It was comforting to feel his lips on mine and his hands holding my wrists against the bed. I felt wanted and needed, and I had never felt anything similar before. It was a thrilling feeling of power. I had something he wanted. I freed my hands, pushed him away, and jumped up from the bed.

He chased me around the room until I let him catch me and kiss me again, this time crushing me against the wall.

"Be still," he whispered. "Don't struggle so, like a wild frantic bird that is rending its own plumage in its desperation. I will not hurt you."

I stopped resisting and let him take over my lips and my mind once more. When I dropped back into reality and remembered that he was engaged to another woman, I pushed him away, "John, you are engaged. Please leave me alone."

"I will not be married for at least two years." He laughed.

"But you will marry her?"

"Of course, and you will marry, too."

"I will not marry anyone I do not love."

"Neither will I."

"But we cannot be married."

"Of course not."

"So, why do you want to kiss me?"

"Because I like you."

"You like me?"

"Yes, I like you very much."

"So, you kiss all the girls you like?"

"Only the girls I run over first."

"Everything is a joke for you. You're toying with my feelings."

"I'm not toying with you. I'm getting to know you. We are getting to know each other, aren't we?"

He brushed his fingers along my face, and I felt soft and safe once more. "I'd like to get to know you. I don't know anyone in England." I whispered.

"You will be safe here at Eyre Hall."

The second interruption was my uncle, who knocked on the adjoining door. "Annette, are you ready? We will be going down to dinner in half an hour."

"Yes, Uncle, I will be ready on time." I shouted back.

I turned to John and admitted yet again of being terrified of meeting his parents. John was surprised at my misgivings and tried to comfort me, assuring me his parents were the kindest people in England.

Before leaving he took my hand, kissed it, and said, "Whatever happens, Annette, remember this: we are more than friends, and more than husband and wife, we are family. My father, my mother, Adele, you, and I, and even your uncle, Mr. Mason, we have a bond which will never be broken. You are part of my life, and you always will be, and that makes me very happy." Then his head leaned against my forehead, where he dropped a soft, warm kiss, as if it were the most natural thing in the world, and whispered, "I will see you later, Annette," before sliding out of my chamber.

I dreaded meeting my father and his wife. I was terrified of not being up to their expectations, of being dismissed or ridiculed, and of losing everything I had, which was nothing of my own. I had nowhere to go back to, neither had I any means of returning home. Where was my home? Would this house be my home from now on? What would I do here? What would become of me, if they threw me out? My uncle was ruined, and we had nowhere to go in Jamaica, or in England. My future lay in the hands of the people who had ill-treated and killed my mother, and I had to be amiable to them. Would I ever have to bear a greater humiliation? I cried bitterly.

Chapter XXI

The Last Supper

My wife has insisted I come down to dinner. I have decided to humour her on this occasion, as I will not have many more opportunities to do so. My time here is coming to a close, and I am grateful for it. What kind of a life have I been living these past months, alone in my room day after day, haunted by devilish creatures of the past? Even Jane seldom comes to see me, and when she does, it is to vex me with accusations. She will never understand how much I have loved her and needed her, or she would not speak to me in that manner. I fear my angel no longer loves what is left of me. My authority is waning, and the worst of it is that I do not care. I am weary of plotting, scheming, lying, and pretending, and all of it to protect her! I require a peaceable existence in my final days.

But she will not allow me peace! She wants me to meet Bertha's daughter! A monstrous creature I never had any wish to see, let alone meet. Why must she be thrust upon me? I had nothing to do with it, but I did not abandon it. I sent money regularly. Mason, her only living relative, insisted on taking care of it in Jamaica, its rightful place, but I cannot argue anymore. I can no longer impose my will. He has brought the thing back, and Jane has become a tyrannical hag, who refuses to respect my wishes or understand that everything I did was to protect her.

So, here I am being carried down the stairs by my son and my valet. The master of the Rochester Estate is an infirm and feeble old man. I am experiencing one humiliation after another, and in my weakest moment, the ghosts have returned to haunt me. I willingly confess my one and only crime: I loved Jane Eyre too much. I lied and plotted and even killed for her. It was all for her.

I took a last look around the house that Jane rebuilt, as I was carried along shorter and breezier corridors than those my grandfather had originally built. I glimpsed the sturdy brick walls and large casement windows along the gallery and smirked at the lavish dark red carpets leading down the stairs. Mrs. Fairfax would never have allowed such a dazzling display at Thornfield.

Downstairs we crossed the dark panelled hall, and my valet pushed open the dining room door, disclosing a glittering Aladdin's cave. Dozens of candles and chandeliers illuminated the crystal wine glasses, polished porcelain dishes, and shiny steel cutlery, while rich, dark velvet drapery hung loosely around windows, tables, and armchairs. The guests sat gravely around the table: my Last Supper. As I was wheeled in, Jane, my graceful seraph, greeted me affectionately at the threshold, and I was seated at the head of the table.

"Good evening ladies and gentlemen. It is my pleasure to have what may be my last public dinner with all of you. I welcome you to my home, and hope you enjoy your stay and each other's company."

I waited for the guests to mumble their thank yous and continued speaking, "I would like to thank my wife, Jane Eyre Rochester, for her love and devotion to me, even when I did not deserve it, which has been too often. Jane, I also ask your forgiveness if ever, in an excess of love, I have offended you."

Once again, I waited for her to acknowledge my comments. She smiled and nodded demurely, but I could tell she had not forgiven me yet. Would she ever?

"I am here tonight to please you, Jane. Everything I have ever done has been to please you. Can you find it in your heart to forgive me?" I insisted in the hope that she would acquiesce for the sake of our guests. Her jaws set firmly and her eyes darted fiery sparks. I thought she would chastise me, but the sound of some glasses tapping stole her eyes away from mine. Her brow relaxed, and she smiled sweetly at someone else, although her eyes turned quickly back to mine, as she finally spoke, "I thank you for allowing us the pleasure of your company and dining with us this evening, Edward, and I dutifully forgive all your minor offences, as I hope you will forgive mine."

The stern look returned, as she finished the sentence, "Our Lord must forgive the rest."

I looked out of the corner of my eye, only Simon and the other young valet were standing behind me. I wondered who had made her smile and forget her anger, but I had no answer.

I looked back to the table at my son, as handsome and confident as I had once been, "John, my only son and my worthiest asset, I entreat you to follow your mother's advice to the letter. She knows best. She always knew better than me. You will be the greatest Rochester, if you do as she bids, and it is my wish that you obey her. Do not neglect my words."

"Rest assured, Father, I will be loyal to Mother, and to my gracious surname and heritage."

"My dearest, lively and loyal, Adele, I should have allowed you to use my surname and you might have married. Jane tells me you have a new suitor, no doubt this gentleman sitting to your left, Mr. Greenwood, I believe. Good evening, sir. You will not toy with my ward, or I shall pursue you from Hell, if needs be."

"Mr. Rochester, it is an honour to be your guest tonight, and I assure you, sir, that my intentions are honourable. We will be departing for Italy shortly, with your permission, and when we return, you will have news of my intentions."

"Jane will have to deal with that matter, because I fear I shall not be here on your return. She will know what to do. She will be the head of this family and this Estate and will be respected as such by everyone in this room."

I waited once more for everyone to nod and mumble agreement.

"Bishop Templar, I thank you for counselling and guiding my son. You have been a great influence in his academic and spiritual progress. I trust you will continue to do so, in a disinterested manner, when I am no longer present."

"Naturally, Mr. Rochester, John is one of my most valued pupils, and I will always watch over his advancement and advise him in spiritual and academic matters."

I turned to the devil at my table, "Richard, we meet again. I see you are in better health than me, for the moment. Beware, you are observing what lies ahead, and not too far away, I fear. You are welcome in this house because Jane, who is a far better person than I am, wishes it to be so. We both did what we had to do twenty-three years ago, and here now sitting beside you I observe the results of our deeds. We each fulfilled our duty, and my wife, who is the most generous person on Earth, because she is not bound by any obligation, wishes my duty to be continued, even after my death. Jane will see to it that Miss Annette Mason is procured a dowry and a husband, and anything else she needs forthwith."

"Thank you, Edward. Miss Annette Mason and I both appreciate your kindness and Mrs. Rochester's generosity."

"So you should." I mumbled loud enough for all to hear before adding, "Can she not speak?"

"I am most grateful and honoured to be your ward, sir."

"Let me look at you. Yes, you remind me of her. That dark, beautiful, and quite ..."

"Edward!" Jane interrupted me before I could tell them that she looked just like her mad, enticing mother, and that she was a fatherless wench, who had come to steal my last peaceful moments.

"She has returned to haunt me!"

"Edward, you are looking at Annette. She is not a ghost. Annette is our guest at Eyre Hall. Naturally she looks like her aunt, but her looks are not her election. None of us decide what colour our hair or our eyes are, do we, dear?"

"You are too good for me, Jane, too good for all of them." I mumbled helplessly.

"Nonsense, we are all good Christians sitting around this table. Please, Edward, let us have our first course together, peaceably. Bishop Templar, would you be so kind as to say Grace, please?"

I turned to the ambitious clergyman, wondering wretchedly if he would dare to court my widow.

"Naturally, Mrs. Rochester. It is an honour to be present on such a special occasion with the whole Rochester family together. I will gladly say a very special Grace at this extraordinary table we all have the privilege to be sharing."

He joined his hands and closed his eyes, as if God could really hear him, and I wished I believed. I wished I had believed in God for one single second in my life, so I could grasp that second and believe again, but I couldn't. I saw nothing. I felt nothing. Nothing more. Just death, quiet, and blackness. No guardian angels. No demons. I closed my eyes and listened to his prayer, in case he had the power of summoning God to come to me, but why should He answer my call? After all, I had ignored Him all my life.

"Dear Lord, we ask you to be present at our table tonight, and we thank you for all these gifts, which we are about to receive from thy bounty. We also thank you for all the blessings conferred upon us throughout our lives and humbly ask forgiveness for all our sins, so that we may feast in Paradise with thee, Amen."

When I opened my eyes, Jane was staring at me, "Are you all right, dear?" She asked.

"Perfectly." I lied.

"Thank you, Bishop Templar." Everyone else mumbled their thank yous once more, as Jane nodded to the servants. "I think we can start our meal now."

I was trembling by the time the food arrived, but Adele squeezed my hand. "It's all right, Annette. It's all over now. He will not speak to you again. Breathe or you'll suffocate!"

I smiled, speechless, as the soup was poured into my bowl.

"Napkin on your lap, elbows away from the table, big spoon across the top for the soup, and bread roll to your left. Come on eat up, it's warm and delicious." Adele prompted helpfully.

Water and wine were poured into the sparkling crystal glasses. I sipped slowly, as I watched John chatting to his father. The old man smiled dotingly at his jovial son. They obviously understood each other, like the fish and the sea. John was so innocent and naïve, he obviously knew nothing about his parents' sins, or was he one of them, out to break my heart and my mind?

My uncle sat opposite me to John's left. He conversed with Bishop Templar, who was sitting on his right. They made an unusual couple, the jovial, pious clergyman, and the grim, business-minded settler. Men always seemed to get on however different they were, not so for women, who choose their conversation partners far more carefully.

Adele was easy to converse with. She was a merry and loquacious lady, who had no doubt wasted her youthful years in this dreary mansion, probably helping Mrs. Rochester bring up John and look after her ailing husband. Having been deprived of her rightful surname, as I too had been, she must have had a hard time finding a suitable husband. Technically speaking, she was my half-sister. I knew little of her mother, a French harlot my father had met while he was still married to my tormented mother, according to my uncle. What kind of a man had my father been? An irresponsible lecher? A murderer? A thief? A negligent father? A cruel husband? Did he think he could just ask forgiveness and be accepted into the gates of Heaven? I was not prepared to forgive him as quickly as Adele had. She seemed happy enough now that she was going to Italy to meet her mother with the unconventional looking poet.

I had seen unkempt bachelors like Mr. Greenwood in Jamaica and on the ship to England, men with unruly, ragged grey hair, whose waistcoats bloated unsightly under the pressure of their greedy stomachs. They wore soiled trousers and shoes, which needed polishing. The London poet did not seem to have a love interest in Adele, although he was certainly in need of a wife. He was pleasant enough, turning to me regularly and asking if I was enjoying the food or my stay in England, as if both things were equally significant to him.

My gaze bounced back and forth from my father to my half-brother. They both had a similar bone structure and jaw line, but John had a shorter more refined nose, clearer eyes, fairer hair, and paler skin. His features were more relaxed, and his manner was more leisurely than his father's. I could easily trust him. I wondered why my father had tortured and killed my beautiful mother, the mother I was torn away from. John smiled at me frequently, and I wondered if his zealous mother would allow us to be friends. Could we be friends and yet feel such a strong attraction?

At the end of the table to my left and opposite my father sat Mrs. Rochester, majestically supervising the banquet. She smiled stiffly, as she overlooked the interactions taking place at the table. She hardly ate, fidgeting with the cutlery and sipping the wine, while she chatted politely with Mr. Greenwood and Bishop Templar. The Bishop's eyes twinkled mischievously, as they rested on our hostess, and Mr. Greenwood also competed for her attention, no doubt keen to make a good impression.

When we finished the broiled salmon, Mr. Rochester complained of tiredness and was taken up to his room by the two young valets. After her father left, and the roast goose and various bottles of wine had been devoured by the hungry guests, Adele asked me to change places, so that she could discuss her travel arrangements with Mr. Greenwood over dessert. I agreed meekly, delighted to converse with John again.

"Well, it wasn't that bad, was it?" He smiled warmly.

"Your father is very intimidating, fortunately, I wasn't alone with him."

"Count your blessings! He's usually far more talkative and asks tons of questions, but he's not his usual self anymore. Anyway, as I told you, we'll look after you. You're part of the family now."

"Your mother was very kind." I conceded.

"Why does that bother you?"

"I'm not sure what to expect from her. She should hate me."

"My mother doesn't hate anyone, why on earth would she hate you?" He chuckled.

"I must remind her of her husband's first wife, and that can't be pleasing for her."

"My mother is not a resentful or vindictive person. On the contrary, she is an honourable and decent person. She has devoted most of her life to helping orphans and setting up charity schools. Why wouldn't she help you?"

"I suppose you are right."

"You look so beautiful when you are worried. May I go to your room tonight after dinner?"

"Of course not!"

"Just to get to know each other."

"I wouldn't trust you in my room again."

"I shall try anyway. My room is next to yours."

"Your mother is watching us, please stop looking at me like that."

"Like what?"

"Like I'm seducing you."

"Aren't you?"

"Of course I'm not."

He smirked, rubbing his knee against my thigh.

"Is this your first dinner party, Annette?"

"I'm afraid so."

"Well, then you've done very well indeed!"

"Stop laughing at me!"

"I'm not. I'm impressed by you. Brace up now. I think my mother wants to talk to you."

Mrs. Rochester suggested the ladies move to the drawing room for coffee while the gentlemen remained at the table, conversing over brandy and cigars. I asked John if I would see him the next day, and he laughed saying he would see me in half an hour after coffee. He guessed I had gasped at the thought of being alone with her. "Do not worry, Annette, my mother wants to help you. She will want to sort out your future, what you'd like to do. Remember to tell her you've worked as a teacher. She loves teachers."

"Don't be too long over the coffee." I begged.

"You miss me already, don't you?"

"Don't be silly! It's because I will be alone with her."

"Adele will be there, too."

The gentlemen stood up as I followed Mrs. Rochester and Adele out of the dining room and into the drawing room, still terrified of the woman who had destroyed my mother and wrecked my childhood.

Chapter XXII

The Reconciliation

I followed the woman, who was both my tormentress and my benefactress into the adjacent room. The valet drew the curtains, which were hung back behind us as we passed through. Jane sat down first on the divan and waved her hand towards the couch, where she wished Annette and me to sit. We could hear the men chatting noisily and chuckling congenially in the dining room while we sat solemnly facing each other in the drawing room. I smiled uneasily and waited for her to speak.

"Annette, I would like to speak freely and honestly with you, do you agree?"

"Yes, Mrs. Rochester."

"We can speak frankly, now that we are alone. Adele knows all the facts, but I would like to spare John the knowledge of the extent of his father's misconduct. I need to know if you are prepared to keep our conversation secret, for John's sake."

Her lips curled into a smile and her impassive eyes pierced into mine. Probing, questioning, judging, and... hating me? I shivered and spoke hesitantly, "Sometimes the truth makes life easier."

"Well, I think we both know life isn't easy. John is young and impressionable. I don't want him to bear his father's guilt." Her eyes smiled gently for the first time, "I want him to live his life without carrying anyone else's burden. Don't you agree, Annette?"

Her features softened, when she smiled, and her look brightened, when she spoke about John. At that moment, she was exactly as I had imagined an English lady would be: elegant, aloof, and demure. She was also beautiful and very rich. It was not surprising that my uncle had decided it would be more advantageous to become her friend instead of remaining her enemy. I wondered how my relationship with her would develop, once my father died. In any case, there was no point in becoming her enemy, was there? She was John's mother, after all.

"If you think that is best, Mrs. Rochester. I am thankful that you have accepted me as your ward."

She smiled triumphantly, "I was an orphan myself, Annette, so I can understand how you may have felt during your childhood, and how you may still feel now, alone in the world. I spent my early years with an aunt, who had no affection for me, and later at an institution where I was not very happy, especially when I was a child."

Her eyes wondered to the window and rested on one of the casements, her thoughts far away, as she continued speaking, "I devote a great deal of my time to helping orphans. There are far too many children who suffer in England."

She looked back at me fondly, "I cannot change the past, but I can do my best to make your future as pleasant as possible."

I was surprised and disarmed by her kindness, "That is very generous of you, Mrs. Rochester."

"I consider it my Christian duty, Annette. Would you not help others, if you were in a position to do so?"

I remembered John's words, "I was a music teacher at the convent school, where I was brought up, and I felt it was my responsibility to help the children, who were mostly orphans, like me."

"It pleases me that you are a beautiful, intelligent, and kind young lady. I am sure we will understand each other."

Her thoughts travelled once again to a distant time and place, "Your mother would be proud of you."

Her unexpected words shook me out of my seat. I stood by the fireplace, breathless. "You knew my mother?"

She sighed, tilting her head towards me. "We will not be having this conversation again, Annette, so I will tell you all I know, or at least all I remember. It is very painful for me, but whatever happened was not your fault, or your responsibility. You are innocent, just as John is. It pains me greatly to bring to mind the tragic events, but I am anxious to share my recollections with you, and feel relieved once and for all."

She also stood up, walked towards the casements, and started speaking to the acquiescent trees, "I arrived at Thornfield to be governess to Adele. I was eighteen years old, and I fell in love with Edward. We both fell in love. He always told me he was a bachelor, and when he proposed, I naturally accepted. On our wedding day…"

She stopped speaking to dry her tears, and Adele jumped up and flew to her side, embracing her fervently. "You don't have to remember all this, Jane, what's the point?"

"I want her to know, to understand what happened." She mumbled, as they both cried in each other's arms until Jane straightened and continued, "On our wedding day, your uncle interrupted the service to inform the Vicar that the groom was already married. Nobody can imagine how devastated I felt. Of course, I didn't believe him until we returned to Thornfield and were introduced to your mother. She was in a deplorable condition, enclosed like an animal, and hidden from the rest of the world. I will spare you the details, suffice it to say that her presence was a shock to all of us. Edward tried to convince me to stay, but I left the following evening and vowed never to return."

We heard the murmur of the men in the other room and the wind whipping the bare trees. I waited impatiently for her to resume her account. Could she be telling the truth?

"A year later, Mr. Briggs informed me there had been a fire and Thornfield had been burnt down. I returned to discover your mother had fallen off the battlements. Edward was alive, although crippled and blind. We married and I nursed him back to health. Eyre Hall was built shortly after John was born, with the money I inherited from my uncle, John Eyre, who died in Madeira without direct descendants."

Tears welled up in my eyes and rolled down my cheeks. Adele rushed to my side to embrace me.

"I'm sorry, Annette, but you have to know what happened. I must tell you what I know, then we can all continue with our lives. Do you understand?"

I nodded, unable to control my tears.

"Four days ago, when your uncle came to Eyre Hall, I discovered your existence. Your mother was married to Edward, when you were born, so you must be his daughter. Edward has paid for your upkeep at the convent, and as soon as your uncle made it known to me that you wished to pay your respects, I made some enquiries with Dr. Carter, who confirmed the events pertaining to your birth. Rest assured, Annette, that I will look after you from now on, if you should so wish. You will be procured a suitable husband, dowry, and residence in the meantime."

If she was telling me the truth, it meant that John was probably my brother, my half-brother, so our feelings were impure. Mrs. Rochester confirmed what my uncle had told me, that Mr. Rochester *was* my father. However, his version was different. He had told me that Jane and my father had planned my mother's death, so they could be free to marry. Had Jane been his accomplice, as my uncle had told me? Perhaps she was not aware of his plans. Perhaps it happened, as she had just told me, and my mother's death had been an unfortunate accident. Who was lying? Who was telling the truth? Who knew the truth? Who could I believe?

Jane returned to the divan and sat down before continuing, "I have only two requirements of you, and I am afraid they are not negotiable. Firstly, my son and everyone else must continue to believe that Mr. Rochester is your uncle. Secondly, you will go to a finishing school in Belgium for a year, where you will complement some of the gaps in your education. Your stay abroad will enable you to have a more satisfactory life when you return to England."

She paused once more, as if she wished me to digest the information gradually. I looked into the hearth, where the flames rose, fell, and tangled into a macabre glowing dance.

"When you return, you will stay at Eyre Hall while we decide your options."

I wondered what it would be like to live in this remote, vault-like house permanently. Would I have to make polite conversation with John's fiancée? Would I have to marry a man I did not love? Or remain a spinster like Adele? She seemed to read my mind.

"You will not be forced to marry against your wishes, although you will be advised as to what is best for you, but you will be allowed to choose how you live. Do you agree?"

I nodded. What else could I do?

"Have you any questions?"

She watched aloofly while Adele consoled me. I suddenly realized how much I missed my life back home at the convent. I wished I could return to the order, the regularity and the security therein. I wanted to recover my previous life, the life of a boring music teacher within the safety of the convent walls. The idea of returning and recovering my innocence empowered me, and I was finally able to stop crying, "Mrs. Rochester, thank you for your kindness, but I miss my school and my life at the convent. I fear I will be unhappy in England, as my mother was…"

"I promise, you will have a more pleasant life than Bertha Mason."

The voices in the next room were noisier and merrier while in the drawing room the silence was broken only by the crackling coal. She was silent and I dared not speak. I wondered if our conversation had concluded, but Mrs. Rochester spoke once more, "I cannot promise you a happier life, because happiness is something you must search for within yourself. Nevertheless, I hope you will find peace and contentment at Eyre Hall."

I smiled, but she was wrong. I had found happiness in another person. He would be sitting with me, chatting amiably in a few minutes. His eyes would be searching for mine, as his hands had been chasing my waist in my bedroom just a few hours earlier. What would she say if she knew?

"If you accept my proposal, Annette, it would please me greatly."

I was trapped. Under the circumstances I had no alternative. They all wanted me to stay. Perhaps I should learn to make the most of my captivity. Perhaps I could be happy at Eyre Hall, although I could never marry John.

"Thank you, Mrs. Rochester. You are most gracious."

"You have made a wise decision, Annette."

It seemed to me that I had not made any decision myself. I had only agreed to my uncle and Jane's wishes. I remembered my uncle's financial worries and instructions.

"May I ask you for something, Mrs. Rochester?"

"What is it?"

"My uncle has been the only relative I have ever known. He is the person who saved my life. I would like to be able to repay him. I understand his finances are precarious…"

"Your concern for your uncle is touching. Rest assured I will not abandon him, either."

I had signed my life sentence. My future lay in her hands. We watched each other's faces for a few minutes, searching for the words we had not spoken until she broke the silence, making an effort to reassure me once more.

"You have suffered enough, Annette. I hope you can find some happiness here in England. I will certainly do all I can to make your stay as pleasant as possible. Remember, I am not your enemy, and I trust we can understand each other."

I had not yet decided whether she was telling the truth or whether I could trust her, but I had realized she was my only option, so I smiled and nodded. She suggested we should have some Madeira wine before the gentlemen joined us, and we toasted to the year ahead, which Jane predicted would be, "Full of joy, travel, and pleasant surprises."

I surrendered to the sound of her voice and the warmth of the wine, and allowed myself to imagine an eventful and pleasant future at Eyre Hall.

Chapter XXIII

Expiation

It had been done. It was not the first time I had killed someone who deserved to be dead. I remembered the beast at the workhouse, who had tried to take my sister by force. I was just a boy then, but I knew what I had to do to protect my only sibling. Once again, I felt the relief and satisfaction that justice had been done. The demon was dead.

I had followed his own instructions: *any discreet means, such as suffocation, will be sufficient,* and covered his face with his own pillow. As he had predicted: *he is old and weak, therefore, he will not resist.* He offered no opposition, saying only, "You have come at last," when he saw me approach his bedside, closing his weary eyes.

The worthless, worn cadaver, which lay limply before me, would soon be buried and forgotten. I hated him for having had the most magnificent woman in the world and not honouring her as he should have. She did not deserve such a heartless companion, and I had mercifully put an end to a life, which was already in its last moments. I had merely anticipated what would have been a reality in a matter of days.

I had restored the balance. He was at rest and my mistress was free, so I would be able to claim her for myself, at last. The moment I had dreamed of for five years was approaching. All the hardship and humiliations I had undergone, since my parents died, seemed insignificant. I would go through it all again a thousand times to feel her hand on my face and her lips just a whisper away from mine. She was the goddess of my dreams, and I would be her slave for the rest of my days.

I walked out of the room and down the stairs light headed. My feet floated over the dark carpet, as if I were alone in a soundless dream. When I opened the drawing room door, the brightness and hubbub shook me back to reality. The moon cast its strong white beam through the casements and onto the floor, challenging the furious flames, which radiated a golden glow from the hearth while the chandeliers and candlesticks illuminated all the corners of the room. The dinner guests were all conversing congenially in their diverse selected nooks. I walked over to each group offering to refill their glasses, inadvertently overhearing fragments of superficial conversations.

Surprisingly, Mr. Mason and Mr. Greenwood conversed amiably, drinking brandy and smoking in the corner, discussing business opportunities in the colonies. Adele and Annette were sitting on the couch, chatting unenthusiastically about fashion and cosmetics, and my mistress was standing by the fireplace, talking to John and the Bishop about the success of the Ragged Schools, but her heart was not in the matter, as it usually was. She spoke distractedly, looking relaxed, no doubt because the evening had run smoothly, in spite of the tensions Mr. Mason and Miss Mason's visit could have provoked.

I approached my mistress and inquired as arranged, "Pardon me, Mrs. Rochester, will you need the hearth in the library?"

"Yes, Michael, I shall be writing a letter shortly." I heard her speak to the Bishop, as I walked away, "Please excuse me, Bishop Templar, but I must write a letter to my cousin, Diana, Mrs. Fitzjames, who is expecting news, and I cannot postpone it any longer."

Minutes later she walked into the library while I was poking the coals. She locked the door and put the key in her skirt pocket.

"Michael, please draw the curtains and put out all the candles, except the one on the desk." I complied.

"Now come here." She added, and I moved to her side by the hearth, looking into her restless eyes.

"Show me your hands, Michael." She turned my palms upwards and held them for a moment before kissing them.

"You have soiled them for me."

"Nothing I do for you is soiled."

"Did you tremble?"

"My hand will never tremble in your service."

"Was it… hard?"

"I think he was grateful. He was suffering physically and spiritually. Nothing unexpected or unnecessary happened. He was compliantly expecting death."

"Did he speak?"

"As I approached his bedside he called, "Jane Eyre, is it you?"

"Did he say anything else?"

"He said, 'Can you forgive me, Jane?'"

"And then?"

"And then he said, 'Find my little Jane, your little Jane.'"

She broke into tears, "I can't believe he's dead. What have I done? I can't live without him. I'm lost."

I embraced her, asking her not to cry, but she was taken over by dismal feelings, "How can you love me any more, after what I have asked you to do? I shouldn't have asked you to commit such a sinful act. How could I spoil you like that?"

She moved nervously towards the desk, leaning forward distressfully. "Michael, I can't breathe."

I realized there was no advantage in saying the truth, so I stood behind her and told her what she wanted to hear, "Don't cry, mistress. I killed no one. When I approached the bed, he gasped three times and stopped breathing."

"He stopped breathing?"

"Yes, he did. He asked for your forgiveness and died."

"Then what did you do?"

"I approached his side."

"How do you know he is dead?"

"His eyes lost expression and his body flattened. He became as white as snow and as cold as ice within seconds."

"Did you see his soul leave his body?"

"I heard his last breath."

She gasped, "Did he suffer?"

"He did not. He embraced death willingly, and then his soul was taken away."

Tears continued to rush down her face, "Michael, I'm so cold."

I felt her trembling uncontrollably in my arms, "Sit by the fire, mistress. Have you a shawl I can bring you?"

"Look in the cabinet."

I found a woollen mantle, which I wrapped around her shoulders, then I brought her a glass of brandy and sat down beside her. "This will warm you. Try not to worry, believe me, he is at peace. Simon is bound to find his corpse shortly, when he goes up to put out his candle and kindle the fire."

She coughed and breathed with difficulty, "I can't do this. I can't go up and see his dead body. I killed him."

"I told you, you killed no one. It was his time to leave us. He was called."

She broke away from me and stood up impatiently.

"What about John? How will his father's death affect him?"

I stood by her side, "It is you John needs. His father has been unable to help him for some time."

"How will I have the necessary authority?"

"You will, you already do. You have been dealing with the house, the tenants, and the administrator for the last year."

"What about his sins, Michael? Who will pay for his sins?"

Her brow was furrowed, and her eyes shone in the dark room. I knew what I had to say to ease her pain, "The soul who sins shall die. The son shall not suffer for the iniquity of the father, nor the father suffer for the iniquity of the son. The righteousness of the righteous shall be upon himself, and the wickedness of the wicked shall be upon himself."

"But I killed him!"

"Nobody killed him. He died because his time had come. He was called by our Lord, that is why he died."

"If only I could believe it."

"Believe it. It is the truth. You must be strong. Mr. Rochester is in the past. Helen is your future. She needs her mother. We must find her. We will find her."

"I know you are right, but I feel so terribly guilty."

I took her hands and spoke quietly, "You cannot feel guilty for his death or for his sins. They are his sins, only his."

She kissed my hands once more, and I moved them up towards her face, her cheeks were flushed, "You look warmer. Are you feeling better?"

She nodded and put her arms around me. I held her tightly, closing my eyes, imagining a world in which we were alone together. Seconds later, Simon's unintelligible screams startled us. As he rushed down the stairs, his words started to make more sense, "Master is dead! Mr. Rochester is dead!"

She gasped, "Oh my God! Simon has already discovered Edward's corpse."

Her fearful face looked up to mine urgently, "What shall I do now?"

"You must accompany your son upstairs to pay your last respects."

"I can't do it."

"John needs you, you must be strong. It will be a very long night, Mrs. Rochester."

"The longest night of my life." She whispered.

"I will be by your side."

Minutes later, I watched her leave the room tearfully and walked behind her quietly.

Chapter XXIV

Deceased

"Mrs. Rochester! The master is dead! We must stop the clocks and drape all the mirrors in the house, or his spirit will be trapped. He will not be able to leave Eyre Hall, so he will haunt us forever! The windows must be opened and the curtains drawn to let the good spirits in to look after him and keep the malignant out. We must bring ice from the kitchen to put under the bed, or malignant life will crawl out of his mouth and ears."

Simon had reached the bottom of the staircase, as I stepped out of the library into the hall with Michael. The drawing room door opened and Adele screamed, "Simon! For goodness sake be quiet, you will wake all the dead in the graveyard!"

John was standing behind Adele looking bewildered, "Mother, what has happened?"

His face white and his expression quite horrified. I rushed to his side, "John, he is at peace at last. There is nothing we can do, except pray."

"Father!" He shouted, as he pushed past me and rushed up the staircase.

"Wait!" I screamed and turned to Michael, "Michael, go with him! He can't be alone now!" Michael obeyed at once.

Bishop Templar turned to me and spoke gravely, "Mrs. Rochester, may I suggest we follow John and say some prayers by his bedside?"

"Of course, my Lord, let us go upstairs together." I took his arm and beckoned to Adele, "Adele, darling, will you come up with us?"

"Not yet, Jane. I can't bear to think of his lifeless body! I can't go up now."

She seemed so distressed that I had no choice but to agree, "Well, wait here. Mr. Greenwood, would you be so kind as to accompany Adele in such a painful moment for her and console her as best you can?"

"Of course, Mrs. Rochester. Come, Adele, let us wait in the drawing room."

"Mr. Mason, Annette, will you be so kind as to wait a few minutes while I go upstairs with Bishop Templar?"

"Mrs. Rochester, I would like to go up with you, if you don't mind." Annette was looking at me earnestly. I told her Edward was her father. She had just met him, and he was dead, quite a dreadful succession of events for an evening. "Of course you can. Are you sure you won't be too distressed?"

"Quite sure."

"Then come with us. Mr. Mason, would you kindly wait with Adele and Mr. Greenwood?"

"Of course, madam. Accept my most sincere condolences, and if I can be of any use, please let me know."

"Thank you, Mr. Mason."

Before heading up the stairs I turned to Simon, "Please see to the clocks. Go down to the kitchen to tell the rest of the household what has happened, and bring some drapery to cover the mirrors, and of course, the ice."

"Yes, madam."

"I will tell Michael to fetch the undertakers at Millcote and Dr. Carter."

"Yes, madam."

"I understand you worked for an undertaker in London before working at Eyre Hall, is that so?"

He nodded proudly, "Yes, madam."

"Could you dress Mr. Rochester when…?" Tears came to my eyes, as I said his name. My feet softened and floated, and my hand slipped from the Bishop's arm. The floor swayed and I lost my balance. I felt rough, sturdy fingers clasp my waist, as I fell backwards and looked into Mr. Mason's furrowed brow.

"Mrs. Rochester! Are you unwell?"

"Thank you, Mr. Mason. I am feeling a little dizzy."

"Please, allow me to accompany you upstairs." I nodded, and he held out his arm for me to cling to. "Thank you, Mr. Mason."

When we arrived at the top of the stairs, the gallery seemed darker and narrower than usual and the floor was rolling, as if I were walking on waves. Tears were running freely down my cheeks, and I was still having difficulty breathing.

Mr. Mason took my hand in his and squeezed it hard, "Unfortunately, Mrs. Rochester, this is God's plan for all of us." I cringed at his touch, which fortunately brought me back to reality.

Inside Edward's chamber, our son was kneeling down on the floor by his father's side, holding his hand and kissing it. Annette was kneeling down on the opposite side of the bed, doing exactly the same. Bishop Templar stood behind John with his hands on his shoulders, attempting to comfort him, while Mr. Mason left my side and stood vigilantly behind Annette.

The Bishop was speaking, but my heart was thumping so loudly I could not hear what he was saying. The room was hot and the air was thick and putrid. I looked at my husband and gasped. Edward's eyes were frighteningly open, as if he had seen a ghost, and his mouth was wide open, too, as if he had gasped for air before dying. His face was as pale as death itself, and his chest crushed and lifeless. He had gone.

Once more I felt my legs bend into the floor. The hexagonal forms on the carpet were sliding into squares as my stomach churned. Michael rushed to my side and I managed to say, "I'm going to be sick," just before he carried me to the toilet table. When I finished, he took the ewer and poured some water on my hands and I washed my face, then he led me to a chair at the foot of the bed.

I heard the distant voice of the Bishop saying some prayers to bid him farewell and facilitate his transit to his new abode in the Kingdom of Heaven, but I was not sure if that would be his destination. He had not confessed his sins. He had not repented for his misdeeds. He had not made his peace with our creator before dying, and he might not be allowed to leave Eyre Hall yet.

I stood up and turned to Michael beckoning him to follow me. We walked out of the chamber and turned into the shorter gallery and the stairs leading to my chamber, where we could not be seen. His eyes shone in the unlit passage. I reached for his hands, and he pulled me closer whispering, "Are you all right, Mrs. Rochester?"

"Yes, I shall be all right."

"You look unwell."

"Michael, please go to Millcote and bring the undertaker as soon as possible. There are many preparations that need to be attended."

"It shall take more than four hours. Will you not need me here?"

"Simon will attend to matters here, in the meantime. He knows what to do."

His concerned eyes bore into mine, "But you will be alone."

"Only for a few hours."

He moved closer, "Before you go, Mrs. Rochester, promise me something."

"What is it?"

"Promise me you will not take any of Mr. Rochester's drops."

He was right. I had thought of succumbing to the easy comfort of the miraculous drug. I put my arms around him, "Hold me, Michael."

He spoke into my hair, "I cannot leave, if you do not promise. I saw you looking at Mr. Rochester's medicine cabinet."

"You are right, the temptation is great."

"It is very harmful. Think of John, he needs you, so does Helen... and so do I."

I pressed my face into his chest, praying I would be strong enough to get through the wake and the funeral without breaking down, or relapsing into the comfort of laudanum once again. It was a pleasant and swift evasion, but I shuddered at the thought of its dire consequences, which I had already experienced. Michael was stroking my hair, waiting for my reply, "Promise me." He insisted.

I broke away and smiled, "I promise. Now go, and please be careful, Michael. It is very late and there is a full moon. Last month a pack of foxes attacked a farmer."

He told me he would be back as soon as possible, and I returned to the death chamber. They were all looking at Edward and listening to Bishop Templar's prayers, except Mr. Mason, whose dark ominous eyes were fastened on me, as I entered the room. We listened in solemn silence to the familiar words of Christian consolation, "Yea, though I walk through the valley of the shadow of death, I will fear no evil: for thou art with me; thy rod and thy staff they comfort me..."

Minutes later Simon arrived with drapery for the long mirror. He told me he had covered all the other mirrors in the house and had stopped the clocks. I told him to bring the ice and wash, shave, and dress Edward in his best clothes. We all left when he returned to prepare the corpse.

Downstairs in the drawing room, Adele was still distraught and being consoled by Mr. Greenwood. I excused myself and went downstairs to discuss arrangements with Mrs. Leah.

I had been waiting for Mrs. Rochester's instructions, so I was not surprised when I heard her tread heavily down the stairs while I was sitting in the kitchen, having a cup of tea with cook, Beth, Christy and Susan. The maids we had hired for the dinner had already left, Simon was preparing the corpse upstairs, and Michael had gone to fetch the undertakers. She walked in sorrowfully and spoke slowly, "Mr. Rochester has died." We stood up and expressed our condolences tearfully, and then she addressed me personally regarding the arrangements for the following days.

"I'm afraid it's going to be a long night. We will not be sleeping. We will need food and drink upstairs for tonight. Tomorrow we will have more guests coming to express their condolences, so please make sure there is someone in the drawing room and a footman at the door all day. There must be enough food and drink for everyone who wishes to pay their respects. Employ extra staff. If you found the young girls, who were here yesterday satisfactory, call them back for the week. I leave it to your judgment, Mrs. Leah."

"What can I do, Mrs. Rochester?" Volunteered Susan. "I could help in the afternoons, after school."

"Very well, Susan. You can help the footman receive the visitors at the door and take care of the cloaks, umbrellas, hats, and bonnets. Prepare the dining room for that purpose, as we will all be eating and receiving guests in the drawing room."

"Would you like me to prepare cake and sandwiches, madam?" suggested cook.

"Yes, please, and roast fowls, which can be served cold, potted meats, bread, and whatever else you think will be needed. Make sure there is plenty of food and drink for everyone at all times."

"What about spirits, Mrs. Rochester? Shall I prepare some decanters with Madeira?"

"Yes, and don't forget some water, and some lemonade."

"Shall I serve it on our best blue and white china dishes and cut glass wine glasses?"

"As you wish."

"We will need fruit bowls, tablecloths, napkins, and…"

"Leah, I leave the selection of cutlery, crockery, and the rest to you. Use the best we have, just make sure it is not too colourful." She broke in, clearing the tears from her cheeks.

"Mrs. Rochester, would you like some tea? You look very tired." Said cook with concern.

"Yes, I feel very tired." She acknowledged and sat down wearily, holding her head in her hands. I watched some tears drop from her cheeks onto the table and wondered why she was crying. I knew she had stopped loving him a long time ago. I handed her a kerchief and busied myself pouring her tea.

⌒◟✿◞⌒

"Is there anything to eat?" I asked, suddenly hungry, remembering I had not ate anything during the meal.

"There are some soul cakes I made with cook, madam. They are delicious!" I smiled at Beth, such an attractive and lively girl. I wondered if Michael had ever considered her as a girlfriend. Her long curly blonde hair was tied back in a bun and her large blue eyes smiled easily, brightening her cream complexion. She was much younger and prettier than I had ever been. Was I prepared to suffer once again the torment of love with its doubts, jealousy, and insecurities? Could I surrender once more to the whims of another person? Yet I must. Michael was the only person I could trust. He gave my daughter a name, and he has given me a purpose in life, but what future was there in our relationship?

I pushed away my conflicting thoughts and forced myself to eat and drink while the girls chattered and cook and Leah discussed the groceries and wrote lists of products to buy for the following hectic days ahead.

Simon came down and told me everything had been prepared in Mr. Rochester's room, "Madam, we should put flowers and more candles in the room, or it will start smelling soon."

"No doubt the undertaker will see to it tomorrow, meanwhile, take all the flowers in the house up to the room. I believe Adele has some scented candles, which she brought back from Paris, and she may also have some flower essences, ask her to give them to you and use them."

"We will need a black crepe ribbon for the door," added Leah.

"I can make the ribbon for tonight, Mrs. Rochester, with an old black dress someone discarded years ago." Beth volunteered helpfully.

I remembered it was the dress I had worn after my daughter died, "Yes, it is about time it was put to good use." I sighed.

"Who will watch Mr. Rochester tonight?" asked Simon.

"What do you mean, Simon?"

"While the undertaker brings the mutes to stand outside his door, someone must protect the deceased. I can do it tonight if you like, madam." I nodded.

"Mrs. Rochester, I can also stand by the front door in case we have visitors tonight," volunteered Susan. I nodded once more.

Nobody slept that night. Simon stood by the chamber door, and the rest of the residents in the house took turns to sit by his bed, pray, and console each other. Susan stood by the front door, in case anyone came to pay their respects. The others were busy in the kitchen. I found shelter in the library to think about what would happen after the funeral.

My turbulent mind could not settle down or think clearly. I knew I had to go to London, and I knew Michael had to come with me, but I had no idea where my daughter was. I knew where she had been taken nine years ago, but I did not know where she had been removed afterwards. Adele would be in Italy, and John would return to Oxford. Annette would be travelling to Belgium, and Mr. Mason would hopefully return to Jamaica, although I may have to give him some funds to help him on his way, but I was prepared to do anything to get rid of him. I would have to wear widows' weeds for a year and make sure the Estate was well attended.

I was lost in my thoughts when Susan showed the undertaker into the library, "Mrs. Rochester, Mr. Tempest from Tempest Undertakers to see you."

I looked up to see an elderly gentleman with unkempt frizzy white hair, bushy grey eyebrows, shifty black eyes, and a chalky complexion. He was wearing a black suit, cloak, scarf and gloves, and held a black hat in his hands. His excessively thin, pale blue lips remained perfectly straight, as he expressed his condolences in a stiff, monotone voice. He looked like the bringer of death itself.

"Thank you, Mr. Tempest. Please sit down and we can discuss arrangements."

I informed him of the duties Simon had already performed and he sneered displeasingly, "While no doubt your employee has acted with the best of intentions, an employee of mine will do the job properly tomorrow by injecting arsenical salt and alcohol, which will greatly reduce the odours…"

"No injections, Mr. Tempest. My husband's body will not be further disfigured. He has been cleaned and dressed to my pleasing. We will use ice, scents, and flowers to cover any unpleasant odour."

"As you wish."

"I would like the interment to take place as soon as possible."

"Shall we say in four days' time? Sunday the 5th of November? Sooner might be considered inappropriate, no doubt all of the tenants, neighbours, friends, and relatives will need time to pay their respects to such an esteemed gentleman."

He took out a notebook and pencil and started taking notes of my instructions. "Have you decided in which church?"

"The interment will take place in Hay church and be officiated by Bishop Templar who is, I mean was, a personal friend of Mr. Rochester's. Mr. Wood and Mr. Blake, the Vicar at Millcote, will assist in the ceremony."

"Very well. I suggest the funeral should be advertised in the local and national papers. All residents and tenants are welcome to visit Eyre Hall and pay their last respects to Mr. Rochester before the funeral. Is that correct?" I nodded.

"Will you require food or servants for the occasion?"

"My housekeeper and cook will make the necessary arrangements."

"Would you like any personal invitations sent?"

"Yes, to the Ingrams, the Leas and Eghams, to his London Traveller's Club in Pall Mall, and to my editors in London, Mr. Spencer at Barnes & Spencer in The Strand. That will be all."

"May I suggest some flowers for Mr. Rochester's chamber and the reception room?"

"Of course."

"And keepsakes? We have many types of lockets available, which we can fill with locks of Mr. Rochester's hair."

"No keepsakes, Mr Tempest. He is in our hearts."

"Any photographs? We have an excellent photographer who…"

"No photographs!" I surprised myself by raising my voice. "Thank you," I added more calmly.

"Mourning clothes?"

"I have asked Miss Adele, a close friend of the family, to make arrangements for the purchase of mourning clothes from her London milliners."

"Then the matter of the funeral itself. I suggest a hearse with four horses, four mourning coaches with forty-three plumes of ostrich feathers…"

"Mr. Tempest, the very best hearse and carriage."

"How many carriages will you require for the mourners?"

"No carriages. We shall walk to Hay church. As you may be aware, it is just outside the gates of Eyre Hall."

"But it is cold, and it may rain…"

"No carriages, Mr. Tempest."

"As you wish, madam. Do I understand the coffin itself should also be the best? That is strong elm shell, with mattress, lined with…"

"Mr. Tempest! I said the best of everything. It is displeasing for me to discuss these details."

"I was an apprentice in the firm when his father, God rest his soul, was buried. That was a grand ceremony. No Rochester has died since then, thirty-three years ago."

"Then do whatever you have to do to make it a grand ceremony, too."

"Madam, the mutes, the pages, the feathermen, the coachmen…"

"For God's sake!" I stood up exasperated, and Michael knocked on the open door, "Can I help you, Mrs. Rochester?"

"Mr. Tempest, could you excuse us for a few minutes please? Perhaps you would like a refreshment in the drawing room?" He walked out curved like a hook over his notebook, mumbling disapprovingly.

I put my arms around Michael and closed my eyes, as he stroked my hair, "That man was driving me quite mad."

"He is only doing his job."

"Hold me tight. I'm completely useless without you by my side. I could fall asleep right here, right now." I felt so safe with him, as if we were alone in the world. "Tell him to go away." I moaned.

"Have you finished making the funeral arrangements?"

"No, I haven't. Where were you, Michael? Why did you leave me with him? I needed you." I reproached him.

"Eating. I was famished. I hadn't eaten in hours. It's raining and muddy. It took hours to get to Millcote and back. It's four o'clock in the morning." He complained quietly.

"I'm sorry, Michael. You must be exhausted, too."

"Shall I help you with Mr. Tempest?"

"Thank you, Michael. Tell him to come back and we'll finish with this as quickly as possible. Can you deal with him?"

I watched carefully, as Michael discussed all the details and negotiated the price, looking at me, when he was unsure. I smiled or nodded when I agreed, and looked serious or shook my head slightly, when I wanted him to negotiate or dissent. He understood my gestures and less than thirty minutes later Mr. Tempest read a summary of our purchase.

"Perfect, Mr. Tempest," I smiled, as I extended my hand, "a pleasure to do business with you. Thank you so much for your kind help and useful suggestions."

"Mrs. Rochester, the pleasure is mine. We are most honoured at Tempest Undertakers to be able to include the Rochester family as our most distinguished clients."

Susan showed him out, and we were alone again. I held him close, breathing deeply to inhale the safety he radiated, "You know, Michael, you are very good at this."

"At embracing you?"

I could feel his smile, "Yes, you are good at that, too. But I meant at organizing and negotiating. You're clever, quick and intuitive, and you have a talent for dealing with people calmly and persuasively."

"I do?"

"You do. You did it with Dr. Carter and now with Mr. Tempest. I'm sure you get your own way with Mrs. Leah, Simon admires you, and I bet the girls eat out of your hand. Adele asks you to help her write her letters and poems. You are such a resourceful person."

"If you say so, but my only concern is to serve you, as best as I can."

"You are like a hidden treasure. You were right next to me for years, but I had never really seen you."

He held me tighter in silence. I had almost relaxed into slumber, when he spoke softly into my hair, "I knew you were the brightest jewel in the world the first day I saw you."

No one had ever shown me such tenderness as Michael. Edward had loved me, as honestly and completely as he could, but he was anything but gentle. Edward had been forceful and demanding, both physically and emotionally. He enjoyed lively discussions, where he always claimed the upper hand, and he was most commanding in the bedroom to his own needs and desires. He was generous and loving, but demanded absolute obedience and submission on my part. I complied at first, but when I was no longer totally submissive, our relationship disintegrated. My submission had kept us together. I had to make sure our relationship was not based on Michael's submission to me. I wanted a companion, not a dutiful servant.

"I should go upstairs and get an hour's sleep, and you should too, Michael." He nodded, and we walked into the hall, and then took our separate ways upstairs and downstairs

Chapter XXV

Blackmail

I watched her walk up the stairs strenuously, slowly pulling her meagre weight, and hoped she would be able to sleep. I knew tomorrow would be an even more arduous day. No one at Eyre Hall slept more than three hours that night. The extra kitchen hands and servants arrived before dawn. As the sun rose, the bells tolled nine times in the churches at Hay and Millcote, announcing Mr. Rochester's passing, followed by sixty-four peals ringing relentlessly in honour of his years among the living. An hour later, the first townspeople wishing to pay their last respects arrived at Eyre Hall. We were all busy until after lunch, when another batch of helpers arrived, and Mrs. Leah allowed us a few hours rest while they took over the chores. Susan, Beth, Christy, and cook retired for a nap. Simon said he had to go to Hay for an errand, and I went to the library to oversee the accounts, as Mrs. Rochester had asked me to do. Before dinner, Leah called me down to the kitchen, because Simon had returned in a deplorable condition.

I entered the drawing room to the unusual humming sound of the guests eating, drinking, and mumbling. In spite of the overcast evening, the room was aglow with the furious fire and the plentiful wax candles scattered around all the tables and shelves.

Mrs. Rochester was standing by the mantelpiece conversing with a solemn looking elderly couple dressed in black. The gentleman stooped crookedly over his short plump wife, who was holding a black kerchief to her red eyes. I recognized the Mayor of Millcote and his wife, because they had been dinner guests at Eyre Hall on several occasions. I approached my mistress and asked her if she needed the library.

She turned her worn and weary eyes towards mine, making an effort to smile, "Yes, thank you, Michael. I shall be using it shortly."

It pained me to bring her more bad news, but the situation was serious, and her intervention inevitable. I drew the heavy curtains, kindled the fire, and lit the oil lamps and candles. Moments later she followed me into the library, "What is the matter, Michael?"

"You are in danger, Mrs. Rochester. We both are."

"Why? What has happened?"

"Last night someone attacked Simon, and two of his fingers were amputated."

She jumped towards me and screamed, "Heavens! Why has no one informed me?"

"He has just returned from Hay. Mrs. Leah and Christy tried to alleviate his pain and cure the wound, but he needs a doctor."

"Dr. Carter must see him at once, but why are we in danger?"

"When old Mr. Raven died, some months ago, Simon was helping his son clear out his father's possessions, and he found a pretty jewel-encased box, which he took without permission. When he arrived back at Eyre Hall, he found a letter inside. He can't read, so he asked me to read it for him. I lied. I told him it was a letter from Mr. Rochester to you, he put it in your diary three days ago, and I replaced it with the letter you received from me."

"Why did you do that?"

"I did not want to upset you any further with Mr. Rochester's letter, so I took it away."

"I still don't understand, Michael. Why did they amputate Simon's fingers? How did they find out about the letter?"

"Some days ago, Simon went out to enjoy himself at the inn and offered the box to a young lady as a present. She showed it to Mr. Raven's daughter, Shirley, who recognized it as being her grandfather's and accused the young lady of theft. The girl admitted Simon had given it to her. The person who has amputated Simon's fingers will be looking for you. He thinks you have the letter and he wants it back."

"What is this letter, and why is it so important?"

"It was written thirty-three years ago in Spanish Town, Jamaica."

She walked to the heavy curtains covering the window, then held her hands to her temples, "Not again! Not Jamaica again! Damn the place. Why did he ever go there?"

I continued, because the situation was urgent, "It is from Mr. Rochester to a certain Mr. Fairfax, his uncle."

She turned away from the window, sat on the chair by the desk, and sighed, shaking her head, "After all these years, I can't believe it…Have you got this letter?"

I sat down on the chair in front of hers on the other side of the desk, "It is a dreadful letter, Mrs. Rochester. I would have liked to spare you the contents. I suppose Mr. Raven came by it and must have been blackmailing Mr. Rochester."

I took it out of my pocket and laid it on the table in front of her. Her fingers gently pulled the manuscript towards her and unfolded the letter. I watched the lines across her brow deepen and a dark shadow cross her face. When she finished reading, she dropped the letter o the table, and spoke quietly, "I was indeed married to a monster, but it is over. He is dead."

I knelt beside her and held her hand. I had to make her understand the urgency of the situation, "Mrs. Rochester, we are still in danger. Mr. Raven knows you have the letter, and he knows I have read it, too."

Awareness struck her at once, "Michael, thank goodness they didn't do anything to you!" She clutched my hands tightly. "What would I do without you?"

She had to understand that she was the person in danger, "Mr. Raven is determined to get the letter back, and he knows you have it. You are not safe."

She pulled her hands away from mine, stroked my cheeks with her fingers, and then told me she needed to think, and asked me to draw the curtains.

"Can I do anything else for you, Mrs. Rochester?"

"Dr. Carter is in the drawing room, make sure he sees to Simon's wounds at once, and then come back."

I sat down, reread the letter, and pondered on the situation at hand. I had to destroy it and put an end to the blackmail and the innkeeper's threats, once and for all. I jumped out of the chair restlessly and walked back to the damp casements. Winter snows were drifting through the grey evening air, silently resting on the gravel. Soon the Estate would be covered by its white mantle. It was a serene view. I could have watched the snow falling for hours, but the furious gusts of wind whipping the snowflakes mercilessly into whirlwinds reminded me that I had to act.

I recalled the other crucial moments I had experienced. The humiliations suffered at my Aunt Reed's house, the misery at Lowood, the death of Helen Burns, the hapless wreck I had been after learning that Edward was already married, how distraught I had felt wandering around the shattered walls and through the devastated interior of Thornfield Hall, after it had been burnt down, how I crumbled and disintegrated when I thought my daughter had died, and how I discovered Edward had selfishly and cruelly ripped her away from me. I wiped the tears away from my cheeks and wondered when my life had been pleasant. I could only remember a few brief months after my marriage, before John was born. His cheerful image brought a smile to my face. He was such a wonderful boy!

I turned back to my desk. Michael had returned and was sitting by the hearth, watching the flames with a furrowed brow. I could count on his loyalty, and my daughter, Helen, was alive somewhere. I could not abandon her again. I had to find her. I also had to make myself respected on the Estate and act firmly with Raven. Edward's misdeeds should be buried with him. I had to take control of my life, or I would be crushed once more by the cruel force of fate or the whims of evil doers.

I looked back towards the hearth, where Michael was now standing. Our eyes met and he walked to my side and asked softly, "Can I bring you something to eat or drink?"

"Not now, Michael."

"Have you decided what should be done?"

"Yes, Michael. Have the carriage prepared and tell Mr. Briggs I wish him to accompany us on an errand. We shall go to the inn and solve this problem, once and for all."

I had received a telegraphic message before sunrise informing me of my client, Mr. Rochester's death, and requiring my presence at Eyre Hall at once. I had collected all of Mr. Rochester's papers in my offices in St. Martin's Lane as required, and then taken the Scotch Express from King's Cross at ten o'clock. I had arrived at York at four o'clock, exhausted and famished, not having taken a morsel to my mouth, since the previous evening. Fortunately I had satisfied my hunger and quenched my thirst with the banquet splendidly laid out in the drawing room at Eyre Hall. I was sitting comfortably by the fireplace, smoking my pipe, and conversing with Mr. Cooper when the young valet, carrying my coat and hat, informed me that Mrs. Rochester was waiting for me in the carriage and wished me to accompany her on an urgent errand forthwith. I had no choice but to force a smile, bid good evening to Cooper, and follow the young man out into the bitter night.

The snow had set. It was an icy evening, as the three of us sat inside the swaying carriage. Mrs. Rochester's stern face was looking directly at me. Her eyes were covered by the dark shadow her bonnet cast, but her jaws were tight, and her lips pressed and thin. Whatever business we had to deal with was most definitely not pleasant. She was silent, however, I ventured to ask where we were going.

"To the Rochester Arms, in Hay." She answered drily.

"May I ask why?"

"Mr. Briggs, I am being blackmailed."

"By whom?"

"By Mr. Raven. He had a letter my late husband wrote many years ago to Mr. Fairfax from Spanish Town, Jamaica."

"Good God!" I gasped. It must have been the letter he wrote regarding his father's death! But how could Raven have got hold of it?

How did she have it in her possession? I looked at the valet uncomfortably.

"You must be aware that this is a very delicate and private matter, madam."

"I have complete confidence in Michael." She snapped. "He came across the letter and recovered it for me."

In spite of the cold, heat began to surge from my churning guts, up towards my brows. I took out a kerchief and wiped the sweat away before speaking, "I can explain everything…"

"I want no explanations, Mr. Briggs, I leave that matter to your own conscience, and in any case, the matter is not of my encumbrance. It occurred years before I met Mr. Rochester. I don't care about the gossip, but I will not allow the matter to be known to my son. Do you understand? He must never know who his father really was. I do not want him to feel responsible for his father's crimes."

"Yes, Mrs. Rochester."

"When we arrive, you will tell Mr. Raven that he will receive us immediately in private rooms to discuss his tenancy, and this matter will be sorted out, once and for all."

I nodded and wiped the sweat away again. The ghosts of the past were back. Old Mr. Rochester was claiming his vengeance. His son had died, and the gates of Hell had opened to receive him and his accomplices, "The dead should not be troubled, or the consequences could be devastating, if…"

"Mr. Briggs, I do not believe in ghosts, and in any case, I have harmed no one. I have nothing to fear, neither has my son, is that clear?"

I nodded, but I knew demons had been set loose on the Rochester Estate, and the consequences were unpredictable.

Inside the inn, Michael and I waited patiently by a table while Briggs arranged our meeting with the host. I remembered the last time I had entered the inn, after discovering the burnt ruins of Thornfield Hall, twenty-two years ago. It had not changed much, the large figured papering on the walls, the flowered patterns and colour of the carpet looked familiar. It was vulgarly decorated with dark wooden furniture and large tinseled ornaments on the tables. The portrait of George the Third and another of the Prince of Wales were still there, but a larger painting of Queen Victoria and Prince Albert had pride of place over the mantelpiece. All this was made visible by the light of the same oil lamp hanging from the ceiling and the same blazing hearth.

Minutes later we were ushered into a small, cosy room at the back of the inn, "How kind of you to see us at such short notice, Mr. Raven."

"The pleasure is mine, madam. Please, sit down. Perhaps your valet will wait outside."

"He certainly will not!"

"As you please."

I sat down next to Mr. Briggs and Michael stood behind my armchair, facing Mr. Raven.

"Now that Mr. Rochester is deceased, I will be taking over the management of the Estate until my son is thirty years old. I will be responsible for your tenancy agreements, is that not so Mr. Briggs?" The lawyer nodded nervously.

"Mrs. Rochester, I trust our agreement will continue as usual."

"Better than usual, Mr. Raven, I am in a position to offer you a ninety-nine year renewable leasehold on this property for you and your descendents."

"That is very generous, Mrs. Rochester."

"The rent will be ten percent lower than the current rate, and it will not be raised in twenty years. Can you write that down Mr. Briggs?"

"Indeed I shall, if Mr. Raven is kind enough to bring a pen and some paper."

The host went out of the room and returned shortly with the required utensils. I spoke firmly, "Please start writing, Mr. Briggs. I want this contract signed today."

He put on his spectacles and carried out my orders obediently.

"Mr. Raven, I would like to discuss a letter, which belonged to the late Mr. Fairfax, my husband's uncle, and was in your father's possession for reasons unknown to me. As I believe you know, this letter is now in my possession. My employee, whom you ruthlessly attacked, has informed me that you are looking for the letter."

I took out the epistle and showed it to him, "Is this the document you were looking for?"

He nodded, and I continued, "As you are aware, although the letter was in your father's possession, it did not belong to him, nor does it belong to you. It was a private and personal letter addressed from my husband to his uncle. I would not like anyone else to read it or disseminate its contents, so I wish to burn it this very moment in your fireplace."

He hesitated and held my look defiantly. I felt Michael's hands pressing the back of my chair, "Do you have any objections, Mr. Raven?"

He spoke at last, "None, madam."

I turned to Michael, giving him the letter, "Michael, would you hand this letter to Mr. Raven and accompany him to the fireplace while he burns it, please?"

"Gladly, madam."

I watched as both men approached the small fireplace and sighed in relief, as the flames destroyed the wicked words and sinful deeds described on the worn parchment.

"I would like to discuss another important matter, Mr. Raven. I understand you have severely attacked one of my employees. Your behaviour has been intolerable."

"I apologize, madam. It was an … accident, an unfortunate accident."

"Please bring a Bible."

He obeyed, taking a ragged copy from the bookshelf and placing it on the table.

"You will swear that you will not spread any gossip related to the Rochester family, nor will you allow it in your inn. You will not attack any of my employees again. You will pay for Simon's medical costs, and he will be your guest at the inn, whenever he chooses to come."

He put his hand on the book, "I swear, madam."

"And in case the Bible is not sufficient deterrent, allow me to further inform you that should there be a breach of contract, my reaction will be devastating. Do you understand?"

"Madam, I would not dream of not keeping my promises to you."

"Mr. Briggs, have you written the leasehold contract for Mr. Raven according to the terms we have just discussed?"

"Yes, madam. Here it is."

"I shall sign it now and it will take effect next month. Mr. Briggs will bring you a copy tomorrow."

He thanked me, as we got up to leave, "Good day, Mr. Raven. It has been a pleasure doing business with you."

"Good day, Mrs. Rochester."

<hr>

I helped my mistress into the carriage and jumped in beside her. As we rode back, she slipped her hand through my arm, and her fingers restlessly squeezed my sleeve, "Are you well, Mrs. Rochester?"

"My legs are trembling. I can't believe I just did what I did." She whispered, "I'm so cold." She pulled me towards her, pushed her hand through my arm and into her muff.

"How do you think that went, Michael?"

"I think it went very well, Mrs. Rochester. You were most persuasive."

"I feel drained. It is so exhausting to play the villain."

"You are indeed a convincing villain, Mrs. Rochester." She smiled at me, then turned to the lawyer sitting in front of us, "Mr. Briggs, you should know I will not tolerate any gossip in my employees. Everything that you have read, seen, and heard this evening will remain undisclosed."

"My lips are sealed, Mrs. Rochester." He answered stiffly, looking at me disapprovingly, but she did not ignore the gesture. She shouted his name angrily, and he turned his eyes away from us towards the window. She moved even closer to me, and so we had another witness to our complicity.

When we arrived back at Eyre Hall, Briggs returned to the drawing room. Mrs. Rochester took off her bonnet and coat and asked me to bring some warm milk and brandy to her room. I went down to the kitchen. Simon's hand had been bandaged by Dr. Carter. I told him that Mrs. Rochester herself had made Mr. Raven apologize and compensate him for his attack. It gave him some comfort, but he was in bed, looking poorly, although the doctor said he would be fit for work tomorrow.

When I arrived at her door, it was open. I pushed it and saw her standing by her wash stand in her nightdress, washing her face. She turned when she heard me come in.

"Please bolt the door and put the milk on the bedside table."

I obeyed. She dried her face and walked towards me.

"Michael," she whispered, taking my hands and pulling me towards her, "I am no longer a married woman." Her look was alluring and her perfume overwhelming.

"May I?" I implored, spellbound.

"You may." She whispered, "No man has ever been inside this chamber," she continued appealingly, "so please tread softly."

I freed her hair and peeled off her layers gently and leisurely, cherishing each one of her sighs and smothering her moans fondly with kisses until my lips travelled down towards her treasure. I nuzzled my nose in her soft curls and heard her gasp rhythmically. Her scent was in my mind, as my lips felt her softness swell and stiffen while she dug her fingers through my hair. At last she moistened and relaxed, and I knew it was time to fill her with my love. She was pliant and supple, as I became her pulsating master for a few brief moments before dying in her mellow kernel. We finally lay limp and soothed, heart next to heart, our fluids mingling, and our limbs entwined. We had been one. She was mine to worship, and I was hers to be commanded. She smiled languorously and drifted into sleep almost immediately, so I was able to gaze at every curve of her anatomy and admire every pore on her skin at my leisure, before reluctantly pulling up the bedclothes and returning to my lodgings downstairs.

My sister was waiting for me in the kitchen and sowed the seeds of doubt in my mind. I did not mind feeling like my mistress's puppet. I was happy to serve her, but I was worried, because our relationship had gone too far, and there was no place for us to go. If we were discovered, it would be embarrassing for her and disgraceful for me. There were already too many people who guessed we were lovers: Susan, Mrs. Leah, Dr. Carter, Mr. Briggs, and Adele. Too many people knew how we felt and more would know soon. I would lose my job, but what tormented me most was the possibility of not seeing her again.

I would have been happy to gaze at her, caress her hand, smooth her hair, and embrace her. I should not have taken our relationship any further. I had crossed a boundary into no man's land and there was no going back. I was terrified of the thought that there was no future for us. Had I condemned my love? Was I feeling guilty because my sister had guessed what happened, or because her husband was still lying in his bed, in his chamber, just a few feet away from us while we made love? Had we made love or had she satiated her desire? Did she love me, or was I just a pastime? I slept restlessly, drifting in and out of nightmares until the light of dawn shook me back to reality.

Chapter XXVI

The Sin-Eater

Michael came down to the kitchen in the early hours of the morning. When I asked him where he had been, he said he couldn't tell me, but he embraced me and cried on my shoulder, as he used to do when he was a boy. I guessed where he had been, as soon as I saw his guilt-ridden face, and I knew it was true, when I smelt her perfume on my brother's skin.

"She will torment you, Michael. You are an amusement for her."

"She's not like that, Susan."

"You don't know what she's like. You look at her as if she were a goddess and she's not. She is the mistress of the house. She will never marry you. Is that what you want, to be used by her until she is bored or tired of you? It is not godly. You are acting in an unholy manner. Mother…"

"Please don't mention our mother. I can't bear to think she would not approve."

"She would not, I am sure. You must either stop being her lapdog, or leave this household."

"You are wrong, Susan. She loves me and I love her."

"I wish I could make you see the truth. What are you going to do from now on? Steal in and out of her room every night she wants you to warm her bed?"

"Susan, it's not like that. You make it sound vulgar."

"Isn't it? Tell me, how is it? She calls you and you follow. She bosses you around and controls your heart and soul. If you want a woman, Christy is your age and she's mad about you. Beth is a few years younger and she thinks she loves you. She's boasting that you kissed her on All Hallows Eve. What are you playing at?"

"I tried to comfort her. Adele had slapped her and I kissed her cheek, but I don't feel anything for Beth, except… I felt sorry for her."

"And Jenny?" He shook his head, as I screamed her name. "Don't you dare deny it! I know what you were up to while you were teaching her to read."

"You don't understand." He stuttered helplessly.

"What's the matter with you men? Why do your brains soften every time you see a pretty woman?"

"Mrs. Rochester is different. She is not like any other woman…"

"I think she is! And you're just like any other man, taken over by your animal impulses!"

"You're wrong, Susan. We love each other."

"When I come back from Italy, she will have cast you out in the gutter. She's domineering, headstrong, and selfish."

"You can't mean that. She looked after us, after you, too. She didn't want you to spoil your hands cleaning. She has given you a good job. Don't you remember when we were in the workhouse, what would have happened, if we had stayed there?"

"She should have remembered her place and yours. She will be your ruin. It's not right, Michael. It can't happen."

"I hope you are wrong, sister, because I don't think I could live without her."

He sunk into a chair, holding his head in his hands miserably. I put my arms around him, "Whatever happens, you can be sure I will never abandon you, Michael."

We embraced and I felt his spasms, as he cried. I knew he would not be able to sleep. Neither could I. I heard him wrestling uneasily in his bed all night, as I tried to find comfort in the Bible. "Blessed are those who hunger and thirst for righteousness, for they will be filled. Blessed are the merciful, for they will be shown mercy. Blessed are the pure in heart, for they will see God…for theirs is the Kingdom of Heaven." I knew their relationship would never be blessed. He would never marry her. A governess could marry her master, as she once had, but a valet would never be allowed to marry his mistress. In any case, I knew I would always look after him, whatever happened. Together we would start a new life, if needs be. This last thought consoled me, as I finally drifted into sleep.

The next morning we all had breakfast together in silence. Michael was quiet and glum. Beth sat next to him and tried unsuccessfully to cheer him up. Simon was a little recovered, but Mrs. Leah said he should stay in bed and rest this morning. Christy cleaned, bandaged his wound, and gave him his medicine most kindly while he complained, but he put on his uniform and refused to stay in bed. Cook was busy arguing with the butcher at the back door while Mrs. Leah gave the newly employed servants instructions for the morning's work. The school was closed in mourning. So after breakfast, I went up to stand by the door inside the hall while the footman accompanied the mutes outside on the doorsteps.

It was early yet, so few people had arrived and were solemnly chatting in the entrance while I took their coats, bonnets, hats, and umbrellas into the dining room. As I returned into the hall, the heavy front door screeched eerily and a gush of chilled fog came flowing into the hallway. A pounding thump resounded and suddenly out of the dense cloud emerged a faint, dark shadow, which gradually solidified into a human shape, while a breath of frosty wind poured in and enwrapped those of us who were standing in the hallway.

"Mr. Rochester has sent for me."

His grating voice echoed the words ominously. I heard some frightful cries around me. Some people ran away into the adjacent rooms, swearing they had heard him say the words three times. Others said he was death, who had come to visit the just dead, and if anyone looked at his eyes they would be taken, too. Everyone disappeared. I stood alone with him. His glazed eyes stared at the only person who had remained. Nailed to the ground, my back had stiffened, like a stick. I felt my jaw drop, as he added in a low frosty voice, "I have a message for Mrs. Rochester."

Someone shouted from inside a room, "No! He has come to take her with him."

I plucked up the courage to approach him and speak, "I'm afraid Mrs. Rochester cannot see you, sir, but I will take your name, if you please, to inform her of your visit."

His frozen features set on my face, and I noticed his eyes were red, all red, and his lips mauve. The rest of his face was a cemented gravestone carved with long creases down his flat cheeks, which looked as sharp as flint. His towering black figure was like an unearthly leviathan. My legs were shaking, and I would have run away had I not decided I had to protect Mrs. Rochester from the omen of death.

Disquieting words rang out of his lips, "I am the Sin-eater. I have come to bestow the wisdom of my ancestors upon the cadaver that is laid in this house, so that he may not become an undead."

I was speechless, motionless, and breathless, as he continued with his foreboding address, "Time is short. His evil deeds have chained him to this world to roam and torment the living until the Last Judgment. I must see him today, or he will never rest, and his soul will wander in anguish around this house and his loved ones."

Who was this unearthly monster? What did he want? What could I alone do to fend him off? His threats persisted, "I must see Mr. Rochester immediately, or leave his soul to roam in this house until the Day of Judgment."

I forced myself to breathe in and managed to raise my right hand up to my neck and clutch the tiny cross hanging from a gold chain, the only possession I owned, and mustered all my strength to reply feebly, "Please leave, sir."

Miraculously, he walked backwards towards the door, gradually devoured by the persistent fog that had accompanied him like an entourage.

"Stop, sir!" I turned to see Simon's distraught face run up from behind me. I had not seen him during the episode. Someone must have run downstairs and informed him of what was happening.

"Please, wait. I will inform Mrs. Rochester of your presence. Your name, please, sir?"

"Mr. Isac das Junot, from the Netherlands."

The figure became larger again, as it walked forward, appearing even taller than before. I noticed he wore no hat and his slimy jet black hair was pressed down with a wide middle parting and tied back into a short greasy pigtail.

"Please wait here in the entrance." The intruder nodded, as Simon continued, "You will be eating and drinking later, I expect." The unearthly visitor smiled, showing a fistful of teeth, which were as black as his hair.

He looked down at Simon's bandaged hand and spoke again, "You have lost two fingers, but found two loyal friends for life. The loss will be compensated."

I turned away from the monster and asked Simon if he had lost his brains. How could the mistress see such a frightful being? He answered that he knew what he was doing, because it was a necessary procedure. His father had told him about sin-eaters. They ate the sins of the dead, so they could enter the Kingdom of Heaven guiltless. I told him he was mad and that it was an unchristian thing to do. I was sure the Bishop would not approve, and neither would Michael or Mrs. Leah. He ignored me and went upstairs to inform Mrs. Rochester.

I was alone with the apparition once more. I had recoiled to the wall by the stairs to the kitchen, in case I needed to flee swiftly. He did not move, but seized my eyes with his stare. I could not look away! He was peering into my heart. I felt an icy shiver enter my soul and gasped for air. He moved close to me and whispered in my ear, "Fear me not. I have not come to take you, yet. Fear not your future. You will travel to a warm distant land, where you will find sweet love and bitter sorrow." Then he moved away back to the entrance. I could see the heads of the other visitors peeping out of the drawing room with terrified expressions.

Too many minutes later, Simon walked down with Michael. I rushed to my brother, embracing him with all my strength. He kissed my forehead and told me not to worry, because everything would be all right. I relaxed, because I believed him. Michael always knew what to do and had protected me from all evil. He had once even killed a man to protect me from his lecherous claws.

"Mrs. Rochester will see you upstairs, if you will accompany us please, Mr. Junot." Michael spoke politely, but just a little too firmly. I noticed he did not like the idea of taking him upstairs any more than I did, but I knew my mistress would be safe with Michael.

Then he turned to me and spoke, "Susan, could you bring up some food and drink from the kitchen? The best meat and drink cook can give you, on wooden plates." I nodded without asking. I imagined it was for him.

I was quivering at the foot of my husband's bed. Edward was flanked by John and Adele embraced and kneeling on one side and Annette and Mason on the other side. Bishop Templar was sneering disapprovingly, facing the door.

As soon as the Sin-eater crossed the threshold, the Bishop spoke, "I must reaffirm that in my name and in the name of the Church of England, I am absolutely against this person's intervention in this house. He is a liar..."

"Bishop, please. I understand your position, but I must remind you this gentleman is a guest in our house. I have opened the doors to everyone, who wished to pay their last respects to Mr. Rochester."

The man smiled and spoke, "Thank you, madam. My ancestors can be traced back to Judas Iscariot, who was condemned to eternal resurrection after his first suicide. After his first resurrection, he used his thirty gold coins to travel to the north of Europe and set up a new religion of adorers of Satan. We cannot die, but we are not the undead. We fear not God and seek not Heaven, because we have been condemned never to enter therein. We must absorb the sins of the sinners, because the more sins we have, the stronger we become. I am the strongest member of our order. I came as soon as the looming herald clouds brought me the news of his death. His sins must be mine."

"Can you not see it, Mrs. Rochester? He is a charlatan and a devil worshipper..."

"He will stay and do whatever it is he came to do. It will harm no one except himself, and it may do some good."

The Bishop stormed towards the door, shouting, "This is outrageous!"

The ghostly figure leant towards him, as he reached the door, "Good day, Bishop. We will meet again, when you are Archbishop."

Bishop Templar looked at him shocked and inquisitively before marching out of the room most displeased. I would deal with him later, but now I had to go through this ceremony. I could not risk a ghost in Eyre Hall, haunting its residents. Edward had sinned, and sinned greatly, and if this man were to devour his sins and let him rest, I was prepared to accept his intervention. The rest of those who were present consented with their silence, although not with their looks of disgust, as the intruder approached the bed.

"May I please ask you to move away from the deceased? I need to speak to him directly."

We all obeyed, taking a step backwards. I broke the silence, "Mr. Junot, I would like my husband to know that I humbly and dutifully forgive him for *everything*, and likewise, I ask his forgiveness, if I ever failed him in any way."

He nodded, "You may stay if you wish, all of you, but I would ask you to turn away and close your eyes, lest his spirit should decide to resist and enter one of you by seeping through your eyes into your hearts and souls."

Adele gasped and embraced John, both turned to face the heavy drawn curtains, which trembled against the open window. Mason put his arm around his niece and turned her away towards the open door leading onto the sombre gallery. I turned away with Michael and Simon on either side. Michael bent down and asked me if I was sure I wanted to continue. I nodded. I looked for his hand and squeezed it tightly, he moved closer. I wanted to lean on him, to close my eyes and bury my head in his sturdy chest, but I knew I could not succumb. I could feel Mason's devious sideways glance at Michael. I wanted to tell Mason to close his eyes, in case death entered his soul, but I dared not move, as I closed my own as tightly as I could manage.

Mr. Junot started speaking his incantation, which sounded like a strange form of Latin, but I did not understand any of the words. Perhaps he was a fraudster and was just pretending to speak Latin, or perhaps it was another ancient tongue I had never before heard. Finally he spoke in English, "I absorb thine sins thee great sinner. Thou shalt not enter through the gates of Heaven, but thou shalt not wander with the undead on this earth. Thou shall first purge the trail of thy sins in purgatory before thou canst enter the Kingdom of God."

He then instructed us to turn around, which we did apprehensively. Edward's eyes and his mouth were open. I screamed in horror. Michael and Simon held my arms, as my legs weakened.

"He tried to retain his sins and escape my purge. He wanted to be an undead and torment the living, but I was stronger than him. He has now left this body, this room, and this world, forever."

"Simon, please can you close his eyes again!" I screamed.

"At once, madam, I must get some paste." He rushed out of the room.

"Do not fear his eyes. He can no longer invade another living body."

We were all dumbstruck, as he continued with his frosty words, "His sins were so great, he cannot be absolved, but he will not stay here. He will not be a walking dead."

I stumbled again, grabbing Michael's arm and summoning all my strength to remain upright. The devil's apostle added disturbingly, "The next Master of Eyre Hall is in this room. His surname is not Rochester, but has number eleven times three, that is thirty-three. The number of years Christ walked upon our earth, but he is not innocent as Christ. He has already killed twice, and his killings are not over yet."

I managed to speak firmly, "Thank you for your help, Mr. Junot. Do you require any payment for your services?"

"None, madam. I have received more than enough already from Mr. Rochester. He is most thankful for your forgiveness and says he has nothing to forgive you."

"Can my coachman take you anywhere?"

He smiled sardonically. "No, thank you. I will return in fourteen month's time, to relieve the next soul to depart this house."

I gasped and he smirked, "There is no need to worry, it will not be you, Mrs. Rochester. You will have a long and eventful life." He moved towards me, but Michael stood in his path.

Abruptly he turned to John, "You will not marry the woman you love. You will not live where you were born. You will not live as you would choose."

"Mr. Junot, please leave, your services are no longer required."

He ignored my words and turned to Adele, who was still perched on John's arm, "You will marry the man you love, but the man you marry will not love you."

I insisted, "Please, Mr. Junot. You must leave now."

He turned to Annette, who was the only person who seemed not to be terrified of him and smiled at her, "We meet again, Antoinette." She gasped, and so did Mason.

She replied hoarsely, "I have never seen you in my life."

He ignored her words, "Perhaps you will be happier this time. You will have everything money can buy."

I had to stop him. He knew too much, "Mr. Junot, will you be taken out by force?"

He turned to look at me over Michael's shoulder, "Good day, madam. I have told each one of your guests their destiny, but I have other important news for you."

I recoiled behind Michael, who made sure he stood between us until he reached the door and accompanied him along the gallery to the staircase. I watched them go down, so I relaxed and turned back into the room. John, Adele, and Annette were crying in a circular embrace while Mason looked on dumbfounded and distraught.

Blood froze in my veins. The Sin-eater was back in the room, standing next to me. He could not be here! I had seen him walk down the stairs! Where was Michael? Junot pulled my arm and whispered in my ear. When I turned in bewilderment at the four words he said, he had vanished. I shouted, "Michael!" and a black curtain covered my eyes and smothered my mouth.

Chapter XXVII

Mourning Weeds

When I woke up, Adele was looking at me anxiously, but where was I? I looked around. I was in my room fully clothed on my bed. The fire glowed and the candles on the mantelpiece were inciting the playful shadows dancing around the room.

"Jane, Mon Dieu! What a spectacle! However did you let that madman with his ravings into the house? The chanting, the conjuring, and fortune telling... Bishop Templar is most upset. I had to persuade him not to leave Eyre Hall. That Mr. Junot said terrible things to us. We are all troubled. It was a bad idea, Jane, a very bad idea. If I were you, I would dismiss Simon for convincing you to let him in. How could you let yourself be persuaded by that half wit of a valet?"

I remembered what Junot had said to me, those four words. Could it be true? Yes, it could be true. What could I do? I was feverish, almost delirious with expectation. I felt a mixture of fear and hope. I had to tell Michael what Junot had told me, but what had Junot told *him*? He said we had each been told our destiny. I was too excited to think.

"Where is Michael?"

"Michael! Michael! Michael! I think it is better that you don't see Michael for the time being. There is enough talk going on. You should have seen Michael, when he rushed into the room and saw that you were in Mr. Mason's arms! He told him to get his hands off you. Can you imagine that! A valet threatening Mr. Mason! They were glaring at each other. Mason could easily have caused a scene, or Michael could have killed him. There was murder in his eyes. Michael wouldn't let anyone near you until I told him to bring you to the bedroom, then he sat there holding your hand and looking at you as if... as if you were his beloved. Mon Dieu! He said he couldn't leave you. Can you imagine that, too! Thank God I calmed him down and convinced him that I would look after you. You will ruin his life and Susan's, if you don't leave him alone. He is not for you, Jane."

"Adele, I must see Michael, I must! You don't understand. I must see him." I sobbed uncontrollably. What was happening to me? What kind of desire had he sparked in me that I had not felt in years? He was the centre of my universe, my present, and my future.

"Jane, you will pull yourself together. You remind me of the time you were ill with the laudanum. Don't look so surprised. Of course I knew what had happened to you. How Dr. Carter and Monsieur got you used to it and you couldn't stop, and you weren't yourself at all, Jane, like now. Thank God Mary and Diana nursed you back to health, away from both of them. Then it was laudanum and now it is Michael, the same obsession. He will be your ruin, or you will be his. You must forget him! You could have any available Lord, Count, or Bishop you choose. Don't you dare throw it all away on a valet, however attractive or clever he may be."

"Adele, I feel quite possessed. I don't know what has happened to me. It's too late, now. I'm trapped, deliciously trapped." I sobbed into my pillow.

"You are delirious!"

"You don't understand, Adele..."

"We will find him a good position in another household. Perhaps Bishop Templar can help us, or Judge Harwood in London."

I cried even louder into my pillow and babbled, "I can't live a single day without him. I can't. I can't."

"Sleep now, Jane." I thought my mind would never rest that night, but I must have cried myself to sleep, because I woke up gasping for air in a cold dark room, and I had dreamt I had a baby girl in my arms. I had to leave Eyre Hall as soon as possible after the funeral. I needed to find Helen. God could not keep her away from me now. I had forgiven Edward and would be allowed to start a new life, without any bitterness or remorse.

When I woke up the next day, Adele told me the mourning weeds had arrived. I howled at the ugliness and heavy burden of the clothes I had to wear for the following six months: a weighty black crepe dress with a stiff white collar and white muslin cuffs. The cloak was black and the bonnet had a long black veil to cover my face. The underwear was also black and stiff. Adele said she would wear the same clothes to accompany me. She had ordered black suits for the servants and for Annette, too. I agreed to wear the clothes for this week, but I warned her I would not be wearing them for longer.

"You must order black silk dresses, capes and bonnets, but pretty ones. I won't have you and Annette looking like old wives, and I won't do so myself, either."

"But what will they say? Everyone will think we did not love Monsieur enough!"

"Nonsense! What has love got to do with stiff crepe! Adele, you must travel to Italy as soon as possible, as arranged with Mr. Greenwood. Your mother is not young, she is Edward's age, or older, she may not live another two years. You will be leaving next week, as planned. You will take black and grey dresses, mantles and bonnets. It will not make a great difference in winter. When summer comes, we will buy new frocks. Annette must go to finishing school in Belgium. She will also wear black and grey silk gowns."

"But, Jane, I cannot leave you here alone!"

"I will not be alone."

"You will be alone! John will be at Oxford, so you will only see him in the holidays."

"Do not worry about me. I am not staying at Eyre Hall. I have plans."

"Mon Dieu! You are not leaving with Michael! I will not allow it!"

"I will be all right. I will tell you my plans shortly. In the meantime, you must tell Mr. Greenwood to secure your passages, and Susan's, as soon as possible."

"I think I know what you are up to…"

"You do?"

"Mr. Greenwood told me you were most interested in his house in London and said he was going to offer it to you while he was away with me in Italy."

"Oh, that is good news, Adele! How charming of him!"

"Yes, he is very thoughtful. I am so very glad he came to Eyre Hall!"

"So am I, Adele. You have made a good choice, for once."

"You think so?"

"Of course." I replied, but I was thinking about Junot's prophecy, he had said she would marry someone who did not love her. Perhaps Mr. Greenwood was still in love with his deceased wife and would never be able to love anyone with that intensity again. He did speak of her frequently with watery eyes. However, I was sure he would be a good, caring, and honourable husband for Adele.

"Come on, Adele, help me get dressed. We will be leaving for the funeral after lunch. Let us eat in my chamber, Adele. I don't want to have to talk to all the visitors downstairs. Tell them I am unwell."

"Very well. I will go down and excuse you from the others and order lunch." She kissed me and walked to the door, telling me she was happy I was feeling better.

I lay in my bed planning and plotting my next moves. Tying all the loose ends was giving me quite a headache. There were so many people who depended on me, and there were so many decisions to make in such a short time. I thought about Junot's predictions. I needed to write them down, so I sat over at my writing desk and took out my diary, which I had brought up from the drawing room, and started making notes.

Adele: She will travel to a distant land and marry the man she loves, but he will not love her.

Well, that is obviously Mr. Greenwood, who is unable to love her completely, because unfortunately all his love has been spent on his first wife.

Annette: She will have everything money can buy.

She's beautiful enough to marry the richest man in London. Once she has been groomed, I'm sure she will be clever enough to know what is best for her. That pleases me. Her poor mother was such an unhappy lunatic.

John: he will not marry the person he loves, and he will not live as he would choose.

He may move away from Eyre Hall, probably to London. Dear John destined to fulfil an arranged marriage and recover the Rochester name and honour.

Me: I would live a long eventful life, and the last prophecy, the one which makes my hand tremble with anticipation... I cannot even bring myself to write the words...

There were two more: someone will die this time next year and another will be the new Master of Eyre Hall. One must be for Mason and one for Michael. He said something about numbers: eleven times three and thirty-three. I was too excited to think clearly.

A knock on the door startled me out of my reverie. I heard Michael's voice, "Mrs. Rochester. I came to see how you were."

I rushed towards the door, "I'm very well, Michael, much better."

"May I come in?"

"Of course. But be careful, Adele will be back in a few minutes and will want you to leave. She is very upset with you. She says you caused a scene."

"Do you remember what happened before you fainted yesterday?"

"Vaguely." I only remembered the four words Junot had whispered.

"Junot was walking down the stairs with me and suddenly he was no longer there. He vanished, and I heard you shout my name. I ran back to the room, and he was in the gallery, and when I reached him, he vanished again. He wasn't there. Was he human or a malevolent spirit? What did he say to you before you called me? Mr. Mason said he appeared in the room and whispered something in your ear before you shouted my name. Tell me what he said."

"I can't tell you now, Michael."

"You can't tell me now?" He repeated my words, and I shook my head.

"Why not? What did he say?" He insisted, and I was silent. He looked enraged. I had never seen him look at me gravely. Was it anger?

Michael angry with me? Impossible. I walked over and put my hand to his face, he took it, kissed my palms, and then my wrists.

"I missed you, Michael." I told him, "But Adele said there was gossip, and she wouldn't let you come. I was too tired to argue with her. She told me you caused a scene and threatened Mason."

"I'm sorry, Mrs. Rochester, I couldn't help myself. You screamed my name, and when I saw you on the floor unconscious, and Mason was bending down touching you, I couldn't let him touch you."

"Well done, Michael." I put my arms around him, "Hold me, please, hold me tight." He did and I slid into an unreal timeless world, where only the two of us existed. I buried my face in his chest and knew that everything would be all right.

He spoke quietly into my hair, "I haven't slept or eaten. I was sick with worry."

"I'm all right. Don't worry about me. Adele has been looking after me."

"What did Junot tell you?"

"I will tell you what he told me tomorrow, after the funeral."

"Why tomorrow?"

"Trust me." I kissed his cheek softly, and I felt a tremor in my stomach. I winced uneasily.

He noticed. "What's wrong? I know something is worrying you. Something he told you. I cannot leave until you tell me. Please, tell me. How can I help you?"

I promised to tell him after the funeral, and finally managed to convince him to leave. I spent the rest of the afternoon at my desk puzzling with numbers, trying to work out Junot's prediction, until we dressed for the walk to the church, where I had married Edward, twice, where John had been christened, and where Bertha and Edward's ancestors were buried. A little girl was buried there, too, an unknown corpse, not my daughter. Helen was alive, waiting for me to find her. A weight had been lifted from my shoulders, and a radiant beam was guiding my path towards a new beginning with Helen and Michael.

Chapter XXVIII

The Funeral

The gruff old church bells in the single belfry have been tolling ceaselessly all morning in the ancient tower, heralding my funeral. The coffin, where my acquiescent corpse lay, was carried down the stairs and through the front door to my hearse by eight sombre pallbearers. The same men who would later carry my coffin to its final repose and deposit it in the church vault with the rest of my kin. There is only one horse drawn feathered carriage, which bears my magnificent hearse. Behind me the black train of friends, neighbours, relatives, tenants, and servants are solemnly walking the quarter of a mile from Eyre Hall to Mr. Wood's modest temple.

The Hay district church stood just beyond the gates of Eyre Hall. It is a small village place of worship, which had been erected in my grandfather's time, almost a hundred years ago, on the site of an older derelict building. It is the church where my grandparents are buried, where my parents married and were buried, and where my brother was buried, too, in the family vault at the front of the altar. It was the same altar where I had married Jane, almost twice, and christened my only son. My unfortunate first wife was buried anonymously in the graveyard, and Jane's daughter's tomb lay empty in the vault.

It is the church where kind-hearted Jane started a Sunday school for the children of the farmers, tenants, and young people who were employed during the week. The church where Jane would attend mass almost every Sunday, often alone, because I had other matters to attend, or because I was away with other occupations. I was not a faithful husband. It was not in my restless nature. I wish I had stayed with her at Eyre Hall more often. I wish I had stayed with our children, the children we could have had, should have had, but I realized too late that I should not have neglected my family. I was too selfish, too greedy, and too profane.

I have arrived. Mr. Wood is wearing a purple surplice and standing at the church door with a prayer book in his hand, he speaks as my hearse approaches, "We receive the body of our brother, Edward Rochester, with confidence in God, the giver of life, who raised the Lord Jesus from the dead." Seconds later Mr. Blake, the Vicar at Millcote, sprinkles some water and speaks, too, "With this water Edward was called to baptism. As Christ went through the deep waters of death for us, so may he bring us to the fullness of resurrection life with Edward and all the redeemed."

Inside the temple I can hear some people crying, most have bowed heads and solemn expressions. My wife is covered in mourning weeds. No part of her countenance is visible, but I can see her shoulders trembling. Adele is standing beside her, weeping loudly, she was always far too expressive and excitable. My son is struggling to keep a straight upper lip, but I can see the tears streaming down his face, too.

The coffin is open, facing the altar. Bishop Templar is reading the introductory psalms and leading the service. The organ Jane persuaded me to generously donate is playing the funeral march. They are all seated now, my good friends the Eshtons and the Ingrams, Jane's cousins Mrs. Fitzjames and Mrs. Wharton with their husbands, the Mayors, Members of Parliament and factory owners, and of course, the tenants and labourers. Nobody wanted to miss out on such a grand event.

Life is too short. I would have needed more time to repent and repair my deeds. I used to think I was immortal, immune to death and decay. I believed I was above any law, man-made or divine. I was used to getting my own way and giving orders, which were unconditionally obeyed, so I imagined my life would continue thus forever. I was naive enough to ignore the scriptures. God's plan was never in my mind, and now that my carcass is dead and buried, I have nowhere to go.

⸻ ❦ ⸻

It was a ghastly cold funeral. Jane made us walk the freezing and drizzling five hundred yards to the church. We were all soaked and shivering, as we paid our hundredth respects to the deceased. How I longed to be back under the Jamaican sun.They morbidly insisted on having an open coffin with wreaths of iris, blue thistles and eucalyptus, and bunches of roses and chrysanthemums at the altar, so the whole church stank of wet wilting flowers and decayed flesh.

I had never seen so many people dressed in black pressed together in such a reduced space. The women's heads and faces were draped in black with black veils, as if they were all wearing widow's weeds. Some idiot at the organ played the death march time and time again, and when that dreadful bore Mr. Greenwood read Tennyson's *In Memoriam* and the poems by Swinburn and Browning, I would have gladly fallen asleep, if my feet had not been so damp and cold.

Back in the house I decided the time had come to speak frankly to the prosperous widow, so I asked Mrs. Rochester for a private meeting. Surprisingly she agreed at once and asked me to accompany her to the library.

We sat comfortably, sipping tea by the fireplace. I decided there was no point in beating about the bush. I did not want to be overtaken.

"I can see you are not lacking suitors Mrs. Rochester, or should I say vultures? You have Mr. Greenwood eating out of your hand, and the Bishop's timely visit cannot be attributed to mere chance, can it? I also noticed your editor, Mr. Spencer, was most solicitous…"

"Please, Mr. Mason, do not offend me. Mr. Greenwood is courting Adele and wishes to gain my approval."

"Of course he does."

"And Bishop Templar has been a dear friend, since John was at Rugby."

"Quite!"

"Mr. Spencer has been trying to persuade me to write another novel for some time, I assure you that is his only interest in me."

"What then are your plans, now that you are a free woman?"

"I am in mourning Mr. Mason. But I have thought about busying myself with a new novel, continuing my charity work, and parish schools. I have my son, I have Adele, and now Annette's finishing school and husband must be procured, too. I assure you, I have no time for suitors."

"I have noticed that John is quite taken with Annette."

She shot a frozen look at me, which I naturally ignored and continued, "You need not worry. She is keeping well away from him, and it is not easy, because I think she has quite taken a fancy to him. Such an attractive boy, and Annette having spent her life in a convent has no doubt a great deal of contained amorous zeal, which could leash out any moment, I fear."

"Mr. Mason, mind your language, she is your niece!"

"John is constantly reminding her that their relation is, "bloodless," shall we say? Of course, she thinks she knows better, doesn't she? She is conveniently convinced they share the same father, and that little, white lie is the only thing that is keeping them apart."

"You know my views on the matter. I will look after her. She will be conveniently educated, and she will marry a man of substance."

"Indeed. I wonder if you had thought of investing in Jamaica?"

"Jamaica?"

"I owned a plantation, which I had to sell, but it is well worth recovering. There are massive gains in sugar exports from Jamaica."

"I am not well enough informed, enlighten me, and explain why you sold it, if it was so productive."

"I have a little vice, Mrs. Rochester. We men are prone to one type of excess or another, as you well know."

"And what is yours, Mr. Mason?"

"Cards. I enjoy playing, and sometimes, inevitably, I lose."

"You lost your plantation playing cards?"

"I'm afraid so, and I'd like to buy it back. We could be business partners, fifty-fifty. You would earn a great deal of money. I would take care of all the work, and you would receive high interest at the end of the year, and of course, the plantation would always be ours."

"Go on, please, I am interested. Tell me more about Jamaican plantations. Do you still use slaves? Do children work?"

"Slavery was abolished in 1833, over thirty years ago. The workers who wish to continue working on British plantations are no longer flogged, and they have fair wages and conditions. Indentured workers from India are also arriving of their own free will to work in the new advantageous conditions. Children work, as they do in England, but I assure you, Jane, they are not able to learn even the most rudimentary intellectual skills. Not a single one of them has ever learned to read or write. They are only capable of menial repetitive tasks, such as plantation work. If you had ever seen one of them, you would understand. They are not animals, and although they have some sentiments, neither are they totally humans."

"Is the plantation a lucrative business?"

"Sugar is the most important crop in the West Indies, which produces over eighty percent of the amount consumed in Europe. My plantation is on flat land near the coast, where the soil is fertile and sugar is best grown. It is a safe and profitable investment, Mrs. Rochester, and Antoinette would no doubt enjoy having a house on the plantation to go back to with her future husband. She might enjoy spending time there, who knows?"

"Can I trust you not to gamble it away again?"

"I will not be the sole owner, so I cannot sell it without your consent. I would benefit by using the property, being the master of the plantation, and receiving half of the profits."

"I think that can be settled, Mr. Mason."

"You have made a wise decision, Mrs. Rochester, which you will not regret."

"I hope our collaboration will be advantageous to both of us, Mr. Mason."

"This brings me onto the next matter. I would also need to have my playing debts covered at my club in London."

"How much does that amount to?"

"Five thousand pounds."

"Heavens! How long did it take you to work up that debt?"

"Several years, I'm afraid."

"Very well, Mr. Mason. I will be your business partner in Jamaica, and I will cover your debts in London."

"I'm afraid, that is not all. I have one further requirement."

"I think it is quite sufficient."

"I would like to be the next Master of Eyre Hall."

"Your greed and ambition have no limits, sir."

"Let me explain, Mrs. Rochester, may I call you Jane?" She looked surprised, but she did not answer, therefore, I continued, "I would be most gratified if you would do me the honour of marrying me."

She stared at me coolly, "I'm afraid I am in mourning, Mr. Mason. I cannot marry anyone for at least two years."

"One year will be sufficient mourning, I'm sure."

"In any case, I am not planning to marry anyone, Mr. Mason."

"If Annette marries John, I will have the Estate under my supervision. Annette trusts me completely. She knows she is alive, because I made provisions for her. She owes everything to me, and she will repay me with gratitude."

"John will not inherit until he is thirty, it is in Edward's will."

"Of course that is a drawback, but are you sure you are willing to have us all here living with you under the same roof? John with Annette, and of course, me, too."

"I have offered to buy the plantation, leave it in your hands, and share the benefits. I am also prepared to pay your debts. Finally, I can also offer you a house, wherever you wish in England, Millcote? London? Anywhere you would like to live."

"How generous of you, madam. Unfortunately, if we are married, it would be even more advantageous for me. It's quite simple, either John marries Annette or you marry me. It's your choice. I'm sure we both prefer the second option, don't we?"

"Why have you never married, Mr. Mason?"

"I had never met the right woman, until now."

"I am sure you are mistaken. I am not the right woman for you."

"Oh, but you are, madam. My brother-in-law was a wise man. You are rich, generous, understanding, intelligent, and the most beautiful widow anyone has ever seen."

"Do not flatter me, Mr. Mason. I do not wish to remarry."

"It will be an honour to be your husband. Mrs. Jane Mason. The name becomes you."

"Please, do not insist. I will not marry you, or anyone else."

"Well, then, that is settled. I will have a long talk with John and Annette."

"You will not!"

"Will you risk it?"

"They will not believe you!"

"Who can tell? In any case, you will have a lot of explaining to do. I would not advise it."

"Never!"

I held her hand firmly, "You will never be rid of me, and I can do a great deal of harm. It would be wiser to buy my silence and have me on your side, don't you think?"

She screamed and pulled away from me. Perhaps I had pushed her too far, too soon. Although I had calculated she was too tired and vulnerable to resist.

"Only on condition that we will draw up a marriage contract."

"Naturally. State your terms."

"Separate bedchambers and separate finance. You will run the plantation and have an allowance of 12,000 pounds a year. You will not interfere with my social work, my son's education, marriage, or career. You will be discrete. You will not embarrass me in public with your mistresses. You will not interfere with my literary career. I plan to have a house and residence in London, you will not interfere, nor visit me there. We will be civil when we are together at Eyre Hall on social occasions."

"That is satisfying for me, however, I would like to add one more point. I'd like extra expenses paid, as well as the allowance."

"Which extra expenses?"

"The voyage to Jamaica is expensive, and I will have to travel at least twice a year."

"Agreed."

"And one more thing, the insolent valet, Michael, he will leave your household."

"He will not!"

"What is it with you and that impudent boy? He is too clever for his own good, and too damned young and attractive. Do you think he will be faithful for long? He is only after your money."

"I brought Michael to Eyre Hall with his sister when he was a young orphan. He is absolutely loyal to me. I need people I can trust completely at my side, and I am very fond of both of them. In London he will be my personal secretary, he will assist me in my literary pursuits."

"You are taking him to London? You should have a female secretary. It will not be acceptable to have a male secretary. I have heard there are women in London, who call themselves journalists and offer their services in newspapers and magazines. I am sure you could employ any of them."

"I want Michael."

"I object."

"Michael is not negotiable."

"Very well, I also have a non-negotiable requirement."

"Pray, what is it?"

"A wedding night, and to share your bed whenever you are in Eyre Hall."

"We have already decided on separate bedrooms."

"I will return to my bedroom when we finish the act."

"You are disgusting! You will not dare come near my chamber!"

"Come, come, my dear, you are hardly an innocent damsel. I am negotiating your son's and your lover's future. I am prepared to turn a blind eye in London, if he is prepared to turn a blind eye in Eyre Hall. We will share you. He will get the better part of your anatomy, and I will get the better part of your finances."

"Mr. Mason, I suggest you find it in yourself to be a gentleman and refrain from entering my chamber, or addressing me disrespectfully."

"Except on our wedding night and our honeymoon?"

"There will be no honeymoon."

"Surely we must have a wedding night. What will people think?"

"Mr. Briggs will write up the contract. We will marry next year on All Hallows Eve. May I ask you to wait six months to make the official announcement?"

"Naturally, madam."

"In the meantime, I will speak to Mr. Briggs to act on my behalf by purchasing the plantation in Jamaica and cancelling your debt as soon as possible, Mr. Mason."

"Thank you, Mrs. Rochester, it is a pleasure doing business with you. I shall be delighted to carry out the transactions on your behalf in Jamaica, as soon as possible, and I shall return to Eyre Hall in April to announce our engagement and marriage."

Chapter XXIX

Confessions

When Mason left the room I felt the weight of Eyre Hall sinking all my plans. How could I have agreed to marry him? But what else could I do? Was he the new Master that Junot had predicted? Did that mean that Michael would be buried next year? Tears welled up, choking my dreams. I could not breathe! I coughed, pushed the window, jutted out my face and opened my mouth, inhaling the icy air, which shook me back to life. I was drying the rain and the tears off my face with my shawl, as Adele entered the room.

"Jane, what is the matter? Close the window, or you will catch your death of cold!"

"Adele, I could not breathe. I needed some fresh air. I am not feeling well. I think I shall retire."

"Do you need Dr. Carter?"

"No, I just need some peace and quiet."

"Jane, but everyone is waiting for you in the drawing room. They have come a long way for the funeral. You must make an effort and thank them for coming."

⁂

I returned to the drawing room without Jane. She had asked me to allow her some minutes of solitude before greeting the visitors. The food was laid out on the tables and the guests walked around eating and drinking, except the older ladies who sat on the couch. Michael came into the drawing room and busied himself with the fire. Captain

Fitzjames, who had been conversing with his brother in law, Mr. Wharton, about the end of the war in America, approached him speaking loudly, so everyone could hear his words.

"Your father was the bravest soldier in the Royal Navy. I would have given my right arm to have ten more like him."

"Thank you, sir, Captain Fitzjames." Michael reddened and bowed.

"Midshipman Kirkpatrick lost his right leg, developed gangrene, and died after fighting bravely against the Russians off the coast of Odessa. He was given an honourable burial in the distant land."

John tapped his shoulder affectionately, "I had no idea, Michael. What an honourable death. You must be proud of your father."

"I am very proud of my father, but I also missed him. I was seven years old when he died."

Captain Fitzjames shook his head, "Such a pity. A great loss for all of us. Have you not thought of joining the Navy?"

"No, sir."

Much as I wanted Michael to keep away from Jane, I did not want to see him in battle, "Captain Fitzjames, you will keep away from Michael." I teased.

John supported my plea adding, "I'm afraid he can't leave. What would Mother do without him?"

Thankfully Jane had not arrived yet and I added jokingly, "What would all of us at Eyre Hall do?"

The Captain ignored us and insisted, "What do you say, Michael? I could speak to Admiral Wellesley and you'd be at naval school in a couple of weeks."

"That's a most generous offer," started Mason, "one this young man should not reject."

"Pay no attention to him, Michael!" I shouted.

"Miss Adele, do not worry about Eyre Hall, there are plenty of young valets to be found in London." Mason insisted and turned to Michael, "Well young man, can you reject such an opportunity to better your station in life?"

All eyes were on Michael, whose nonchalant expression made it clear he was not impressed by the offer or by all the fuss. He replied calmly, "I'm afraid I must reject your generous offer, Captain Fitzjames, for a personal reason, sir."

"Personal? Your sister? Another woman?" Enquired the Captain.

He nodded, "Yes, a woman. When my father died, my mother made me promise never to join the Navy."

Fortunately, Diana, the Captain's wise wife, sentenced, "The conversation is over then."

"Thank goodness for that." Said John.

"Well, I tried." The Captain threw his arms into the air and shook his head in disagreement, as he looked at his wife.

Jane walked in moments later, mingling politely and thanking all the guests for their attendance at the funeral. I heard Michael ask her if she would be returning to the library, she nodded and followed him out of the room. I wanted to stop her, but Mr. Greenwood was reading some of his late wife's poems, and I felt it would be rude to interrupt him and leave the room.

⁕

I followed him into the library and sat down quite exhausted, "What is the matter, Michael?"

"Mrs. Rochester, there is something I must speak to you about, because I would not like you to believe I have lied to you. I know how important it is for you to trust me. I have never lied to you and I would not like to start now."

I wanted to tell him that I was upset, exhausted, and that he should not vex me, but he looked so worried that instead I asked, "What is it that troubles you?"

"I believe my sister has recommended a lady by the name of Jenny Rosset, and Mrs. Leah has informed us she is to be employed at Eyre Hall."

I watched him carefully, as he spoke nervously and confirmed the information, "Mrs. Rosset will visit the hall this afternoon, and I may decide to employ her. As you know, she has two children to feed on her own."

His expression was one of confusion, as I waited for him to continue.

"Did Susan mention to you that we know Mrs. Rosset and her family?"

"Yes, Susan has told me you are acquainted with her. Susan taught her children to read, because they had to work and could not attend Sunday school. If I employ her, the children will move in, too. The boy will start working with Simon, and the little girl will go to school until she is twelve, and then she will work here, too."

He moved about the room restlessly yet he did not speak, so I insisted, "What is it you would like to tell me, Michael?"

"I taught Jenny how to read."

I was silent, waiting for him to continue. I suspected there was more.

"May I speak freely, Mrs. Rochester?"

"Of course. I prefer to hear the truth. Don't lie to me, please."

"I... we have been intimate."

I gasped and he knelt down beside me taking my hand, "Mrs. Rochester, it was some time ago, before I declared my love to you, before I ever touched you."

"Do you love her, Michael?"

"I never loved her, not then, and not now."

"Why then?"

"I had no experience of women and I needed to be instructed."

I sighed with relief, "Would it be a problem for you, if she were to work here?"

"No, of course not. She needs a proper job for her children. I promise I will never love any other woman, only you."

"That is a difficult promise to keep."

"It is an easy promise for me to keep."

"There is just one thing I'd like you to promise me, Michael."

"Anything."

"Promise me you will tell me when you stop loving me."

"That will never happen."

"Never is such a long time. Promise."

"I promise, if I ever stop loving you, I will tell you, but I also promise you that it will never happen."

I looked into his eyes and I knew he was telling me the truth, "I'm glad you told me. We both have a past. The past no longer interests me. We will make our future together."

"Will you tell me about Junot's words now?"

"Michael, I am afraid I have had an unexpected complication and bad news today. My mind is distracted with many unpleasant matters, and I need some time to disentangle the mess. Please be patient for at least another day."

I moved down and sat beside him on the floor, "Embrace me, Michael. I need your comfort."

∼∾⌇⌇∾∼

When Mr. Greenwood finished his wife's poem, I returned to the library, where I hoped to find Jane. I stood at the door shocked at what I saw. Jane's arms were around Michael, her eyes were closed, and she was whispering in his ear and kissing him. I rushed in and slammed the door behind me, which made them move apart and look at me in astonishment.

"Michael! How dare you! Get out at once!" I cried.

"Adele, you will refrain from speaking to Michael in those terms."

"Jane, your house is full of guests, your husband has just been buried, and you are in mourning. Have you lost your mind?"

"Adele, I trust you will keep our secret for the time being. I think you already know what Michael and I feel for each other."

"It is unnatural! Impossible! You must stop!"

"Adele. You will not speak to us in that manner. You will respect our feelings, as we respect yours. Remember you are going to Italy with a man you have just met."

"But he is your valet, and he is your son's age!"

"We are all leaving Eyre Hall shortly. You are going to Venice with Susan and Mr. Greenwood, John is returning to Oxford, Mr. Mason is returning to Jamaica, Annette will be going to Belgium, and Michael

279

and I are going to London. Mr. Rochester has died, but for the rest of us, life must go on. You will not judge anyone's behaviour, except your own."

Jane stood up and took Michael's hand defiantly, as I left the room in a huff. She was playing a very dangerous game.

Chapter XXX

Lovers' Parting

Last night I dreamt I was in Coloubri again. It seemed to me I stood by the shackled gate leading up the dusty path to the sea-blue veranda, which embraced the house. There was a rocking chair still swaying to the memory of its last occupant. Was it my mother? I called her name. No one answered. I entered the house. It was unfurnished and uninhabited. Tethered curtains hung and blew over the empty windows. Splintered floorboards cracked under my cautious feet. It was empty, but not lifeless. I could see the shadow of my mother's dress twist along the weathered walls. I heard her voice laugh, as she twirled to the music.

"Come back!" She shouted. "Come back to Coloubri!" But Coloubri had disappeared long before she died. Long before I was born. There was no going back.

I woke up to the rhythmic tapping of bare branches mercilessly beating my chamber wall. I lifted my eyelids warily. Where was I? The waning moon magnified and distorted by the latticed window shone on my face. The same ruler of the night, but a different place. The same lovers' mirror, where I now saw his face reflected, instead of the sea. The same bright colour, but a duller shine did I perceive in this cold distant land.

Back home I could taste the moon, fresh like salt, yet gritty like sand. I often heard the moon whispering, like creaking bamboos. I remembered Mother Angela had told us it was very bad to sleep in the moonlight, when the moon is full, because madness could creep in and torment our souls. A cloud crept past and brought back the dark night. I felt safe again.

I had only met my mother's husband, her cruel husband, and my absent father, once. Our eyes had locked for a few brief seconds across a dining table, surrounded by dinner guests. I had only spoken one terrified sentence to him. And minutes later, he was gone. The man who had incarcerated my mother and estranged me was dead. Yet I did not understand why I should be sad. How could I feel anything after what he had done? But I did. Once more, I felt the burden of abandonment and loneliness.

We paid our last respects by his corpse. I held his icy, stiff hand, and watched my brother, his only sanctioned son, do the same, shedding silent tears, and avoiding my gaze. Why? He had not spoken to me since the dinner party, when he had promised to invade my chamber once more that very night. The night our father died. Suddenly his look had become as aloof as his father's. His eyes lost their sparkle and his contour sagged under the weight of the loss.

I longed to hear his enticing words in my mind, and feel his fingers around my waist, but he was silent and withdrawn, and as cold as the ice on his causeway. His brow was rutted with the pain and anger of death. Throughout the prayers, he was silent. While the atrocious sin-eater performed his unholy ritual, he was silent. When the mourners expressed their condolences, he was silent.

What would happen to me now? Would my stepmother honour her promises? Or would I be cast away, like an unwanted burden? Only Jane Eyre seemed to be in calm control of the situation, which did not seem to surprise me. She supervised all the arrangements with cool efficiency, sliding from one room to the next, giving orders softly yet confidently. She dealt with the undertaker, the staff, the mourners and guests, paying attention to the smallest details, from the draped mirrors to the lemonade and the flowers. I had to admire her elegant command of the situation.

Only once did I see her wane. After the sin-eater's ghostly visit, she cried out her valet's name and fainted. When I saw him carry her away, I understood the reason for her composure: she was in love with another man. I did not think it odd, or even wrong. It was a just chastisement for her husband's crimes. However, I was surprised and shocked when my uncle told me he would be marrying her the following year, but he convinced me it would be advantageous to both of us, and I was not in a position to argue.

Everything changed at Eyre Hall, after my father's death. Faces became taught and grim. We all avoided each others' eyes, keeping our sorrow to ourselves. Sadness was not to be shared. The house itself was in mourning, smothered by the putrid, sickly-sweet smell of death mingled with the scent of flowers and perfume. The incessant murmur of the mourners could be heard through the walls, galleries and staircases, and their shadows quivered on the ceilings, rehearsing their dance of death.

My father's death transformed John. He lost his good humour, and his interest in me. He became taciturn and locked in his thoughts, avoiding me and the rest of the guests, and refusing to greet the visitors, although he was obliged to accept condolences curtly. I had lost a friend, and spent most of my days alone in my room, or wandering around the grounds by myself.

The funeral had passed, and the mourners and guests had left. It was my last night at Eyre Hall, for the time being, and it was my last chance to say farewell to John. I did not want our parting to be cold or unfriendly. I needed a happy memory to pull me through the lonely year ahead. I wished he would write to me, and hoped we could be friends again, when we returned to Eyre Hall. I tapped on his bedroom door.

"John, are you there?"

He did not reply, yet I knew he was inside, so I knocked again and spoke, "John, I wanted to say goodbye. I'm leaving England tomorrow."

He did not answer, so I returned to my room, sat on my bed, the bed where he had kissed me, and looked out across the fields, wondering when I would see him again. Minutes later I heard a knock on my door. I rushed to greet him, "Please, come in."

He made a negative gesture with his head from the doorway, "I was wondering if you would like to come for a walk with the dogs?"

"Of course, let me get my cape and my bonnet."

We walked downstairs and into the garden in silence. I walked quietly by his side, wondering where he was taking me, "Are you all right, John?" He nodded.

"Do you miss your father?" He nodded again.

"Do you want to talk about your father, or how you feel?"

"No." He was looking at the ground, absently observing his boots crushing the damp grass. The dogs jumped along, carelessly sniffing the bushes and trees. I took his hand. It was limp and cool, but he did not pull it away.

"I'm leaving Eyre Hall after lunch, today. I must return to college, although I have no wish to do so, but my mother insists."

"It is your final year. It would be a pity not to finish what you started."

"I do not like to think of my mother alone at Eyre Hall during the long winter. She will miss my father terribly."

"John, your mother is a very strong person. I'm sure she will manage."

"But she will be alone!" He insisted, "She has never been alone before. Never."

"I would offer to stay with her, but she was most insistent that I should go to finishing school this year. Adele has also offered to postpone her journey to Italy, but she will hear none of it." I paused before continuing and squeezed his hand, "You know, I think she may want to be alone."

He looked at me for the first time inquisitively, "Why would she want to be alone? Has she told you something?"

"Not exactly," I started, "but she did say she wanted to write another novel. Perhaps she is looking forward to some peace and quiet. It has been a busy fortnight."

"I cannot imagine Eyre Hall, or my mother, without my father. It would be like a tree without branches, or a horse without its mane."

284

"She will recover, in time." I tried to comfort him, although I knew she had recovered already. I had observed how the valet's eyes followed her like a hawk all day, and the way she hazily searched for his gaze made it so evident. I could not understand how everybody in the Hall had not noticed. She wanted to be alone with him. It was obvious.

It started to rain more heavily, and John suggested taking cover in the nearby stables. He pulled my hand and we ran in. The strength of the tug and the short run energized me. When we arrived, we laughed nervously, and I put my arms around his neck and kissed his cheek. He grimaced, pulled my arms down gently, and looked towards the haystack, "Let's sit down." I obeyed.

"Elizabeth and her father are not well. I'm afraid they are in bed with the flu. It is a shame you did not meet her. She is a wonderful person. Truly wonderful. She will be a good wife and mother, that is why my mother chose her for me. I cannot let my mother down, do you understand, Annette?" I nodded.

"I cannot behave as my father did," he continued, "I am no longer Master John. I am Mr. Rochester, now. I will be the owner of the Estate soon, and I must behave honourably, as my mother would wish. I'm sorry I misled you, when you first arrived. I am engaged, and we can only be friends, and family, of course. Nothing more. It was improper of me to make any other suggestions to you. Please accept my apologies."

My silence suppressed the turmoil and pain I was feeling. Needles pierced my eyes, as I held back the tears. He misunderstood my feelings.

"Please do not be angry with me, Annette."

I was not angry. I was distraught. He was my only friend at Eyre Hall, and I had fallen in love with him. I knew I would never love anyone else, but I also knew I could never tell him how I felt. Over the last few days, I had convinced myself that although Mr. Rochester had been married to my mother, he was not my father. Mrs. Rochester and my uncle were both lying to me for their own purposes. Mr. Rochester had abandoned my mother in the attic. He hated her. Why would he visit her and make love to her, especially when he had already met Jane

Eyre? He was not my father. John and I were not related. We could be married, but of course, he was already engaged, and he could not break his promise. And I had also promised Mrs. Rochester I would pretend to be Mr. Rochester's orphaned niece.

"Do you like me?" I asked him.

"Of course I do." He answered earnestly, "I like you very much, but I must to do what is right, what is expected of me."

"And if you were not engaged to Elizabeth?" I started speaking and took both his hands in mine, "Imagine that you were not engaged, imagine that." He looked into my eyes and smiled, I knew he had imagined being with me. I pulled him closer and whispered, "Would you..."

But he did not let me finish, he covered my lips with his hungrily, pulling me into his desire. We tumbled on the hay and kissed until we were breathless. He held me tightly, kissing my hair, and I melted into his embrace.

"If I were not engaged, I would kiss you like that every day, and I would ask you to marry me." He held me closer, "But I am engaged, and that is not possible, so this must not happen again, my dearest Annette."

I understood the finality of his words, but they made me so happy that it did not matter. I knew he loved me the way I loved him, and for the moment, that was enough for me. We were destined to be together, as family, as friends, as lovers. I did not care whether we were married or not. I needed to be with him, on any terms.

He rocked me in his arms until it stopped raining, and we walked back to the house holding hands carelessly. His hands had warmed, and his arm swung loosely with mine. He was smiling and calm, at last. The weight was slowly lifting from his shoulders. I knew I could make him the happiest man on Earth, if he let me, as he had just done.

"Will you write to me, John?"

"Would you like me to write to you?"

"Of course, I would. I will be so lonely in Belgium. Please, write to me." I begged, as we approached the house. "I will write to you, Annette." He promised, squeezing my hand.

He stopped, as we reached the top of the stairs, which led to the front door, "We should say goodbye now. I will be having an early lunch with my mother and Adele before leaving."

"Take care, John." I was not going to say anything else, but he smiled, pulled me closer, and brushed his lips against my cheek. I held his arms, so he could not move away and whispered, "I will miss you, terribly. Make sure you write to me, soon, very soon. Remember how lonely I will be without you."

"I will miss you, too." He whispered back, and I moved my lips to his and said, "I love you, John."

He was about to speak, when the door was pulled open, "Good afternoon, Master John, Miss Mason," greeted Simon. I broke away and rushed up the stairs to my room.

I threw myself on the bed, face down on my pillow and cried. I could not believe what I had said! What had possessed me to say something like that? "I love you." I told him I loved him. How would I survive a whole year without him?

⸺ ⟡ ⸺

Chapter XXXI

Lovers' Quarrel

The days after the funeral had been long and lively. I had spent most of the time getting to know Mr. Greenwood and planning our journey, which he had promised would be memorable. The drawing room was full of people most of the day, indulging shamelessly in roast meats, pies and Madeira, although conversations were hushed and glum. Jane had confidential conversations in the library with many of the guests. I was duly informed of all of them, except one. She had spoken privately to Mr. Mason and remained quite secretive about the subject discussed. She also made final arrangements regarding Annette's finishing school in Belgium, after which she promised to introduce her to English society and procure her a husband.

John was urged to finish his studies and resume his courtship of Lord Harwood's daughter (neither of them had attended the funeral due to influenza) with the intention of officially announcing their engagement the following spring. The Bishop informed Jane that he would move to London to work at the Bishopry, and he did not hide his aspirations to contend for the seat of Archbishop of Canterbury. Mr. Greenwood was given many recommendations regarding how I should be looked after and treated, and she was also adamant that Susan should be well cared for and suitably chaperoned.

Her cousins Mary and Diana and their husbands also conversed privately and amiably with Jane, offering their support and help in the following months. Jane promised to visit them as usual at Christmas. She informed her delighted editors that she would shortly be travelling to London, because she needed to move away from Eyre Hall, in order to write another novel about a poor orphan from the provinces, who is taken to London.

Most of the guests had already left. John had left after lunch, Mary and Diana had returned to Morton with their husbands, and Mr. Greenwood had returned to London to prepare his luggage for the journey. Only Mason and Annette remained in the house, keeping to themselves most of the time, except for dinner. I was sitting in the drawing room after lunch with Jane, when Susan knocked and entered.

"Mrs. Rochester, Miss Adele, Mrs. Rosset is here with her children."

"Where is Michael?" Jane was surprised that Michael had not introduced the guests, as he usually did, he hadn't served lunch either. It was obvious to me that he was avoiding Jane, and I was glad of it. Thank goodness he had come to his senses, even though she was still behaving like a spoilt child with a new toy.

"He's bookkeeping with Mrs. Leah. She is worried about the accounts. The butcher insists there is money owed to him..."

"Very well, Susan. I'm sure Michael and Leah can sort it out. Please tell Mrs. Rosset to come in and bring us some tea and cake."

Jenny Rosset was a fine wholesome looking woman indeed. Her scanty bonnet covered her long, curly, blond hair, which was tied loosely at the nape of her neck. She wore a blue dress with white cuffs and collar stiffly buttoned up to her neck, a thin brown cape and worn old boots, which peeked out queerly from under her skirt. Her large pale blue eyes looked around the room in awe, as her jaw dropped.

Jane greeted her politely while she held out her hand limply, "Good afternoon, Mrs. Rosset." Jenny shook her hand energetically and spoke enthusiastically, "What a beautiful house, Mrs. Rochester."

"Thank you, Mrs. Rosset. Please sit down. Susan has told me you have worked at the George Inn."

"Yes, madam."

"Have you ever worked in a private household?"

"I'm afraid not, madam, but I can cook, clean, sew, and do anything that needs to be done in a house like this one. I'm prepared to work all day, every day."

"What is your salary at the inn?"

"I do not have a regular salary, madam, it depends on the time of year and the days and hours worked. Mr. Earnshaw calls me when I am needed. That's why I asked Susan to speak to you. You see, I have two children to feed and keep warm, and I can't do it with the guinea I get at the inn a month. Other months I just get some shillings or some food for the children. I'd like to offer them something better."

"Where do you live now?"

"We live in a room in Millcote, a room I rent in a small house. The landlady is a widow, she uses one room and rents the other two. The room is getting too small for us, we all sleep in one bed, and I can't afford to rent another room or another bed, it wouldn't fit in the room anyway. I would be most grateful, if I could stay here with my children. Thomas is only twelve, but he can work with the gardener or in the stables, or in the house, if he's taught, he's a clever lad. Nell is nine, she is small and weak, but she can work, too."

"Mrs. Rosset, I do not believe that children under the age of thirteen should work. They should be at school." Jane spoke solemnly. It was a subject she felt strongly about, far too strongly about in my opinion.

"You are right, Mrs. Rochester, I would like my children to go to school and learn a trade, that's why I asked Susan to teach them, and she was kind to do so, with your permission, not charging me a single penny. Don't think I'm not a good mother. I am. I would do anything for my children, and I have done many things for them, things I am ashamed of, but they must eat and have a roof over their heads. If they went to school, if I hadn't done what I had to do, they would have died of hunger and lived or rather died on the streets."

"Surely you exaggerate, Mrs. Rosset." She was obviously being overdramatic, as the paupers so often were.

"I assure you, swear to you, Miss Adele, I do not exaggerate." She spoke forcefully, making me wonder if she would be a good servant.

"Mrs. Rosset, please do not feel offended, I trust you are a good mother and a good person. I am sure you have done what was best for your children." I wondered why Jane seemed concerned that she should not feel uncomfortable.

"Mrs. Leah knows me, so do Susan and her brother Michael, he taught me to read. They know I'm a good mother." She insisted, exaggerating an offended tone.

"I think very highly of the three employees you have mentioned. Naturally, I have asked them for references. Susan and Leah have spoken highly of you, and I am aware of your arrangement with Michael, who has no objections to your working here."

"Thank you, madam."

"He has told me about your reading lessons, just as long as you understand they are a thing of the past, you will no longer have time for them while you live here."

"Of course, madam."

"On the other hand, regarding your children, Thomas will go to school in the mornings, at least until he is thirteen and he will work in the afternoon with Joseph, our gardener and groom. Let's see how he gets on, and we will decide on his future occupation. Do you agree?"

"Yes, madam."

"Nell will go to school every morning and afternoon until she is thirteen, too, then she will follow the same system as Thomas. Do you agree?"

"Yes, madam."

"You will earn two guineas a month, plus board and lodging for the three of you. For the moment, you will have two beds in one room, until other arrangements can be made. You will have Sunday afternoon free."

"Thank you, madam."

"I expect you to behave modestly, reservedly, and refrain from spreading gossip."

"Thank you, madam, for your kindness."

"When can you start?"

"As soon as you would like me to start, Mrs. Rochester."

"Leah will see to the arrangements, please speak to her after we have tea. Now I would like to meet the children. Where are they?"

"In the kitchen with Susan."

She rang the bell and clumsy Simon tripped in far too quickly, as usual.

"Simon, go down to the kitchen and tell Michael to bring the children upstairs, will you?"

"At once, madam."

"Mrs. Rochester, we can have tea downstairs in the kitchen."

"Not today. Today you are my guests, and you shall have tea with us in the drawing room. When you are working at Eyre Hall, you will have your meals in the kitchen with the rest of the staff."

Jane had moved to the window and was absently looking out to the orchard, wrapped in her thoughts. When the door opened, she turned with a smile, which transformed into a stunned expression. I ran to her side.

"Mrs. Rochester, Michael is still busy with Mrs. Leah." Susan informed, as she walked in with one child clinging to each of her hands.

Jane gasped and bent over with pain, her look reminded me of her face, when she had fainted after Junot's visit, a mixture of pain and horror.

"Jane, what's the matter?" I shouted. Susan and Jenny rushed to her side and helped me carry her to the divan.

"Jane, shall I call the doctor?" I asked with concern.

"No. I'll be all right in a moment. I just felt a sharp pain, like a stitch in my side. I just need to sit down."

The children were staring quietly with bewildered faces.

"Jane, you haven't rested since before the funeral. Let me take you to your room." I insisted.

"Thank you, Adele, but I'll stay here for now."

She winced and I knew she was in pain. She seemed to recover, and we all sat down on the couch facing the divan, the table with the tea and cake stood between us. I asked Susan to serve the tea, and we all ate and drank quietly. Jane looked at the children intently while she sipped her tea. Finally she spoke. Her question was as unexpected as the answer.

"Mrs. Rosset, do the children have the same father?"

"No. I had three children, each have a different father. My husband and my first child, a baby girl, died of typhus, when she was a baby. Nell's father is dead. Thomas's father is Mr. Rosset, who left me shortly after he was born. His whereabouts are unknown to me. I tell most people I'm a widow, to avoid gossip."

Jane was oddly quiet, looking at the children intently. They were indeed very different. The boy was tall, dark, and well-built while the girl was fair and extremely pale. Neither of them took after their mother. They were eccentrically dressed with grotesque clothes, which were clean and pressed, but at least two sizes too big for them. The girl's coat swept the floor, like an odd wedding dress train, and the boy's long jacket sleeves were rolled up. They looked quite in awe of Jane, lowering their gaze, as she scrutinized them. She finally spoke.

"I'm very glad you came today, Mrs. Rosset. It will be nice to have children in the house again. You have fine looking children. I would like to offer you a month's salary in advance, in order to buy clothes and anything else you may need for yourself and the children. We must make sure Nell is warm and well nourished, she is too pale and thin for the approaching winter."

"Thank you for your kindness, Mrs. Rochester. Nell seldom has a good appetite and it is in her nature to be pale, unlike her sturdy brother."

"Susan has told me that you read very well, Nell."

The little girl nodded, pushed a piece of cake into her mouth, and smiled amiably at Jane. After that, the conversation continued on civil terms. We discussed the wet weather, the bumpy ride to Millcote, and the children's progress with Susan's lessons. When they left, I sat by Jane while she dozed on the couch, wincing occasionally, as she folded her hands over her waist.

Michael knocked on the door before dinner, when night had fallen. He stood at the threshold, looking serious and asked far too politely, "Mrs. Rochester, are you feeling better this evening?"

"No, she's not." I answered sharply. "She nearly fainted earlier, and I can see she is still in pain, but she won't let me call the doctor. Don't you think we should call Dr. Carter, Michael?"

"What's the matter, Mrs. Rochester? Are you unwell?" He walked in and approached her.

"I'm feeling a little dizzy. I did not sleep well last night, that's all."

"You haven't slept well since the funeral, and you look ill, Jane." I insisted.

"Would you like me to call Dr. Carter?"

"No, thank you, Michael."

"Mrs. Rochester, I heard Christy say you were sick again this morning, perhaps the doctor should see you." I was relieved, but surprised that his tone was distant and seemingly unconcerned. Jane shocked me by losing her temper and shouting fiercely, "Christy is a gossip and I will dismiss her if she dares to..."

"Jane, you will make yourself ill again if you shout like that. It is so unlike you, what's the matter?"

"Just stop fussing and leave me alone, both of you!" She continued with her unexplainable rage and walked once more to the window. After a few moments, Michael insisted again.

"What would you like me to bring you for dinner, madam?"

"I'm not very hungry. Whatever Adele wants." She replied with her gaze fixed on the cloudy sky.

"I can't eat. I'm so excited about my trip to Italy."

"Mrs. Rochester, shall I bring you some fruit?" His voice seemed more concerned.

"Bring whatever you like. I shan't eat it." She snapped, refusing to look at him.

"Will Mr. Mason and Miss Annette be having dinner with you this evening?" He was looking defiantly at her back, as he spoke.

"I hope not!" I shouted. "I have no idea where Mr. Mason is dining today, but I have no patience for his company, I'm afraid."

Jane spoke dryly into the window, "Mr. Mason is packing, because he is leaving for London tomorrow with Annette. They will be making arrangements for Annette's journey to Belgium."

"We will be leaving for Italy next week. John has returned to Oxford. Your cousins, Diana and Mary, left, too. Everyone will be gone soon. Jane, what will you do when we have all gone? I can't bear to think of you all alone. Michael, will you be here to look after her?"

"Mrs. Rochester has made her choices. It is not in the stars to hold our destiny, but in ourselves."

Jane turned around, when she heard his words, with a furious look on her face, "I am very tired and most unwell, Michael, please do not vex me with your riddles, or I shan't be able to sleep tonight either."

"By the way, Michael, did you know that Jenny Rosset was here this afternoon?" I interrupted, changing the subject. "She will be moving in with her children. I thought she was a little uncouth to me, but Jane seemed to like her enough to offer her a job. I can't think why. She had three children with three different men. It seems to me she is some kind of easy woman. I really can't see what Susan, or you, could like about her unchristian behaviour. What is it about her that you liked?"

"She works hard to feed her family on her own and she is truthful. She is what she seems, some women seem truthful and are much less faithful."

"I've heard enough." Jane walked towards us, but had to steady herself, leaning on the back of the armchair, "I do not know what has possessed you since yesterday afternoon, Michael, you have been avoiding me, and now your behaviour is exasperating and driving me close to.... I suggest you reconsider your absurd words and actions. Now, if you will excuse me, I am retiring for the evening."

She started walking to the door, but he stood in her way and spoke sternly, "Mrs. Rochester, you are unwell and you will not see the doctor. You have not had dinner and you refuse to eat. You will make yourself ill."

"Don't you dare speak to me like that!"

There was electricity in the air. They stood silently, looking at each other's sparks flying out of their eyes. I decided to intervene, "On second thoughts, Jane, I'll have something to eat. Let's have something together, please. On this occasion, I think Michael is right."

They had frozen. I was sure I had just witnessed a lovers' quarrel. I spoke quickly, "Michael, bring some fruit and cheese, you know what Jane likes, just go and bring it."

He did not move, and stared at her angrily, yet strangely close to tears.

"Michael, just bring some food, please!"

When he left, Jane slumped onto the couch and sighed.

"Jane, what was that about? Do you know what you're doing? Has he slept with that Rosset woman and are you bringing her here? What is happening, Jane? Do you love him? You must tell me!"

"Adele, I cannot talk now."

I sat by her side while she closed her eyes and looked as if she was in pain. Michael returned and placed the food on the table quietly and left the room. Jane ate half a peach and some cherries silently, her thoughts again elsewhere. I waited for her to speak.

"Adele, would you sleep with me tonight?"

"Of course, Jane. Do you remember the night before you married Monsieur, the first marriage?" She nodded. "Do you remember you slept with me all night? I was a little girl, you weren't much older, but you were a grown woman, who was about to get married. You were so frightened, you held me tight all night and you cried. Were you happy then, Jane?"

"I was very happy. I've never been happier, I think. Perhaps I never shall be happy again."

"Why were you so frightened and crying?"

"Bertha had come into my room. I didn't know who or what it was. I convinced myself it was a ghost, perhaps I really did believe it was a ghost. I knew something was wrong. Somehow I knew it was too good to be true. I couldn't believe I would be marrying Edward the next day, and when Mason and Briggs arrived at the church, I realised I had known all along that it wasn't right. He had lied to me, or perhaps I let myself be deceived. I do not remember any more."

"But finally it all turned out well, did it not, Jane?"

"Did it? Or was it all an illusion. I thought I loved Edward, and I thought he loved me, but he has been so cruel, Adele, so cruel, heartless, selfish, and murderous. How could I not have noticed? Am I mistaken again? Who is Michael? Does he love me? Do I love him, or is it an infatuation? Am I losing my mind?"

"I can't answer that question for you, Jane. I think it would be an unnatural union. Think of John, and Mary and Diana, and the other servants. I cannot see the situation ever prospering, Jane."

"Adele, I have promised to marry Mr. Mason"

"I don't believe you! Have you lost your mind?"

"I had to accept. He threatened to tell Annette that Edward was not her father. He claims John and Annette are in love."

"What are you going to do?"

"He will not announce it until I am in half-mourning in six months' time. We shall be married next year at Hallows Eve."

"Mon Dieu! That is what is wrong with Michael. He must know!"

"He cannot know, nobody does. We were alone when we discussed the matter, and he has told no one."

"Will you marry that dreadful man?"

"No, I would rather die than marry him. I have bought some time that is all. I have a year to think of something. I have many things on my mind, Adele. Things I cannot tell you, things that are tormenting my soul. Please do not ask any more questions. I need you to comfort me tonight."

I hugged her reassuringly. I was glad to be able to repay her generosity and kindness to me. When Michael returned to remove the dinner plates, she took his hand, put it to her lips, and spoke.

"Thank you, Michael. Please don't be angry or distant with me. I can't bear it."

He removed his hand and asked coolly if she needed anything else.

"I will take a whole bottle of laudanum."

"Jane!" I shouted, appalled.

"You will not." He replied dispassionately.

"Would you care?" She pleaded, taking his hand once more.

"Of course, I should be out of an employment." He pulled his hand away again.

"Is that what I am to you? An employment?"

"Can you be anything else?" He was hurt and very angry.

"Will you miss me?" She took his hand again.

"Not more than I do now, this minute."

"Who do you miss, Michael? I am here."

"You are different now." He removed his hand a third time and backed away towards the door.

"Because I am free?"

"Are you free?" He spat the words out fiercely.

"I am free to take my life."

"Jane! You must not speak like that!" I shouted at her.

"Not with the laudanum, I disposed of it."

"Well done, Michael. That horrible, filthy drug," I added, relieved.

She stood up before speaking, "Then I shall walk out in the middle of the night, barefoot in my nightgown, into the moors and never return."

He moved back to her side, took her wrist firmly, and swung it in the air angrily. She winced and I gasped.

"Would you be so selfish as to have me stand at the door all night to prevent you from doing so?"

"Michael, you are hurting me." She whispered.

When he dropped her arm, she closed her eyes and folded down to the ground with a loud thump.

I realized that night no force of nature would keep them apart. Michael carried her up to her room and cried like a baby, as he laid her on the bed. He told her how much he loved her and begged forgiveness with such endearing terms that I felt most embarrassed, yet I was unable to stop him. I was thankful she finally awoke and made us promise we would not call Dr. Carter. I convinced Michael to leave, reassuring him I would look after her. I did not sleep all night, my head was spinning with worry over my poor Jane, who eventually fell asleep cradled in my arms.

Chapter XXXII

Mrs. Rochester's Proposal

"Jane, Mr. Greenwood has ordered our passages to Venice. They have arrived, Jane! Look!" I was so proud to have them in my hands "Miss Adele Varens, Mr. William Greenwood, and Miss Susan Kirkpatrick have tickets for travel from Southampton to Venice. We are leaving in ten days' time. We will be leaving for London a few days earlier. I need to make some purchases for me and Susan. She has absolutely no suitable clothes at all!"

Suddenly Jane went deathly pale, "Don't you dare faint again, Jane! Or I will cancel the journey at once! Whatever is the matter? You look as if you have seen a ghost!"

"Can you show me the tickets, Adele? The three of them, please."

"Of course. If you don't want me to go, I'll postpone the trip."

She took them and looked anxiously through them, reading all the details carefully, then she sighed and whispered, "Oh my God!"

"Whatever is wrong, Jane? You are worrying me." She smiled and closed her eyes.

"I'm all right. Don't worry, Adele. It's wonderful! It's really wonderful that you are going to Venice at last, that's all."

"You don't mind me going?"

"Of course not! I may even join you there later on, in spring. Yes, in March I will visit you!"

"I don't know if I shall stay six months. That's a long time, don't you think?"

"You must stay six months. We will exchange homes. I will stay in Mr. Greenwood's house in London, and when you return, I shall stay in your lodgings in Venice. Where will you be staying?"

"Mr. Greenwood has a palace in Venice, where his son lives."

"Wonderful! There will be room for all of us!"

"Jane, I didn't know you wanted to visit Italy. You never wanted to come to France with me, you used to say there was no country like England."

"How narrow minded I was! Now I will be travelling to Italy in spring."

"We may return for Christmas, won't you miss me?"

"It's a long journey, do not worry about Christmas, if you are having fun. There will be many more Christmases."

"You are speaking most strangely, Jane. Are you sure you are well?"

"Very well. I will give Mr. Cooper instructions to endow you with whatever funds you may need for your purchases and travel, and you must take funding with you."

"We have had a lot of expense lately, how are finances?"

"We have had many extra expenses, and I have discussed matters with Mr. Cooper and Mr. Briggs, we will manage. I plan to make some changes in the financial running of the Estate. We need to branch out and expand our income."

"Where are you thinking of investing?"

"In Jamaica with Mr. Mason."

"With Mason? Are you sure?"

"Quite sure. There is money in Jamaica, honest money to be made, now that there are salaried workers not slaves working the land."

"Do you trust him?"

"He knows Jamaica well. We will be business partners, the more we earn, the more he earns."

"I hope you are right."

"I may invest in industry. Mr. Cooper has informed me that there are many London investors interested in building factories in this area. Now that the American war is over, the mills are flourishing again. More jobs will be available with better salaries and working conditions than farming. The latest transport innovation, the railroad, is making communications faster and more efficient. I may invest in stocks."

"You have been busy planning, Jane."

"I have been supervising our expenditure and bookkeeping, there is a great deal to be done. John will inherit an even greater fortune, and we will all benefit from a comfortable life. I would also like to invest in a residence in London. Nothing too grand, a town house will be sufficient, and I shall write another novel."

"My goodness! You are going to be occupied!"

"I also want to continue with my charity work. We need more parish schools in the area and social reform. Orphans and poor children need our protection."

"You will write to me regularly, won't you?"

"Of course I will."

"And you will tell me if you need me, or if you are unwell?"

"Don't worry about me, Adele, I will be perfectly well."

<hr />

After lunch I was sitting in the library and rang the bell, expecting Michael. When Simon answered my call, I told him I needed to speak to Michael.

"I'm afraid Michael is busy with…"

"No excuses. Michael is to come at once. I do not care what he is doing."

Minutes later when he arrived, I rushed to embrace him. "Michael, I have missed you. Where have you been? I did not see you at breakfast or lunch."

"Working, Mrs. Rochester."

I closed the door and took his hand in mine, it was unusually limp. "Have you been avoiding me since yesterday? I thought we were friends again." I stood close to him, but he stiffened, retrieved his hand, and backed his shoulders away from me.

"Mrs. Rochester, I would like to apologize for my impulsive actions."

"There is nothing to apologize for, Michael. I was speaking and behaving stupidly yesterday."

"I forgot my station."

"Your station is in my heart."

"I am your valet, Mrs. Rochester, and I would like to remain in that occupation."

"Michael, is there anything you regret having done?"

"Mr. Rochester was still in his bed, in this house. It was not right. Our… friendship is …not right."

"What do you mean *not right?*"

"How am I to look at you and be near you, after I have been so intimate with you? Everyone will notice and I shall have to leave. You said so yourself."

"Do you want to stay with me?"

"I cannot pretend all the time."

"Do you still love me?"

"I cannot have you. You are … too much for me."

"You have had all I can give you, and that is more than I have ever given anyone." I took his hand and placed it over my breast. "Listen. Can you hear my heart beating?" He nodded.

"It beats for you."

Unbelievably he seemed unaffected and pulled his hand away from me, "What more can I give you, Michael?" I pleaded.

"Perhaps you belong to someone else now."

"I assure you, I belong to no one else."

"I will not be a ….. an amusement."

"You think you are an amusement for me?"

"Am I?"

"Of course not. You are the reason I smile and I breathe. You are the only person I would trust with my life."

I tried to take his hands in mine, but he backed away. I thought he cringed, but it was not possible. How could he?

"You are to be married to Mr. Mason, are you not?"

I gave a sigh of relief, "So that's it. Who told you?"

"Does it matter?"

"Not really, I suppose a lot of gossip goes on behind my back."

"Is it gossip?"

"No, it is not." I saw him stiffen to contain his anger and take a further step back.

I moved forward, "I wanted to tell you, but you have been avoiding me …"

He looked away from me, "May I leave, Mrs. Rochester?"

"No. You may not leave." He turned to open the door.

"I said you may not leave!" He turned back to me with tears in his eyes. I was devastated, what had I done to him? "Please stay, Michael." I added softly.

"You have thrust a dagger into my heart and you ask me to stay?"

"Michael, do not look at me with those angry eyes. Do not speak to me with such harsh words. You are killing me. If you still love me, come to me and I will explain."

"Do you think that because I am your poor valet I have no feelings?"

I moved closer. He did not move away this time and let me take his hands in mine.

"How would you feel if I told you I was to marry Beth or Jenny?"

Now the dagger had been thrust into my heart, "I would die of grief, Michael. I love you, only you. Trust me."

"Then why are you marrying him?"

"I have agreed to marry him, but I have no intention of being his wife."

"He shall be your master."

"He shall not!"

He shot a perplexed look at me.

"I cannot marry anyone until at least a year has passed. I am in mourning."

"And then he will be your master. He will … be close to you."

I grimaced, "I had to agree, Michael. It was the only way I could keep Annette away from John. Mason needs my financial help. He is ruined. He has lost his plantations and has squandered all his money. John has fallen in love with Annette, but they can't be married! There is a chance they are half-siblings, but he can't know that. I have kept all his father's mistakes and misdeeds away from him. At the moment, Annette thinks Edward was her father, that is why she refuses his advances, but Mason has threatened to tell her that Edward was not her father, if I don't marry him. If John marries Annette, his marriage with Miss Haywood will be undone. Elizabeth will be disgraced, Judge Harwood will be furious, and John's future in Parliament will be thwarted. And worst of all, *she* will be mistress of Eyre Hall. I can't allow it. I can't. She is Bertha's daughter! She is not responsible for her mother's mistakes, and I'm prepared to compensate for her unfortunate childhood, but she cannot be mistress of Eyre Hall."

"If Mason wants money, can you not give him the money he needs?"

"He is so greedy. He wants to be sure he will have all the money and social prestige he needs until he dies. He does not trust me to pay his debts and maintain his lifestyle indefinitely. I tried, Michael, believe me I tried, but to no avail. I am torn between both of you, my son and the man I love. I had to agree."

He looked shattered, but I had to continue and tell him everything.

"We have drawn up a marriage contract. I will only spend one night with him, the wedding night, after that, we will have no further physical contact. We will lead separate lives, and you will be employed by me indefinitely."

"I was part of your negotiation?" He gasped in disbelief.

"He wanted you out of the house. I refused, so he demanded a wedding night in exchange, and I had to agree."

"What kind of a man or woman agrees to that kind of marriage? What kind of a man would I be, if I agreed to a relationship with you while you are married to another man?"

I remembered my conversation with Edward, after I discovered he was married to Bertha and tried to understand how Michael felt. I could not let him go. I had to convince him my marriage to Mason was not important.

"It will only be a formality."

"I cannot stay with you, if you marry him. I will not watch him touch you." He held me tightly for the first time since he had entered the room, and I closed my eyes and listened to his heart beating steadily, and my world was safe again. I had to keep him by my side at all costs. My life without him was an abyss. I had to make him understand that my marriage to Mason was no obstacle for us.

"Twelve months must pass first. I will think of something. We will think of something, but rest assured that you are, will be, my only master." I pulled away gently, taking his hand in mine. "Michael, come here, sit with me on the couch, I have thought of a solution, a temporary solution at least."

He sat beside me and listened attentively.

"We are going to London. You and I are going to London forthwith. Mr. Greenwood has kindly offered me the use of his house at Dougherty Square while he travels to Italy with Adele. He has a permanent housekeeper and a maid, and it is conveniently located in central London. I will tell everyone I am writing a new novel and need to go to London, because that is where it is set. Who knows, perhaps I will really write a novel. In any case, it will be a perfect excuse to move there, and we will look for Helen."

He looked confused. I searched his eyes to hear the feelings he could not express.

"Do you still want to come with me to London and look for Helen?"

"Of course I do, but how? And Mason?"

"Mason will return to Jamaica to recover a sugar plantation he had lost and in which I will be his business partner. I will finance it, and he will run it, which will keep him busy for some time. He will be out of our lives for six months."

"And then he will announce your engagement and you will be his wife?"

"Let's not think so far ahead. Let's take things one step at a time. Many things can happen in a year."

"I shall not, cannot stay with you, if you marry him."

"I promise you, I will not marry him unless you agree. Is that enough to keep you by my side?"

"I will never agree to it."

"Then I will never marry him."

"But you have made a promise. You accepted his proposal."

"You are, will be my only master, and that is the only promise I will never break."

He did not speak, so I continued to expose my plan, "In London, you will no longer be my valet, you will be my personal assistant."

"I have never heard of such a job. What does it entail?"

"I will need someone to copy, revise, and correct manuscripts. As executor of the Rochester Estate, I need someone to help me with the administration of the property, deal with tenants, meet with my agent, overview my finances, hire personnel, and similar duties."

"I am not sure I have enough experience and knowledge to carry out such tasks."

"You have been helping Leah and me with the accounts, you are clever and resourceful. I will show you and you will learn quickly. We will work together, looking for Helen and running the Estate." He looked surprised.

"Well, do you accept the post? Do not look so worried. I trust you. You must trust me. I know you will be an excellent assistant. Would you accept the position?"

"I will try and fulfil my obligations."

"You will have your own room upstairs next to mine with comfortable furnishings, and you will not wear a uniform. You will work office hours, and you will earn one hundred pounds monthly, plus board and lodging, and any other expenses in which you may incur to fulfil your obligations. Do you agree?"

"I cannot accept such a high salary. A hundred pounds is more than I earn in a year at Eyre Hall."

"Your work in London is far more valuable than your work here. You will work hard, and it will entail the responsibility for an Estate, which is worth more than £500,000, and I expect you to help me to increase the revenues. In less than ten years, my son and his family will take over the running of the Estate. I must have my own income by then, and you will help me venture into new business. I want to expand my charity work with more schools for orphans and people in need. I would like you to help me with my projects. Will you help me Michael?"

"What will I be to you? What will people think of me? Of us?"

"I did not think what people think would worry you more than what I think. Does it?"

"What do you think... what am I to you?"

"You know what you are to me. I love you more than you can ever imagine, and I will prove it to you every day of my life."

"I wish I could believe you."

"Darling, believe me." I held his beautiful tormented face in my hands. "Do you believe me?" I sought an answer in his eyes, "I have missed you so much, Michael. Kiss me." I whispered and as he did so, I felt the recipient of his love again and my world was safe once more. I was relieved that he wanted to kiss me again, but I pulled away and continued to tell him my plans.

"When we move to London, we will be working together every day most of the day, or as much of the day as you would want to spend with me. For the time being, when others are present I will treat you as an employee, not as a servant, and you will treat me as your manager, not your master. You are a free man and I am a free woman. We will be equals as children of God, although our obligations and duties are different. I would like you to call me Jane, and I will call you Michael."

"I'm out of my depths. You expect too much of me. I am your valet. I am afraid I will never be your equal, Mrs. Rochester, and I will never be able to call you, Jane."

"Can you say that again?"

"I am afraid..."

"Just the last word. Please, Michael."

"Jane."

"You see, it was not so hard, was it? Try again."

"Jane."

I smiled with contentment. "The time has come to tell you the words Junot said."

I hesitated, unsure if I should disclose such devastating news, if I were still not sure it was true, but I was sure. I knew I was full of love and life, "First, I need to hear you say what you feel for me now, at this moment."

"I love you, but I won't share you with another man."

"Four words."

"Four words?"

"Junot said four words to me."

"Which words?"

I knew the four words would change the rest of our lives. I spoke very slowly, looking into his eyes and revelling in each word, "You are with child."

He gasped and fell to his knees, dropping his head on my lap, and I knelt down beside him, waiting for a response.

"Could it be true?" He whispered bewildered, lifting his face to mine.

"Oh, I'm sure it is, my darling." I smiled with satisfaction, holding his face in my hands.

"I am ... overwhelmed, Jane." His dazed eyes were glowing with emotion. I kissed his eyelids lovingly, as he lowered them, "That makes two of us, Michael."

<hr />

I had never felt so afraid since my mother died and we were taken to the poorhouse. My whole world crumbled then, as it was crumbling now. I had felt safe with my mistress at Eyre Hall. She had taken care of us, and I was happy to adore her from a distance, but I was not ready to take on such serious responsibilities.

"What shall we do?" I asked.

"We shall be together."

"But we are not alone in the world. What about Mason, John, Annette, and Susan? Your family, friends and acquaintances, the other servants…"

"Next week we shall go to London as planned, and we shall look for Helen. At Christmas we shall return to Eyre Hall, and in spring we shall spend some months in France or Italy, where our baby will be born. We shall be back for the harvest moon next All Hallows and we shall be married. I shall be Mrs. Kirkpatrick and you, Michael Kirkpatrick, shall be my master and the new Master of Eyre Hall, as Junot predicted."

"You have planned everything to your convenience, but I am not sure I am ready for such commitment. I have heard many distressing words. I need time to think."

"About what? You said you loved me. You said you would always be with me…"

"That was when I was your valet and you were a widow. The situation is different now. You are engaged to another man, and I can no longer be your valet."

"What about our son?"

"Junot is a charlatan and a devil worshipper."

"But you saw what he did. You saw how he displaced himself without using his feet! You heard the things he said."

"I cannot believe what he said, and I cannot serve you in your new situation."

"Of course my darling, you are so young, so new to these intricacies. You need time to think. Michael, promise me you will think about what we have discussed and everything I have said to you."

"I promise I will confer with God and decide what I must do."

"But make haste in your decision, do not take too long, your hesitation is destroying me. Michael, come to me with your decision at any time, I shall be waiting for you."

Chapter XXXIII

Michael's Decision

I had made my decision before leaving the room, perhaps I had made my decision when Simon told me he had heard Jane agree to marry Mason, two days ago. That very moment I realized I was not part of her world and could never be anything but a servant, or an occasional amusement for her. What a fool I must have seemed! I had imagined she was a pure celestial soul in search of another companion, but I had discovered in the cruellest way that I was deluded. She is a selfish enchantress. I do not understand her world of lies and pretence. It is indeed as Bunyan described and Mr. Thackeray fictionalized, full of vanity, greed, and deceitfulness. She may even be imagining, or worse, still contriving a pregnancy to keep me by her side a few more months until she finally tires of me. I have no choice but to leave at once. I must make my way in the world, away from her and Eyre Hall.

Dearest sister,

Susan, you were right all along. I am only an amusement for Mrs. Rochester. She would like me to be her private toy for a time, and our mother would not like me to fall so low. When we first met her, I thought she was an angel our mother had sent, and now I realize she is a temptress sent by Satan instead.

I cannot undo what has been done, although I truly wish I could. I wish we had never met her, and I had never loved her, or been prey to her whims and desires. She will marry Mr. Mason and together they will no doubt make a great deal of money and fool a great many people on the way. She is quite obsessed with making her son a Lord. She has chosen his wife, his profession, and the life he will lead. He is indeed a sad puppet in her hands, even more than I was. He is destined to live an unhappy, predesigned life, in order to comply with her avaricious needs. I feel sorry for him and for anyone who has ever loved her.

By the time you receive this letter, I will have left Eyre Hall. I am going to join the Navy, as our father did. I know Mother made me promise I would never do so, but she would understand that I cannot stay in England and be a valet any more. I need to make an honest living in a profession I respect. Father would be proud, and I hope Mother can forgive me for all my mistakes.

Susan, you must stay with Miss Adele and make your trip to Venice. It will be good for you. Encourage Adele to marry Mr. Greenwood, who is a good, honest man. He loves her, and he will give her a new life away from the stifling and depraved Eyre Hall. Stay with them and serve her, she will be a good, caring mistress. Do not mind her bad temper, it passes quickly and most of the time, she is affectionate and considerate. She will make sure you are procured a good husband and have your own family one day.

Under no accounts are you to show Mrs. Rochester this letter. I have enclosed another letter I wish you to give her, no sooner than tomorrow afternoon. Do not be taken in by her tantrums and fake tears. She will pretend she is ill, she will threaten to commit suicide, and invent all kinds of scheming manoeuvres. She may even try to bribe you to tell her where I have gone. I warn you, sister, if you ever want to see me again, do not give in to her.

Forgive me for not saying goodbye to you, but I must leave at night while I cannot be seen or stopped. Wish me luck and be

happy, you deserve it. I will come and see you, when you return to England.
Your loving brother,
Michael.

⁓⟳⁓

I recalled his words as clearly as if I had just heard them.

"*You are going, Jane?*" Edward had asked me.

"*I am going, sir.*" I had answered.

"*You are leaving me?*" He had insisted, close to tears.

"*Yes.*" I had been merciless.

"*You will not come? You will not be my comforter, my rescuer? My deep love, my wild woe, my frantic prayer, are all nothing to you?*"

Despite the unutterable pathos in his voice, I found the courage to reiterate firmly, "*I am going.*" He let me go, deeming I would return to him in the morning.

"*Withdraw then, I consent, but remember, you leave me here in anguish. Go up to your own room, think over all I have said, and, Jane, cast a glance on my sufferings, think of me.*"

I had walked away from him, towards the door, while he threw himself on the sofa and cried in anguish, "*Oh, Jane! my hope—my love—my life!*" before breaking into a deep, strong sob.

I couldn't leave him in his distress, so I walked back, knelt down by his side, kissed his cheek, smoothed his hair, and spoke softly, '*God bless you, my dear master!*' I said. '*God keep you from harm and wrong—direct you, solace you—reward you well for your past kindness to me.*'

An angel gazed on me that night, and whispered to my aching heart, '*My daughter, flee temptation.*' I replied, '*Mother, I will.*'

I left Thornfield Hall a few hours later, as the dim dawn glimmered, I stole out of the house, with an aching soul, and only a morsel of bread in my pocket. I took a road I had never travelled, which led me away from the man I loved, to an unkown destination.

I scowled at the epistle on my desk filled with harsh words which stabbed my soul. Would I never be allowed to experience love without anguish? He had betrayed me! Each letter was a blade slitting my splintered heart and shredding my stunned womb. I shed brine and blood, until I was as hollow as Tartarus, where I had been chained, for loving too much.

Dear Mrs. Rochester,

As a result of our conversation this afternoon, I have realized my place is no longer in your service.

I thank you for your kindness to both my sister and me while we were employed at Eyre Hall. I have no doubt that you saved our lives five years ago, when you offered us a job, shelter, and safety in your residence, and I will always be grateful to you for that. I sincerely hope you will not hold my sister responsible for any of my actions, and that her trip to Italy will not be affected by my decision.

I trust you will find the peace and person you are looking for in London, as I must find mine elsewhere.

Yours faithfully,

Michael Kirkpatrick.

Epilogue

Eyre Hall, January 10th, 1866

My Dearest Adele,

St. Agnes Eve has not yet come, but already snowflakes are sparkling to the moon. After your departures, the fang of melancholy bit into my thoughts. Once more, I felt I had been tossed in the storms of an uncertain struggling life. Once more, I had erred and been taught by rough and bitter experience. I remember the lines we once read together, 'But when the days of golden dreams had perished, and even despair was powerless to destroy; Then did I learn how existence could be cherished, strengthened, and fed without the aid of joy'. Do not pity me, Adele, for I shall not resist my fate. I expect little enjoyment in life for myself, yet I feel contentment, when I think of your joyous future.

Mary came to visit at Christmas and longed to take me out for a walk around the orchard, but we were obliged to remain in the drawing room by the hearth, lest we should freeze and crack, like the helpless water in the congealed pond. I yearn after the hour the joyless days should end, the snows of winter should melt, and the frost and cutting winds should cease. I long to smell the pleasant greenness and watch the flowers peep under the hedges . . . I shall continue writing another day, for at present my spirits are too low . . .

January 17ʰ

I have just received your last lively letter, my dearest Adele, which has greatly relieved my melancholy. I'm glad you are having fun and finding Venice so stimulating. I struggle to imagine a city, which has canals instead of streets, and where the ladies wear colourful silk dresses and have ringlet postiches, I had never heard the word before, added to their hair as if they were going to a ball every day. I envy the sunny weather, but make sure you use your parasol, my darling, for I can't bear to think of your perfect pale skin turning dun. The clear, pink and orange-tinged skies you are fortunate enough to regard at dawn and dusk must be delightful. I am impatient to see Dante Greenwood's paintings, whose pallet you tell me is able to entrap and duplicate the colours. Make sure you bring back as many as you can. The moon twinkling on the rippling water must indeed be an inspiring sight, especially if you are holding hands with the man you love, but please be careful and wait for Mr. Greenwood to make his intentions clear. Adele, be kind and expectant, but rush him not, or your impulsiveness may frighten him away!

Mr. Greenwood's son Dante sounds like a lively and interesting young man. I would very much like to meet him. By all means you may invite him to stay with us, whenever he visits England. I would like to renew the paintings and artwork at Eyre Hall, and as you value Dante's artistic capacity so highly, his paintings and advice will be well received.

I was sorry to read that your mother is unwell and can no longer recognise you, or indulge in any form of intelligent conversation. I agree that Edward should have informed you of her existence earlier, but we both know that his idea of what was *best was not always in agreement with our opinion. He is now responding, wherever he may be, for whichever errors he may have committed. Remember that it is not our place to judge him. If we do so, it will only stain our own souls. Take comfort that you finally found your mother, and can make her last moments more pleasing. She is fortunate that her companion, Count Galdini, is looking after her, and although their house is cold and damp, and you tell me she is excessively thin and frail, it is probably due to her cruel illness more than to her living conditions. I know she was not the mother you would have desired, but dearest Adele, remember that you have had a pleasant and happy childhood, and a comfortable and loving life. Refrain from judging Mlle. Varens. She was another of Monsieur's victims. You have not walked in her shoes.*

In your next letter, be sure to tell me more about the ghostly legend of the Palace Hotel. To have stayed at such a mysterious place upon first arrival in Venice—! Perhaps you should write a short story, and I shall send it to Mr. Dickens, who has often asked me for a contribution to his monthly literary magazine, All Year Round. The meagre details you mentioned were absolutely riveting! Creaking floorboards, human-shaped shadows in the corridors, and unexplainable violin music in the middle of the night . . . But Adele, you are impressionable. Do not get carried away, remember ghosts are not to be taken seriously. They are a superstitious and unchristian belief.

You are right, Eyre Hall is a large, lonely house at the best of times, but even more so now that you have all gone. Aside from your time at finishing school, I can hardly believe that is sixteen years past! We've not been apart for more than a few days.

I do miss you terribly, every day, but do not rush back, when you read this, for I would not be pleasant company now for anyone. Make sure you come back for summer, when I shall be completely recovered, and we can view the dense foliage and unclouded skies together. I am impatient to take long walks along the bubbling brooklet by the causeway, as we used to.

I'm much recovered from the unfortunate incident, which overcame me shortly after you all left. Forgive me for not telling you about it at the time. I did not want to spoil your journey or worry you. It served its purpose, which was undoubtedly to punish and purge my soul, and bring me to my senses. Although I was bedridden for the greater part of November and all of December, I am now able to get up for a walk almost every day and write for a short while at my desk in the library. Do you remember little Nell? She has become my faithful companion. After her morning classes, she spends the afternoons reading to me, as she is the only person in this house who can do so fluently and has time to spare, except of course Leah, but she is busy enough, and her company for any long stretch of time would be most tedious. Christy's shrill voice displeases me, and Beth stutters agonisingly. Simon cannot read, cook, Joseph, and Jenny can barely string a few words together, and of course I would not care for young Thomas to spend so many hours in my chamber.

Nell reads exceptionally well, thanks to Susan, although I have no doubt she is a very talented child. Her soft voice is like music to my ears. She has already read the Book of Genesis, but instead of continuing with the Bible, I have decided something of lighter spirits would no doubt cheer me up. I selected George Eliot's riveting novel Silas Marner, at Mr. Dickens' recommendation. I had some concern that the contents might shock the little girl, but there is no point in protecting her from the real world. She will soon grow into a desirable woman, and I am educating her regarding the harshness of life. Tom takes her to school in Hay every morning with her packed lunch, because I insisted that she should not walk alone in such wintry weather, and he brings her back in the afternoon. We have tea together and she reads until I can hear, by the thickness and pastiness of her voice, that she is tired. I trust she will follow Susan's footsteps and become a worthy teacher

No doubt John has written to you from Oxford. He is busy preparing his final papers and very worried about Elizabeth. He must have written you about the vicious flu she caught this winter. It followed a previous malady, the one, which as you may remember, kept her away from Edward's funeral, and has confined her to her bed since. Judge Harwood has written to inform me, and Adele, this is absolutely confidential, that whilst distraught, he is preparing for the prospect that the worst may occur. I cried all day, when I read his letter, and was only comforted by the fact that he suggested his younger daughter, Phoebe, would be happy to replace Elizabeth in seeking John's favours. I know you think she is too young and fickle, and you are right. But she is only sixteen, and no doubt she will soon bloom into a much desired and docile wife. Her father and her mother will see to that. Elizabeth was, I hate to use the past tense, but we must be ready for the worst, a wonderful girl, calm, intelligent, and demure. Her soft, watery eyes were so restrained and attentive to those around her . . . Adele, I have had worrying dreams in the last nights and fear she may have already left us. My hand trembles and a solitary tear slides down my cheek as I write. It has landed on this page, blurring the date. I cannot continue. Elizabeth's memory has made me too sorrowful to hold my pen, and I cannot hold back the shower of tears, which are now splashing my words...

January 20th

This afternoon I have been out for a walk with Nell. A tiny, obstinate ray of sun forced its way between some furious clouds, beaming on the marble bench in the flower garden, where we sat on our cushions (the crimson ones you embroidered so many years ago), listening to the breeze teasing the laurel leaves and watching the brave sparrows jump merrily from twig to twig, no doubt wondering what has happened to the flowers, and longing for the spring to bring some colour to the bleak bushes. I almost imagined I could smell the bees making honey, but of course, that's impossible. A curious robin, perched on one of the empty urns by the barren flower beds, eavesdropped as Nell read. He watched me listening so intently that I am sure his cheerful chirping was a secret message! If only I could decipher its meaning...

You kindly ask about Annette, I'm so proud of your generosity in accepting her as part of our family at Eyre Hall, and I must inform you that I received a letter from her some fourteen days ago, in which she writes of her contentment at Miss Burney's School for Ladies. She is expected to return after the summer, in time for my wedding to Mr. Mason. Adele, I must ask you to make an effort to tolerate Mr. Mason and understand my reasons for accepting his proposal, to be made public after Easter, when he returns from his business, our business, in Jamaica. We shall be married on All Hallows Eve as planned. It will be a quiet affair. There will be no guests, just the family, and Mr. Briggs, who will supervise our contract, which will be signed in the church before the event. I have already explained why this marriage, which is purely of convenience for both of us, must take place. I trust Mr. Mason will not spend much time at Eyre Hall, as I am sure he prefers his London club and his Jamaican plantation.

I never imagined I would be trapped into a loveless marriage, but I assure you I have no choice. I have been immensely fortunate in love. I have been loved passionately and unconditionally, for a short time, on more than one occasion. However, I have also been betrayed, abandoned, and broken hearted. The last betrayal occurred so recently that I still feel numbed. I no longer have a heart. It has been destroyed and crumbled to pieces. I shall never find any type of contentment, other than seeing you, Annette, and John happily married.

Dearest Adele, I always imagined we would plan and organise your wedding together, but I fully understand Mr. Greenwood's desire to have a quiet and intimate ceremony, away from

England and London society, in order not to offend his late wife's family, although I do think he ought to think more about your feelings and less about theirs. I see you have discussed the possibility of marrying in Venice and I do not object. I agree that it is the only way your mother could attend, and I am glad she will be present at such a memorable occasion. On the other hand, I must remind you to wait until I receive a letter with his intentions before making any plans. I will wire you any necessary funds you may need for your own expenses, but Mr. Briggs has recommended that your dowry should not be made effective until your wedding, which should be held six months after your engagement. Although, as you point out, your mother's failing health may require an earlier wedding, to which I will agree. I am sure Mr. Greenwood is aware of these events, so negotiations should not be protracted. Mr. Briggs will draw up a deed of settlement with provisions for you, too. I know you do not think these matters are important, but Adele, believe me, they are. Life in London is expensive. You will have your own household to manage, once you marry, and Mr. Greenwood is not a wealthy man.

I have some more news on financial matters. I have decided I will be selling part of the Estate. This may come as a surprise to you and John, but there is no alternative at the moment. Your wedding, dowry, and settlement, as well as mine, including Mr. Mason's expenses, will be very taxing. John and Annette will not be long in following suit. I have spent the last weeks bookkeeping with Mr. Cooper, and there is no other solution. Mr. Cooper has informed me that there is an American investor from Boston, Mr. Jackson, who wishes to buy land to build a paper mill in the vicinity. Apparently, he has made a fortune as a hatter in Boston, but he wishes to move to England with his wife, as his daughter, Emily, has married an English sugar importer from Liverpool, Mr. Harvey Lyttle. The land to be sold for the mill is mainly hunting ground, which is hardly being put to use, and the mill will bring in a great deal of wealth and employment to the area. I have not met Mr. Jackson yet, but Cooper tells me he is willing to donate a percentage of his profits to fund more schools for children and to train teachers in the county. I hope to be receiving visitors soon and discuss matters further with him.

I must finish this letter now, it is already far too long. I hope I have not bored you too much.

Respectful remembrances to Mr. Greenwood, your mother, and Susan, and please write to me soon. I do so cherish your letters.

Yours affectionately,

J.E.R.

P. S. Finally, Adele, please make sure Susan knows I am well, in case she should be in touch with her brother, which I am sure she will be, one way or another, either now or in the future. You may find my next request unnatural or even deceitful, so please forgive me for asking you to do something almost dishonest, but it would be a small comfort for my worried and weary soul. Worry not, I have understood the irrationality and folly of my infatuation. Nevertheless, I would find great comfort in the knowledge that he is well, wherever he may be. I would never ask you to read anyone's mail, but dare I ask you to observe the postmarks on Susan's correspondence and the return address? The purpose would be to comfort me in the knowledge of his whereabouts and good health. Adele, I trust you will ensure no other eyes ever read this letter and no ears ever hear of its contents.

Acknowledgements

Thank you to my generous and irreplaceable Beta Readers: *Elizabeth, Karen, Roberta, and Tina*, without whose time, help, expertise, and encouragement, this novel would never have been published.

Thank you *David Pedrera* for the original cover design, which has been my novel's distinctive pictographic representation even before it was completed, and special thanks to Melody Simmons at http://ebookindiecovers.com for the unique new cover designed in May, 2015.

Thank you *Alicia Carmical* for proofreading an earlier version of this novel, and special thanks to *Alison Williams* for proofreading the final, print version.

My gratitude to all my friends at *Goodreads*, especially *Indie Author Central, The Source, Beta Reader Group*, and *Making Connections*, and to my friends and followers on my Wordpress Blog, *Rereading Jane Eyre*, on Twitter, and on Facebook, for their generous help and support.

Thanks, too, to *Amazon* and *CreateSpace* for making this venture possible.

Finally, a big thank you to *my family and friends* for believing in me.

Afterword

I would never have felt the power of prose, if I had not read *Jane Eyre,* when I was an impressionable and romantic thirteen-year-old. On the other hand, I would never have fully appreciated *Jane Eyre,* if I had not read *Wide Sargasso Sea* thirty years later, when I was an active and overrun mother of three teenage children. Finally, I would never have had the idea of writing this novel, if I had not taught *Postcolonial Literature in English* to Undergraduates, whose lively discussions and thought-provoking questions ignited my overactive imagination. As a result, both novels merged in my mind to re-emerge by means of my audacious pen. My humble and sincere tribute to both literary giants, who contributed to make me, not only the writer I am, but also the person I have become.

Thank you for reading *All Hallows at Eyre Hall,* I hope you enjoyed it, and that you will read the second volume of the *Eyre Hall Trilogy, Twelfth Night at Eyre Hall,* to be published in 2015.

Visit my blog, *lucciagray.com,* or my Facebook page *Facebook.com/LucciaGray* for updates on the *Eyre Hall Trilogy.* Feel free to contact me via Twitter *@LucciaGray.*

13278056R00183

Printed in Great Britain
by Amazon.co.uk, Ltd.,
Marston Gate.